Charles Shearer Keyser

The bicentennial reunion of the Keyser family. 1688-1888.

The Keyser family, descendants of Dirck Keyser of Amsterdam

Charles Shearer Keyser

The bicentennial reunion of the Keyser family. 1688-1888.
The Keyser family, descendants of Dirck Keyser of Amsterdam

ISBN/EAN: 9783337732028

Printed in Europe, USA, Canada, Australia, Japan

Cover: Foto ©ninafisch / pixelio.de

More available books at **www.hansebooks.com**

THE
Bicentennial Reunion
OF THE
Keyser Family.
1688—1888.

LINUM ET TEXTRINUM
VINUM.
German Town.

THE

KEYSER FAMILY

DESCENDANTS

OF

DIRCK KEYSER OF AMSTERDAM.

COMPILED BY

CHARLES S. KEYSER.

CONTENTS.

ILLUSTRATIONS.

PORTRAITS.

Tobias Goverts van den Wyngaert, Rev. Peter Keyser, Elhanan W. Keyser, Nathan L. Keyser, Peter A. Keyser, Mary Slingluff, William S. Baker, Dr. J. K. Knorr, C. Maris Keyser, Philip W. Keyser, Daniel L. Keyser, General B. F. Prentiss, William Keyser, Julia A. Orum, Dr. P. D. Keyser, Silvester Keyser, Samuel Keyser, Miller Bullard, Charles S. Keyser.

THE BICENTENNIAL REUNION

OF THE

KEYSER FAMILY

IN THE

OLD MENNONITE MEETING-HOUSE,

GERMANTOWN, PENNSYLVANIA,

OCTOBER 10, 1888.

AS the two hundredth year after the arrival of our ancestor Dirck Keyser, in Germantown, was nearing, some time in 1887, Dr. Peter Dirck Keyser, in whose possession much of the family genealogy has been preserved, suggested to the writer of this paper that some commemoration of the event would interest the family generally, and that it was, in a sense, a duty to our ancestor's memory. A year later, in the summer of 1888, it was the subject of further conversation from time to time, Dr. Keyser desiring that a stone should be erected to mark the place of our ancestor's ministry and burial. A committee was formed, consisting of Dr. Peter Dirck Keyser and Charles S. Keyser of Philadelphia, and Romaine Keyser of Germantown, by whom the following circular was addressed to the members of the family whose places of residence could be ascertained:

5

When William Penn visited Holland and Germany, promulgating his doctrines of free religious thought in antagonism to the forms of established churches, he invited all to join him in his settlement in the new country. Accepting his ideas, Francis Daniel Pastorius of Frankfort, Germany, organized a company for taking up land and forming the settlement of Germantown, now part of this city. The Mennonites of Holland and the lower Rhine of Germany joined with him, and among those who came here was Dirck Keyser of Amsterdam. He was a manufacturer of and dealer in all kinds of silk goods, and a man of prominence, but, desiring to worship God in all freedom, he came over with his son, Pieter Dirck Keyser, in 1688. There are many descendants of the family throughout this country and Mexico.

In commemoration of the arrival here of Dirck Keyser, a bicentennial reunion of his descendants will be held in Germantown (Twenty-Second Ward), Philadelphia, in the old Mennonite church, on or near the original ground of said Dirck Keyser, on the 10th day of October next, at 10 A. M., being, according to the present mode of chronological reckoning, the two hundredth anniversary of the day on which he came to the place. It will be a social family gathering on the ground where our common ancestor is buried, and where he built his domicile in the wilderness of the New World. Sketches of the family history will be read, the old family Bible and such other relics as can be obtained will be exhibited.

A cordial invitation is extended to all descendants of the family to be present and bring with them anything they may have in their possession that will throw any light on the history of the family or indicate its progress.

Can you be present on the occasion, with any of your immediate connexions of the family? An early answer will greatly oblige the undersigned.

CHARLES S. KEYSER,
ATTORNEY-AT-LAW,
No. 524 Walnut Street.

PETER DIRCK KEYSER, M. D.,
No. 1832 Arch Street.

ROMAINE KEYSER,
Cor. Main and Rittenhouse Streets
(GERMANTOWN), PHILA.

Philadelphia, August 2, 1888.

It was determined, as the invitation indicates, that the commemoration should be of an historic character. The day selected for the anniversary was the 10th of October, 1888; the place was the old Mennonite meeting-house in Germantown in whose first structure, on the same site, our ancestor had passed his life in the ministry, and in whose ground he was buried. It was determined to confine participation in the ceremonies to the members of the family, embracing both male and female lines, and this was not deviated from, except in that the following gentlemen were invited in their representative characters: Edwin H. Fitler, the mayor of the city of Philadelphia; J. R. Plantin, the consul-general of the Netherlands to the United States; Lars Westergaard, consul of the Netherlands in Philadelphia; Professor Oswald Seidensticker of the University of Pennsylvania; and the Rev. Nathaniel B. Grubb, the bishop of the (present) First Mennonite Church in Philadelphia. An invitation was also sent to Dr. G. De Hoop Scheffer of the Mennonite college at Amsterdam, to Daniel K. Cassel and Abraham H. Cassel, in recognition of their services in the preservation of Mennonite literature, and to Adrian Van Helden, a gentleman of Holland now residing in our city, to whom the committee is under many obligations.

After consultation with those who were to take part in the ceremonies, a programme was arranged, of which the following is a copy:

BICENTENNIAL REUNION

of the

1688   Descendants of Dirck Keyser   1888

in the

Mennonite Meeting-House,

Germantown,

October 10th, 1888.

Programme.

10 A. M.

GIDEON KEYSER, the oldest male member of the family, will preside.

PRAYER, by Bishop N. B. GRUBB of the First Mennonite Church of Philadelphia.

HYMN, Te Deum Laudamus.

THE FAMILY IN AMSTERDAM AND GERMANTOWN, by CHARLES S. KEYSER.

THE HOMES, MEETING-HOUSES AND BURIAL-GROUNDS OF THE FAMILY, by Dr. PETER DIRCK KEYSER,

THE MENNONITES, AND THE MARTYRDOM OF LEONHARD KEYSER, read by JULIA A. ORUM, a descendant of Dirck Keyser.

HYMN, Jubilate Deo, Psalm C.

THE LEVERING LINE OF THE FAMILY, by HORATIO GATES JONES, a descendant of Rosier Levering.

THE PANNEBAKKER LINE OF THE FAMILY, by SAMUEL W. PENNYPACKER, LL.D., a descendant of Henry Pannebecker, the first emigrant.

LETTERS FROM ABSENT MEMBERS OF THE FAMILY, read by ROMAINE KEYSER.

HYMN, Old Hundred.

A dinner was provided for on the occasion. For this purpose Dr. Peter Dirck Keyser tendered the use of his summer residence, then vacant, in Germantown;* a notice, in the following form, was sent to the members of the family:

The Bicentennial Reunion

OF THE

1688   **Descendants of Dirck Keyser,**   1888

AT GERMANTOWN,

WEDNESDAY, OCTOBER 10, 1888.

TO THE FAMILY:

As there are no hotels in Germantown, a dinner will be served in the afternoon at the summer residence of Dr. P. D. Keyser (Tulpehocken Station, Pennsylvania Railroad), who has placed it, for the day, at the disposal of the committee.

* The expenditures for the occasion, beyond the sum which remained after the payment for the dinner, were provided by William Keyser of Baltimore, Dr. Peter Dirck Keyser, Charles S. Keyser, Romaine Keyser and George G. Pierie of Philadelphia.

The members of any family wishing dinner must enclose one dollar for each person on or before the 5th of October to either of the undersigned, when the ticket and programme will be forthwith mailed to them. All tickets must be ordered by that day.

CHARLES S. KEYSER,
524 Walnut Street, Phila.

ROMAINE KEYSER,
Germantown, Phila.

September 29, 1888.

THE MEMBERS OF THE FAMILY participating in the reunion were John Heisler Adams and Mrs. John Heisler Adams, Edgewater Park, New Jersey; T. A. Alexander, Mrs. Kate C. Keyser Alexander, Baltimore, Maryland; George J. de Armond, J. Keyser de Armond, Mrs. George J. de Armond, Elizabeth W. de Armond, Philadelphia; Mrs. Sarah W. Atherton, William Spohn Baker, Philadelphia; Charles M. Benson, Philadelphia; Mrs. Howard Boyd (granddaughter of Mrs. Mary Slingluff), Mrs. Mary Slingluff Boyd, Norristown, Pennsylvania; Daniel C. Bullard, Grand Ledge, Michigan; Samuel Keyser Bullard, Sedalia, Missouri; Mrs. Annie W. Button, Miss Sara R. Button, Miss Jennie Button, Joseph Button, Germantown, Pennsylvania; Charles Keyser Bullock, Mrs. Ann M. Bullock, Philadelphia; Mrs. S. P. Campbell (*née* Mary A. Keyser, daughter of Andrew Keyser), Miss Mary Keyser Campbell, Miss Mayland C. Campbell, Miss Anna C. Campbell, Philadelphia; Joseph Channon, John C. Channon, Charles Keyser Channon, Miss Margaret Keyser Channon, Mrs. Susan Keyser Channon, Mrs. J. H. Clark, Philadelphia; Mrs. Henry Cooper (great-granddaughter of Mary Keyser), Stevens, New Jersey; John H. Cooper, Mrs. John H. Cooper, Miss Elizabeth Y. Cooper, Germantown, Pennsylvania; Mrs. William Cookshott (*née* Mary L. Frick, great-granddaughter of Michael Keyser), Philadelphia; Mrs. Hannah D. Colgan, Elk View, Chester County, Pennsylvania; Mrs. E. E. Cornbrooks, Wilmington, Delaware; Samuel Davis, Mrs. Samuel Davis (Eliza J. Mitchell, granddaughter of Catherine Keyser Lynd), Charles A. Duy, Philadelphia; Mrs. Mary Elton, Tioga, Philadelphia; Miss Miriam Elton Davies, Tioga, Philadelphia; Mrs. Clara Slingluff Pawling Fisher (daughter of Mrs. Mary Slingluff), Allentown, Pennsylvania; Mrs. Rachel Fitler, Philadelphia; Joseph Fitzwater, Port Providence, Pennsylvania; Mrs. Joseph Fitzwater (great-granddaughter of Anneke Keyser), Miss Fitzwater, James H. Flint, Mrs. James H. Flint (Ellen Keyser Mitchell, granddaughter of Catherine Keyser Lynd), Mr. John Michael Fox, Mrs. Anna Childs Fox Dunn, Philadelphia; Mrs. Sallie Steiner Keyser French (daughter of Dr. Peter D. Keyser), Noroton, Connecticut; Jacob Frick, Dreshertown, Pennsylvania; Edwin P. Frick, Mrs. Edwin P. Frick, Mrs. Edwin P.

Frick, Jr., J. W. Gaskill, Philadelphia; Mrs. J. W. Gaskill (daughter of Silvester Keyser), Mrs. Sarah Gorgas, Philadelphia; Joseph Hammer, Mrs. E. L. Hawes, Mrs. Emma M. Hassinger, Charles Hassinger, Samuel E. R. Hassinger, Mrs. Samuel E. R. Hassinger, Miss Mattie L. Hassinger, S. Reed Hassinger, Philadelphia; Mrs. Hannah Heisler, Edgewater Park, New Jersey; Mrs. Charles E. Hires, Clara Keyser Hires (granddaughter of Andrew Keyser), Philadelphia; Mrs. Isabella Keyser Idell, Germantown; Caroline Keyser Inglis, John Auchinclos Inglis, Mrs. Mary Uhle Inglis, Philadelphia; Albert B. Jarden, Mrs. Caroline Marie Jarden, Miss Caroline M. Jarden, Miss Catherine Schmoele Jarden, Miss Katie S. Jarden, Philadelphia; Miss Katie Jackson, West Philadelphia; Hon. Horatio Gates Jones, Roxboro'; Alfred G. Keyser, Alexander Provest Keyser, Mrs. Alexander Provest Keyser, Germantown; Mr. Algernon S. Keyser, Rising Sun; Andrew D. Keyser, Mrs. Andrew D. Keyser, Miss Anna L. Keyser, Mrs. Annie T. Keyser, Philadelphia; Miss Anne Paul Keyser, Germantown; Miss Amelia Snyder Keyser, Philadelphia; Miss Anna Keyser, Germantown; Barton M. Keyser, Germantown; Mrs. Charles Maris Keyser, Sr., Baltimore, Maryland; Charles Keyser, Mrs. Charles Keyser, Charles E. Keyser, Charles Shearer Keyser, Francis Keyser, Philadelphia; Frank Keyser, Germantown; Francis Provest Keyser, Germantown; George Keyser, Germantown; George F. Keyser, Philadelphia; Gideon Keyser, Mrs. Gideon Keyser, Germantown; Miss Harriet Nice Keyser, Germantown; Harriet Davis Keyser (daughter of Andrew Keyser), Philadelphia; Miss Helen R. Keyser, Germantown; Horace R. Keyser, Phœnixville, Pennsylvania; Jacob Keyser, Mrs. Jacob Keyser, Miss Jennette Campbell Keyser, Germantown; John G. Keyser, John S. Keyser, Philadelphia; Miss Kate Keyser, Miss Lulu Keyser, Philadelphia; Miss Margaret C. Provest Keyser, Germantown; Miss Martha Keyser, Germantown; Miss M. Keyser, Newberry A. Smith Keyser, M. D., Baltimore, Maryland; Naaman H. Keyser, Germantown; Nathan Levering Keyser, Philadelphia; Peter Dirck Keyser, M. D., Philadelphia; Mrs. Peter Dirck Keyser, Philadelphia; Romaine Keyser, Germantown; Sylvester Keyser, Mrs. Sylvester Keyser, Germantown; Susan Keyser Keyser (daughter of Charles Shearer Keyser), Mrs. Daniel L. Keyser, Germantown; William Keyser, Baltimore, Maryland; Miss Mathilde Keyser (daughter of William Keyser), William F. Keyser, Mrs. William F. Keyser, Germantown; Albert Kulp, Mrs. Albert Kulp, Mrs. H. K. Kurtz, Mrs. Robert Levick, Mrs. Robert Loughead, Mrs. Marielle Marselis Loughead, Hon. A. B. Longaker, Mrs. Mary M. Longaker (daughter of Mrs. Mary Slingluff), James W. Lynd, Nicetown Lane, Philadelphia; Lillie Lynd, Estell Lynd, James F. Lynd, Earnest L. Lynd, Mary C. Lynd, Robert S. Lynd, M. D.,

Philadelphia; Mrs. Lydia D. Magarge, Germantown; Mary A. McCorkle, Hopewell Cotton Works, Chester County, Pennsylvania; Frank E. McIntire, Mrs. Frank E. McIntire, Philadelphia; Mrs. Grace Keyser McIntire, Baltimore, Maryland; Miss Sarah K. Mears, Thomas Mullan, Jr., Wilmington, Delaware; Mrs. Sylvania McKee, Wilmington, Delaware; Miss Katurah Gorgas McNeely, Philadelphia; Charles Nice, Germantown; Miss Julia A. Orum, Germantown; Mrs Helen Paris (*née* McIlhenny), Philadelphia; N. A. Pennypacker, M. D., Phœnixville; Mrs. D. N. A. Pennypacker, Miss Pennypacker, Matthew Pennypacker, Samuel W. Pennypacker, LL. D., Philadelphia; James Lane Pennypacker, Mrs. James Lane Pennypacker, Haddonfield, New Jersey; Mr. George Gorgas Pierie, Mrs. Elizabeth Pierie, Miss Edith Pierie, Miss Helen Pierie, Mrs. Ann Pierson, E. B. Pierson, Matthew K. Pierson, Mrs. Rebecca Heisler Samson, Mrs. Mary Slingluff Rex (granddaughter of Mrs. Mary Slingluff), Miss Mary Slingluff Rex, Mrs. Sarah Slingluff Rex (eldest daughter of Mrs. Mary Slingluff), Norristown, Pennsylvania; Mrs. Sarah Keyser Robinson, Germantown; C. Henry Roney, Mrs. Catherine Blanchard Roney, Philadelphia; John Richard Savage, John Richard Savage, Jr., Miss Kate W. Savage, Mr. Mahlon L. Savage, Philadelphia; Mrs. Will. Ida Scanlan, Mr. Frank Siddall, Mrs. Frank Siddall (*née* Keyser), Mrs. Catharine Keyser Lynd Schmoele, Mrs. Mary Slingluff, Norristown; Mr. John Slingluff, Mrs. H. S. Smith, Mrs. Rebecca J. Smith (daughter of Andrew Keyser), Philadelphia; Mr. G. W. Turner, Philadelphia; Benjamin Urner, Elizabeth, New Jersey; Mary Unruh, Mrs. Mary A. Vanderripe (granddaughter of Mary Keyser), Stevens, New Jersey; William H. Wallace, M. D. (grandson of Elhanen W. Keyser), Philadelphia; Mrs. Emily F. Wallace, Philadelphia; Clifton P. West, Nelson R. West, Germantown; Cornelius C. Widdis, Mrs. Cornelius C. Widdis, Cornelius C. Widdis, Jr., Edward R. Widdis, Miss Susanna Widdis, Anna Williamson, Mary Williamson, Philadelphia; Mr. G. Banks Wilson, Mrs. G. Banks (Mary J.) Wilson, Chester, Pennsylvania; David H. Wolfe, Mrs. Catherine Lynd Wolfe, William Schmoele Wolfe, Miss Kate Marie Wolfe, Miss Belle Wolfe, Miss Amelia R. Wood, Mrs. J. P. Wright, Anna Yerkes, Martha Yerkes, Mary Ann Young.

The committee received regrets from some and acceptances from others of the following, who are not noted as present on the occasion:

Mr. Richard Engle (son of Mrs. Thirza Engle, *née* Keyser), Mrs. Richard Engle (*née* Lizzie H. Keyser), Mr. James D. Keyser, Philadelphia; Lizzie B. Pierson, Fox Chase; Mr. C. E. Hires, Miss Myra Baker (daughter of Mrs. Ann Baker, *née* Keyser), James R. Pennypacker, Isaac R. Pennypacker, Philadelphia; Peter Keyser Heisler, Edgewater Park, New Jersey; Mrs. George S. McKee, Wilmington, Delaware; Silvester Keyser,

Rising Sun; Benjamin Urner Keyser, Washington, D. C.; Cipriano Canedo, Ameca, Mexico; Mrs. Juan G. Matute (*née* Margaret Canedo), Guadalajara, Mexico; William R. Gorgas (grandson of Johannes Gorgas of Germantown), Harrisburg, Pennsylvania; Mary P. Keyser (daughter of Michael Franklin Keyser of Baltimore, a descendant of Samuel Keyser), Boston; Laura Lynd Hill, Clementine K. Lynd, Merchantville, New Jersey; Mr. and Mrs. Alan Wood, Jr., Philadelphia; Andrew Keyser, Philadelphia; Mrs. Clementine L. Fobes, Baltimore; Mrs. Kate Keyser Fracker (daughter of William Keyser, late of Baltimore), Zanesville, Ohio; Alpheus Channon, Mrs. Jane Keyser Channon, Germantown, Pennsylvania.

Among the correspondents of the committee were the following: William H. Fry, Philadelphia; Mr. Andrew Dunlap, Chester County, Pennsylvania; Mrs. Elizabeth Keyser Chambers, Washington, D. C.; Mr. Hugh Dunlap, Harford County, Maryland; Mrs. Elizabeth Tollinger, York County, Pennsylvania; Mr. John Dunlap, Butler County, Ohio; Mrs. Wilhemina Wiley, Harford County, Maryland; Mr. William T. Dunlap, York County, Pennsylvania; Mr. John E. Mullen, Charleston, South Carolina; Mrs. May Ennis, Queen Anne County, Maryland; Mr. Andrew Tollinger, Philadelphia; Frederick Wallace, Washington, D. C.; Margaret M. Pennypacker, Orkney Springs, Virginia; Morgan R. Wills, Norristown; Mr. and Mrs. Henry C. Keyser, Springfield, Ohio; Mr. Daniel Bullard, Independence, Missouri; Mr. William R. Robinson, Washington, D. C.; Mr. and Mrs. William T. Hassinger, Westville, New Jersey; Dr. and Mrs. J. K. Wiley, Springfield, Massachusetts; Mrs. M. A. Goldsmith, Bainbridge, Pennsylvania; M. M. Pennypacker, Mount Jackson, Shenandoah County, Virginia; Mrs. Martha Wilhoite, Shelbyville, Tennessee; Mrs. S. E. Engle, Bainbridge, Pennsylvania; Mr. Rufus Bullard, Cambridge, Iowa; Mr. and Mrs. Edwin Goodall, New York City; Mr. and Mrs. Charles McAllister, Minneapolis, Minnesota; Charles Keyser Urner, Washington, D. C.; Mrs. Rachel Douglas Wise, Elmsmore, Crawford County, New York; Mr. Frank Heisler, Wilmington, Delaware; Mr. and Mrs. Enos F. Erdman, Tarrytown, New York; Mrs. Anna K. Jones, Germantown; Mrs. Sallie E. Heisler, Philadelphia; Mr. and Mrs. Samuel West, Germantown; Mrs. Susan W. Yerkes, Norristown, Pennsylvania; Mr. Thomas S. Keyser, Philadelphia; Mrs. William H. Jones, Mr. William H. Keyser, Philadelphia; Mrs. Hannah Nice, Mrs. George Keyser, Mr. William F. Slingluff, and John H. Michener.

NOTE.—The representatives of the press present were Tunie H. Symonds, of the *Evening Telegraph :* Horace F. McCann, of the *Germantown Independent :* William E. Meehan, of the *Gazette* of Germantown and the *Public Ledger* of Philadelphia, with representatives of the *Germantown Telegraph* and other papers.

THE MENNONITE MEETING-HOUSE.

THE DAY OF THE ANNIVERSARY.—The morning of the day of the anniversary, the 10th of October, was auspicious of the event. It was clear and pleasant, in doors and out, and remained so all day long. Soon after nine o'clock the family began to assemble around the old meeting-house, filled every seat and standing-place, and yet gathered around the door; it was a moment of great interest when we first looked on one another, and strangely-mingled emotion. Aged and young, men, women and children, we saw ourselves repeated more or less, the one in the other —the same features, the height continued so many generations looming up in the assemblage from five feet eleven inches to six feet one inch, two, three and four inches, the blue eyes, the dark hair and the same expression, individuals of one family, long separated, and never to be united again, in all human probability, in this generation, but bound, and yet to be bound, together by a continuous remembrance of that ancestry in whose name we gathered there, for yet longer generations.

The church had been suitably set, as for a festive occasion, with flowers, and a choir engaged, selected from the churches of Germantown. On the pulpit was Van Bragh's *Book of Martyrs* brought here by our ancestor from Amsterdam, and the family Bible brought at the same time by him, in which were contained the marriages and funeral notices of the family there—these and the Bible used by Peter Keyser, the preacher, in Germantown.

THE OPENING PRAYER.

The REV. NATHANIEL B. GRUBB at half-past ten o'clock amid a solemn silence made this prayer:

Almighty God our heavenly Father, we bow in humble submission before Thee, the great and eternal God. We magnify Thy holy name and adore Thee as the Father of our blessed Lord and Saviour Jesus Christ, in whose name we now draw nigh with confidence and say, "Abba, Father!"

We bless Thee for our creation and preservation, and for all things bestowed upon us by Thy grace. We lift our hearts in grateful praise to Thee for the inestimable love to us made manifest in the gift of Thy Son the only begotten of the Father, through whom we are redeemed and in whom we have a Mediator between Thee and us.

We come humbly confessing our sins, and do earnestly beseech Thee to grant us Thy Holy Spirit as the pardoning Comforter, and to lead us in the path of truth and holiness. Enter not, we pray Thee, into judgment with us, but grant us Thy favor and Thy help.

Blessed Saviour and Redeemer, we praise Thee for the work of redemption and the institution of Thy Church on earth. We rejoice with grateful hearts that we have received into our own souls the light of Thy gospel, and that we may stand in holy places and partake of holy things.

We thank Thee for the blessed boon handed down to us by our fathers, some of whom have sealed the covenant with their own blood and sacrificed their lives at the stake. We thank Thee for the noble and self-sacrificing life and testimony of Thy servant our father in Christ, Leonhard Keyser.

We rejoice to-day with grateful hearts that Dirck Keyser, Thy faithful servant and minister, the descendant of that faithful martyr, came across the waters into this new world and rallied around the banner of the cross erected at this very spot. We lift our hearts with grateful praise unto Thee, the Father, Son and Holy Ghost, that we may stand on the spot made sacred by his life and deeds, and we are happy to-day to be enabled to rejoice in the same blessed gospel and gladly bear testimony to its gracious power.

While we rejoice and bless Thee, we would earnestly beseech Thee to come and bestow upon us Thy heavenly benediction; and grant that we may walk in the footsteps of our fathers, as they walked in the footsteps of Christ.

Help us now, Father, that we may so live, and by Thy grace so lead those around us, and especially our children, that in years to come they too may be found faithful as defenders and upbuilders of the cause of Christ. May we truly rejoice to-day as children of our heavenly Father, and may the exercises of this hour and day prove a lasting blessing to us and result in good to others, and may it all redound to Thy honor and to Thy glory!

Lord, we look to Thee for help and earnestly beseech Thee to make us humble in spirit, grateful for every blessing and zealous to serve Thee with all our God-given powers, that by Thy divine benediction we may continue to faithfully rally around the banner of the cross and be ever truly the bearers of the image of Christ, unto whom and through whom shall be honor and glory to God the Father, the Son and the Holy Ghost in a world without end. Amen.

We come yet in the name of Jesus, and desire as a congregation to unite our hearts and voices as one man and pray as Thou hast taught Thy disciples to pray:

Our Father which art in heaven, Hallowed be Thy name. Thy kingdom come. Thy will be done in earth, as it is in heaven. Give us this day our daily bread. And forgive us our debts, as we forgive our debtors. And lead us not into temptation, but deliver us from evil: For Thine is the kingdom, and the power, and the glory, for ever. Amen.

[*The family joined with the Pastor in the Lord's Prayer.*]

THE HYMN, TE DEUM LAUDAMUS, was then sung by the choir.

THE FAMILY HISTORY.

The following paper was then read by CHARLES S. KEYSER:

OUR MEETING.—It has now been two hundred years since Dirck Keyser, our common ancestor with his two boys, from his home in Amsterdam, arrived in this then German town, and we have met here on the ground where in a log house long since passed away he ministered the doctrine of the Mennonites, and, in a house to whose building his grandchildren contributed, and on which it may be worked with their own hands.

On this occasion of so much interest to ourselves it has been assigned to me to relate what is known of the family there, and here; what we have done for ourselves, and for the advantage of the localities where our intentions or our fortunes have located us; what manner of men, women and children we are. And first let me speak of our family name.

THE FAMILY NAME.—The surname of our family is common to

every nation; wherever one obtained distinction above his fellows, to that extent that he could rule, he was by virtue of his place, in its various written or spoken forms a "Kaiser;" as far back as the Hebrew language goes, far back into the Chaldaic, in the Sanscrit, in the remote Hindoo language, to its remotest origin in the Osites, the name in this use appears, and thence down through all following languages to our later civilizations.

THE DERIVATION OF THE NAME.—Syriac—Kesar. Persian— Kaysar, Kayseer or Kisra. Gothic—thzar, tzar, sar, sir. Runic—sir; siar. Old Icelandic—Soera. Punic—Ksar. Hebrew—Sarah, sor, sarr, ser. Arabian—Sary. Chaldaic terminus Zar—King, as Belshazzar, Nebuchadnazzar, etc. Sanscrit—shera, shira. Bengali Moorish—sir. Afghan—sar. Hindoo—syr, sear. Kurdish—ssar. Caucasian (The Osites) —Zer, sser. The zer or sser of the Osites meaning "the head;" the Persian word sâr, etc., was employed to designate the heads or chiefs or princes of Georgia; and by the addition of the initial, forms the Cæsar (Latin), tzar, (Russian) Czar (Illyrian) then Czeszâr (Hungarian). German—Kayser (Kaiser). Bavarian—Kaiser, Keyser. Belgian—Keyser. Holland—Keijser, Keyser.—Tressor des Origines, Porigin, Paris 1819.

THE SPELLING OF THE NAME.—No other man with this surname, as far as we have knowledge, arrived in Pennsylvania prior to the coming of the founder of our family; nor any one very certainly, for fifty years after his coming, so that there is no one living among us, probably, with our name, except in our family, who can trace his line back of 1749. It was as far as the emigration here is concerned a singularly exclusive name; among the list of thirty thousand German, Dutch and Huguenots arriving here since 1688, there were but six with the name and none prior to 1749: Leonard Keyser, September 26, 1749 Joh. George Keyser, 1750, Johan Jacob Keyser, 1752, Andreas Keyser 1753, who might be one of our family returning from a voyage, as also Johannes, 1757, and Philip Keyser, 1773. Another fact I may mention, the spelling of other names, as also of the Christian names, in our family, widely differ * yet by whomsoever written under all circumstances I have found but one spelling of the surname—Keyser, since the arrival of the family in this country and what makes this adhesion to the one spelling the more peculiar is, that it does not indicate the pronunciation.

* To illustrate this I find these spellings, Govertsz, Govertz; Dirrick, Dirick, Dirck, Dirks, Dirk, Derrick; Andreas, Andrew, Anders; Johannes, Johan, Jon, John; Pieter, Peter; Cunnard, Conrade, Conrad, Conerads, Cunard; Pancbacker, Penebaker, Pannebakker, Pennypacker, written in two ways by two brothers on the same paper; so also Ruddinghuisen, Rittenhuises, Rittenhausen; Neus, News, DeNeus, Neiss, Nices, Niece, and so for many others.

THE ARMS OF THE FAMILY.—In connection with our immediate family the name obtained whatever distinction it had in past times, in Bavaria whence the family originally came; the arms on the copper plate our ancestor used, now over two hundred years ago, certainly, and beyond of this of a date yet undeterminable, are the arms of the family in Bavaria. They are described in Rietstap's Armorial Général as follows: Parti d'arg. et de gu.; á un homme naiss de carn. hab. de l'un en l'autre, mouv. d'un tertre d'azur. Supp. de sa main dextre un monde cintré et croise d'or et tenant de la sen. un sceptre du même. C.: un vol a l'antique de gu. L.: á dextre d'or et d'azur. a sen. d'arg. et de gu.

THE ANCESTRY OF THE FAMILY.—The first one of the family in the male line of whom we have certain knowledge is Leonhard Keyser of Scharding in Bavaria. In the early part of the sixteenth century this greater ancestor of ours separated from the Catholic Church and identified himself with the true believers; his story is elsewhere written here. After his death the family went down into the Netherlands, and prior to the emigration here for a century and longer, lived and are identified by association and marriage, as a Holland family. They were manufacturers and business-men in Amsterdam for the four generations of which we have information—say a period of a hundred and thirty years.

Dircksz Keyser, the grandfather of the Dirck Keyser who emigrated here, and himself one of the sons of a Dirck Keyser living there, had two children of whom we have an account—Dirck Gerritsz Keyser, a morocco leather manufacturer of Amsterdam, and Jannetye Gerritsz Keyser. Dirck Gerritsz Keyser, the father of the Dirck Keyser who emigrated here, married Cornelia, daughter of Tobias Govertz van den Wyngaert; she was one of a family of three or more children living in Amsterdam. One of her brothers was Tobias Govertz, Jr., and she had a sister who married Gerrit Gerritsz Vortgens, who died in Amsterdam and was buried in the Norder Kerckhof, June 4, 1662. Gerrit Gerritsz Vortgens' residence at the time of his death was in Korte-lange Street, in the Emerick Arms; he had a brother, Arent Gerritsz Vortgens. Dirck Gerritsz Keyser's sister Jannetye married Galenus (Geleyn) Jacobsz, who survived her husband, and lived in Amsterdam until her death, September 1, 1669. The family were living in 1655 in Elandt Street, opposite the Witte Beer.

Dirck Gerritsz Keyser by his marriage had four sons—Dirck, Gerritsz

The notices of our ancestor's wife's death, his sister Anneken's and a daughter, Elizabet, written by his own hand, I have selected from others in his family Bible; they are reproduced in fac simile on page 18.

ENTRIES IN THE FAMILY BIBLE WRITTEN BY DIRCK KEYSER 1681.

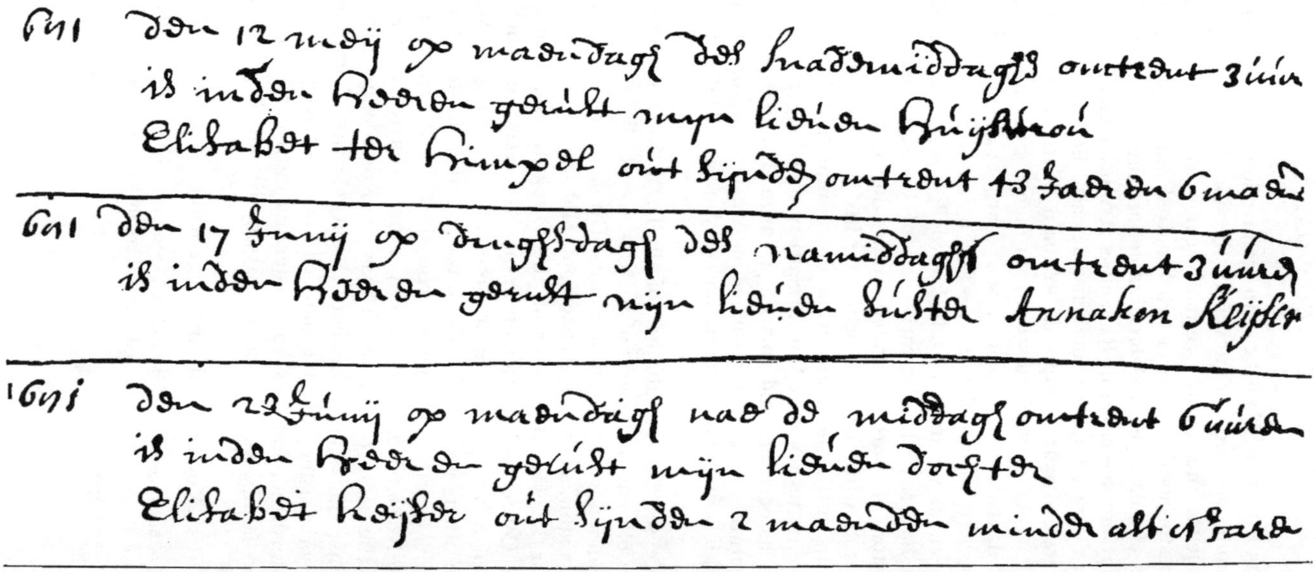

[handwritten Dutch text in three entries]

1681 Monday the 12 May in the afternoon at 3 oclock died my dear wife Elizabet ter Hempel aged 43 years and six months.

1681 Tuesday the 17 June in the afternoon died my dear Sister Annaken Keyser.

1681 Monday 23 June in the afternoon at 6 oclock died my dear Daughter Elizabet Keyser aged seven years and 10 months.

TOBIAS GOVERTSZ. vanden WYNGAERT, Bedienaer des Godelijken woorde, inde Vlaemsche
Doopsgesinde gemeente, tot Amsterdam. Ætatis LXXX.

Dirk, Tobias Dircksz, one other, who was the youngest son, whose name is not given—and one daughter, Anneken. Dirck, the first son, who emigrated here, married Elizabet ter Himpel, daughter of Elizabet, *née* van Singhel, the wife of Pieter ter Himpel of Amsterdam. She had brothers: Pieter ter Himpel, Jr., Aernaut and Dirck ter Himpel. Pieter ter Himpel, Sr., a woolen draper of Amsterdam, lived in the first Lely-dwars Street, by the Bloemgraft, and died December 10, 1680. Pieter ter Himpel, Jr., died 23d January, 1681, and was buried January 25 in the Norden Kerckhof.

Elizabet ter Himpel, the mother, lived in the Halsteegh, in the house ter Eimpel, and had two brothers—Pieter van Singhel and Jan van Singhel. She died October 14, 1657, and was buried in the South Church.

Gerritsz Dircksz, the second son, married Josyntye van Gestel, daughter of Jan van Gestel. She died June 27, 1676. He was then living in Elandt Street, in the Resting Hart.

Dirk Gerritsz Keyser was in 1655 living in Elandt Street, in the Resting Hart. His youngest son was buried from this house, in the Wester Kerk, July 12, 1655.

Tobias Dirksz, his third son, was buried September 18, 1655, in the Wester Kerk.

His daughter, Anneken, died June 17, 1681.

TOBIAS GOVERTZ VAN DEN WYNGAERT, one of the most distinguished of the Mennonites in Holland, was born at Amsterdam in 1587, twenty-six years after the death of Menno, and fifty years after Leonhard Keyser's martyrdom; he was the author of a number of theological works, one of the four representatives of the churches of Amsterdam in the third Mennonite Confession signed at Dort 21st of April, 1632, which has remained unchanged now, for two and a half centuries; and was engaged in the ministry for over fifty years. His biography, will be found in Hermannus Schyns Geschiedenisse der Mennoniten (ed. 1743).

The engraving of which a copy appears in this biography was made about the year 1650 by A. Bloteligh obtained some years ago, by Hon. Samuel W. Pennypacker, in Holland.

The lines under the portrait are—

Tobias Govertsz van den Wyngaert, Minister of the Divine Word of the Flemish Mennonite Congregation at Amsterdam. LXXX. years old.

The old father is thus in copper pictured ;
The Vineyard which for nearly fifty years,
Spent in the service of the Church bears a fruitful harvest,

ANNO 1655.

Tegens Saturdagh, den 18 September.

W Erde U E. ter begraffenisse gebeden , met

TOBIAS DIRCKSZ.

KEYSER, Soon van *Dirck Gerritsz Keyser* Zal: Dochters-
Soon van *Tobias Govertsz van den VVijngaert.* Inde Elant-
straet, in 't Leggende Hart : 's Morgens ten acht uren pre-
cijs, als Vriendt, daer naest, in huys te komen.

Wester Kerck.

Translation: Anno 1655, on Saturday, September 18, you are invited to the funeral of Tobias Dircksz. Keyser, son of Dirck Gerritsz Keyser, late grandson of Tobias Govertsz van den Wijngaert. In Elant-street, in the Resling Hart : in the morning at 8 oclock precisely, as a friend to come in the next door house.

Burial in the Wester Kirck.

As full of good as he is snowed with silver hairs.
This man with uprightness and a venerable countenance
Teaches the unconverted souls their Christian duty.

The engraver's art shows his mortal part only ;
But his humility and unblemished life
Which wholly perfect him, and make all colors pale—
These cannot be drawn, nor be graven in metal.
The immortal part outshines mortality ;
And so he waits life's crown whene'er his days shall end.

J. Antonides.

Translated by Adrian Van Helden 1888.

Wyngaert means Vineyard.—A. V. H.

CORNELIA (GOVERTZ) KEYSER.—Our ancestor, like the founder of our State,* was of a pious Dutch mother whose spiritual influence over us yet remains; and it is from her rather than his wife the daughter of the wealthy woolen draper, our nearer mother, with her grander wardrobe, come the qualities of our race—very certainly it must be that her earlier influence as it is in most men's lives, determined him from the paths of trade with all their luxuries to the Believer's life with all its better tendencies. We may very well imagine that our mother of the house ter Eimpel, I hope I do no injustice to her stately memory, would have said to our ancestor had she heard him propose to leave his ware-house on the broad Printzen Gragt, for the narrow pathway in the German town, what another woman said at the same time ;† and so it was not until after her death, and a second marriage and death had severed these marriage ties to trade, that the promises of the founder prevailed with him, to leave Amsterdam.

ELIZABET (TER HIMPEL) KEYSER.—The Dutch women were lovely, rather than beautiful; fair in their complexions, with regular features, very quiet in manner, taller than the men, many of them. It is quite possible therefore to realize the probabilities of the appearance of this ancestor of our race, at the time of her marriage; of her dress we have a quite absolute assurance; the style was the same for all ladies of her condition, and we have of it the most minute description; our grandmother on social occasions, or calling formally upon her neighbors, wore her hair gathered close to her head; she wore a small cap with lace around it, a large plate of thin gold on each side of, and a plate of the same metal in the middle of

* Penn's mother was Margaret Jasper, the daughter of John Jasper, a merchant of Rotterdam. He certainly spoke German, and probably the Dutch language.—Seidensticker. Pepys Diary.

† Docenius of Cologne would have come with Penn to Pennsylvania, but his wife said, "Let well enough alone, here I can ride in a carriage from one house to another, there I might have to milk the cows."

the forehead; she wore heavy earrings, "ponderous" is the word used to describe them, and a necklace of the same metal. The waist of her robe was of unnatural length and rotundity; over all she wore a hat the size of a parasol, lined with red and set up, like a fan; she also wore, all the ladies then wore them, yellow slippers; this was the costume "de rigueur;" the silk of the dress was heavy and in the case of our grandmother of the best character, very probably, because our far back grandfather was its importer or manufacturer; such gold bands I have seen worn in Holland some years ago but I believe they are confined to the people of the farming districts of the northern part; then, they were worn by every one, by those in very moderate circumstances, as well as by the wealthy; they descended as heirlooms in the family, generation after generation; they were always, and those still worn there are yet, pure gold. There were probably none worn here in Germantown, the costumes while bounteous in their quantities here, were more simple in their character; besides, although they had some gold with them, we have a record that our ancestor paid some accounts in gold, it was a *very* much rarer metal here, than there. *

A M S T E R D A M.

AMSTERDAM.—The place whence our immediate ancestor came, was Amsterdam; I will describe it as it was, the year he left there for America, —a noble city truly as you will say, worthy of the greatest and best men of any age. Amsterdam, as it was first written Amstelredam—the dam or dyke of Amstel, taking its name from the river, was 9 miles around; a great canal 80 feet wide was its boundary; nine magnificent gateways of stone were its entrances—eight looking toward the land, and one, toward

---

* It was said of the women of Amsterdam by a traveller writing about the time of our ancestor's departure, that they had the conduct of the purse and managed it rarely well, and were very capable of affairs beside domestic ; that the good wife got, while the husband spent the money—but that she had this consolation that at his death she could give away half of the estate ; and he also says that they were all for making their daughters and nieces or grandchildren great fortunes, and let the boys shift for themselves, but this may have been only the talk of the traveller ; however it is to be seen in the wills of our family here in Germantown in the early times, they not only did treat their wives with the utmost care and consideration, but also showed their confidence in their ability by giving them their estates for their lives, and making them, their executors.

the sea; it was built on eighty islands, connected by between two hundred and three hundred bridges. Its streets were in concentric lines; three of them were streets of palaces, and of suitable names—the Printzen Gragt or the Prince's Canal, where our ancestor lived; the Heeren Gragt or the Gentleman's, and the Keizer's Gragt or the Emperor's Canal; each of them was 140 feet wide, street and canal together, and 3 to 4 miles long. The streets were paved with pebble laid in sand—the canal in the middle was lined with stone, the pavements were laid in black and white marble; the houses were of equal height with abundance of iron work for ornament, and silver and gilt leather of which we have an imitation in our times, hung on the walls and covered the furniture of their large and stately rooms. Rows of trees were before the doors and lamps which burned through the night, one to every two dwellings. The more notable citizens rode about in chairs and coaches for the most part placed upon sledges. In these they made their calls of ceremony, went to the playhouses or to the churches. The wealthier citizens had also coaches on wheels with horses. The city itself was a congregation of all nationalities, going to and fro continually—a moving tide of work and watchfulness; the people went about the streets, and the watchmen stood in the steeples of the churches and sounded trumpets every half hour, all night long. The houses made an irregular line of gables, roofs, and chimneys, against the sky, through which rose the turrets and towers of the greater structures of the city; among these was the old church (Oude Kerk) with its rich painted glasses and great organ, the warehouse of the East India Company the odors from whose vast stores of spices from the Indies, filled the atmosphere constantly; the new church (Nieuwe Kerk) which when a boy our ancestor had seen burned, and which he had seen rebuilt in greater splendor, with its organ chorus like human voices, and De Ruyter's monument; and last the greatest of these edifices and one of the greatest of the world's edifices—the Stadt House, which he had seen begun when a boy ten years of age and five years later occupied. The stone of which it was built was carried to Amsterdam from other countries; it was, as the whole city built on piles—the trees, or rather the forests of other countries, driven 50 feet into the clay below; of these for this building, there were 13,659; its front was 282 feet long, two-thirds of the length of one of our city's squares; it was 116 feet high, and 238 feet in depth; its cost was computed to have been fifteen millions of our dollars. In the centre of the front at the roof was a piece of sculpture 18 feet high and 28 feet long, wholly of marble in relief, representing the city under the figure of "Cybele" seated on the chair of Neptune—Lord High Admiral of the Seas, and goddesses bearing branches of the olive and palms to this mighty woman; two lions at her feet and Tritons before her sounding their horns. Over it were three statues, the centre one represented "Peace," and on one side of this statue, "Prudence," and on the other "Justice," each 12 feet high. The rear of the building had a similar ornamentation in relief and of the same size—"Commerce," a woman with the head and wings of Mercury seated before masts, sails, the rigging of vessels, and instruments of navigation; two water-gods representing the rivers Y and Amstel, and representations of Europe, Asia, Africa and America bringing the products of these countries to her feet. Over it were also three statues—the centre one was "Atlas" holding a globe of copper larger than that of Saint Peter's Dome, on one side was a statue of "Temperance," and on the other "Vigilance;" on each of the four corners of the building at the roof were four brazen eagles gilt like gold, grouped together; and above all rose a tower 41 feet high, surmounted by a ship— the old arms of Amsterdam, 157 feet from the ground; in the tower were bells, to ring out their victories over the seas; the larger one of the chime weighing seven thousand pounds and the second six thousand pounds. Within, this building was encrusted with marble, floors, walls, and pillars; and the walls again covered with the best works of the greatest painters of the world; the noblest apartment of this building, was the common meeting-room of the citizens; it was 120 feet long, 57 feet wide, and 98 feet high, with galleries and colonnades of red and white marble; on its floor were delineated the heavens and the earth, pictured in three great circles—the middle one, represented the heavens, one of the others the eastern, and the other the western hemisphere, of the earth, with all the isles, promontories, rivers, and seas, in jasper inlaid in marble; the stars were brass, inlaid in marble; each globe was 22 feet in diameter and 69 feet in circumference. Another apartment of this building was the magazine of arms, which contained sufficient to equip in four hours, twenty thousand soldiers. The offices of the great hospitals of the city were also there; and the officers of the Court of Bankruptcy whose duties were not to divide, but to preserve, insolvent estates. In the vault underneath this building lay the vast treasures of the Bank of Amsterdam; two hundred of millions or more of gold and silver bars and coins,* the representative of other hundred millions more. in credit—the greatest treasure of the world, as was believed in those centuries. The whole was the fitting monument of the country, which in everything then dominated and controlled the world; but what seems to me of far more interest than the building itself was an inscription in one of the rooms. In this room

* Sir Wm. Temple writes "in barrs of gold and silver plate and infinite bags of metal;" another authority states three hundred tons of gold.

to which I refer was a pedestal on which was seated a woman representing the city—in her right hand the rod of Mercury, in her left the new arms of the city, and on her head the imperial crown, granted to the city as its privilege to bear alone, of all the cities of the world, by the Emperor Maximilian; on this crown, an eagle with outstretched wings, and on either side the arms of the four burgomasters, under whose rule the first foundation-stone of this building, was laid. On the pedestal was this inscription in Latin, these words which will endure as long as courage and constancy endure upon this earth:

"IN 1648 THE 28TH OF OCTOBER THE UNITED PEOPLE OF THE DUTCH NETHERLANDS HAVING CARRIED ON A WAR COURAGEOUSLY WITH THE THREE PHILIPS MIGHTY KINGS OF SPAIN, BY WATER AND LAND ABOVE 80 YEARS, IN NEARLY EVERY PART OF THE WORLD, AND HAVING ESTABLISHED THE LIBERTY OF THEIR COUNTRY, AND RELIGIOUS FREEDOM, THE FIRST STONE OF THIS CITY HALL, WAS LAID.

GERMANTOWN.—To-day the Germantown road that was here a century ago, is an avenue, paved and lighted from Chestnut Hill to Laurel Street, a distance of nine miles; other avenues cross it many other miles, but the German town itself, is almost hidden in the larger recent structures for business and residence. It has become a part of the city—Philadelphia. It is a part of the Twenty-Second Ward of that city; it is Post-Office Station G in the Nation; but that day our ancestor arrived with his two boys, the younger twelve years of age, it was only an Indian pathway lined with laurel bushes; caves here and there, cellars with some shelter over them, houses as they were called, fifty altogether; one with two stories, and one mill to supply the town with flour. There were here some Huguenots, some Germans, some Holland people of whom our ancestor was one. In these houses were high-backed chairs, round tables, pewter dishes and spinning-wheels. One man's cellar, it might

tree, with its shelter of branches, was one of their meeting-houses; among the first comers, Francis Daniel Pastorius was a man of much learning, he brought books with him; our ancestor also brought books, these books among them, with their leather backs stretched over wood, fastened with brass clasps and hinges, which we have kept in our family to this hour. But it was a town then rather of trees than houses, a new Amsterdam in which the piles were all uncut and above ground; its surveyor in the first line of the patent that year our ancestor came (1688) describes it as beginning at a corner hickeree tree, and ending with a similar tree, in another place; Duy's Lane so called from a female line of our family, now Wistar Street, was its southern boundary; Keyser's Lane, a mile and a quarter in the woods further up this Indian pathway, was its northern boundary; the town was divided into fifty-five parcels of land; but it was not until the year after he came, that they were allotted among the owners, of which he was one. The population was a peculiar one, those here then and those who came here, during our ancestor's life; some of them, far-seeing people of which this Francis Daniel Pastorius, was one; he wrote the first protest against slavery here from which ultimately came the manumission of our slaves, two centuries after; it was signed by him, by the Op de Graeffs—Mennonites, and others of this Germantown emigration; there were some Mystics and Pietists, John Kelpius was one, he, also a man of much learning, waited along the Wissahickon, as so many others have done in other places, for Christ once more to reappear and reign on this earth; with his followers he died waiting there. The Quaker was sitting here in silence, when our ancestor,—separate in sect but united in spirit, came here.* The Mystic Brothers, who built their monastery which still stands on a hillside of the Wissahickon, whose pillows were logs of wood, laid on the ground, and who sought out in that roadless place, a pathway to the far and illimitable; the Brothers from Ephrata, came here sometimes, girt about their waists with ropes, barefooted or in sandals walking in silence, to the old log meeting-house which was here near where this meeting-house stands, slowly, in single file with their long beards hanging down on their breasts. Various languages were spoken here, some French, much German, and much Dutch, and contin-

---

* Barclay writes, "So closely do these views correspond with those of George Fox, that we are compelled to view him as the unconscious exponent of the doctrines and discipline of the Dutch Mennonites."

The Quaker and the Mennonite both lay the greatest stress upon inward piety and a godly humble life, considered all strife and warfare as unchristian, scrupulously abstained from taking an oath, declared against the paid ministry, exercised through their meetings a strict discipline over their members, favored silent prayer, and looked upon the established churches as unhallowed vessels of the Divine truth.— *Seidensticker.*

ued to be spoken for nearly a century after. Farther from man and nearer to God, seems to have been upon their lips and in their lives, coming to this wilderness. With these peculiar people were the simple workers, toiling in the gardens, weaving in their caves and houses, working from daylight to darkness; these had also their peculiarities, the women went about in short skirts and petticoats; we yet remember, some of us, the old grandmothers or great grandmothers, with kerchiefs snowy white, folded across their breasts, who survived down to the beginning of our passing generation. White linen was worn here and woven here, pure and spotless as the snow, making the town notable; all of these men and women worshipped together, striving to do the will of the Saviour as it is written in the Scriptures, without magistrates and without laws, and without ceremonies, without poverty, and without crime, with an earnest endeavor to conform their lives as far as it was possible to them, to the image of the Saviour on this earth. Our ancestor we have seen, was here as a minister to inculcate and enforce by his life and example the doctrine of the Mennonites, the boys were here to make themselves homes in whatever way that could be done; a wide ocean rolled between them and the warehouse on the great canal, and all their past associations. They were upon the rough hard ground as God had made it and left it here for them; there were stones to be taken from the ground, a place to be set aside for their own and their father's grave and house to be built in which he might set out the way for their salvation, these things they set about to do.

THE CAUSE OF OUR ANCESTOR'S COMING.—The immediate influence toward his coming to Germantown, I take to be the Founder's influence over the Mennonites; William Ames from 1655 to 1662 had already converted many in the Netherlands—Caton preached through the Holland cities in 1660, married Anneke Dirricks a woman of Amsterdam, and died there in 1665; Stephen Crist another of the Quakers, was there from 1663 to 1684, and married Gertrude Derricks, an Amsterdam woman. She was converted to their faith; both in Germany and in Holland the only foothold the Quakers got, was in these Mennonite congregations, the inner life—the divine essence,—the silent seeking, were cognate ideas in both congregations; in July, 1677, the Founder himself went there, he with his companions attended a meeting in Harlem, of Friends and Mennonites; Jan Roeloff, from whom Pieter Dirck Keyser bought land in Germantown, was among these; in August they held a large meeting in Amsterdam. This must have made a great impression on the Mennonites there; a common contempt for the clergy and their formularies, united the representatives of the various sects, who came to Germantown; Penn's doctrines were broad enough for Labadists, Mystics, and Mennonites. "The Founder was at that time thirty-three years of age, in the flush of manly beauty, the graces of the courtly gentleman blending with the fire of the enthusiast, the determined champion of religious liberty out of the walls of Newgate, in the free atmosphere of Holland, and full of the future of this fair province of Pennsylvania," very naturally everything yielded to his power, that had anything in it, worth yielding. Penn returned to Amsterdam on the 8th of September of the same year 1678, remained there a few days, and again returned to Amsterdam, in October. At Amsterdam, he had a public discussion with Dr. Gelenus Abrahams de Haan, a leader of the Mennonites; the first debate was on October 9, and lasted five hours; the second on the 11th, lasted as long. The influence did not end here, he wrote an account of his Province giving his terms of settlement which was published in Dutch, in Rotterdam 1681, and in German in Amsterdam; accounts by other writers followed, one in French was printed in Rotterdam the same year. Another pamphlet was written showing that plantation work was the true work of that generation; in 1684 a letter from the Founder was republished in Dutch, in Amsterdam, and passed through two editions there;* two letters in Dutch were printed at Rotterdam and a Collection de diverse pieces concernant Pennsylvania at the Hague 1684; another, descriptive of Pennsylvania in Dutch by Cornelius Bom in Rotterdam 1685; the same year another account by the Founder printed in Dutch at Amsterdam; and in 1686 another tract appeared in Dutch, at Amsterdam; the advantages therefore of the Province to rear up a family, the character of the Founder, the similarity in their religious views, and a disposition to close his days in a more entire devotion of his life to God's service were very probably the motives which determined our ancestor to make the great change. It is very certain he did not come here to better his fortune as was the case with so many of others coming here at the time; Holland was then the centre of a vast tide of human industry with every business advantage, and he himself

* Missive van William Penn Eygenaar en Gouverneur van Pennsylvania in America.

was socially and financially a man of prominence there; nor whatever the cause of his coming did he, or the Holland emigration generally, come here to escape from persecution—there was no persecution there;[*] Holland at the time of our ancestor's departure had established religious liberty, and that country was the one refuge for the oppressed of all the nationalities of Europe for conscience' sake, in the same manner and altogether as liberally, as it is here. Nor did he nor that emigration generally come here to gain political liberty, that was the possession of the Netherlands by its eighty years of a struggle without parallel in human history. Political liberty was as secure there as it is now here. The Holland emigrants brought with them civil and religious liberty as a part of the habitude of their existence—a part of themselves. They brought with them the great foundation-stones of the structure of our own liberties, industry, integrity, education, and toleration. There was only for them to gain in coming here a larger space for the future outgrowth of these advantages, they brought here; and in this respect the Dutch emigration stood on a higher plane than any other emigration here, it was the first promoter of that education, religious tolerance, and broader freedom, which this country has come at last to enjoy.[†]

---

[*] "The Mennonites, the meekest of all Christians, after suffering much bloody and heartrending persecution, were granted in the Netherlands the enjoyment of all religious and civil rights which pertained to the other citizens of the provinces."—*Barclay, Inner Life, p. 78.*

When they were in Aarenberg (1618) hindered in the free exercise of their worship, the States-General issued in their favor a mandate of toleration—and when subjected to persecution in Zurich and Berne the magistrates in Amsterdam in 1642 and the States-General in 1660 remonstrated with the Swiss authorities.—*Davies, vol. iii. p. 160, and Martyrer Spiegel.*

[†] Among the first inhabitants of Germantown were Claus, Willem and Gerard Rittenhuysen, ancestors of the great astronomer, our ancestor Dirck, Dirck, Jr., and Pieter Dirck, his sons; Cornelis Claesen, of the Mennonite church at Hamburg, Harman Casdorp, Jacob Telner, a merchant of Amsterdam, Jan Roeloff van der Werf, his son Richard van der Werf, Cornelis Siverts, a native of Friesland—Menno Simons' home, Jan and Hendrick van der Sluys, Arnold van Vossen, a Mennonite, Cornelis van der Gaegh, Jan van de Woestyne, Matthias and Isaac van Bebber, large landowners; Aret Klincken, Isaac van Sintern, great grandson of Jan de Voss, a Burgomaster at Hamishooten in Flanders, a Mennonite; Jan Luken (Lyken), Peter Hendricks, and the three brothers—Herman Op de Graeff, Dirck Op de Graeff and Abraham Op de Graeff; grandsons of Herman Op den Graeff, delegate from Crefeld to the Council at Dort 1632, born at Alde Kirk on the border of Holland and married a Dutch woman, Of these, some came in the first vessel which left Rotterdam on the 24th of July, 1683, along with some Germans, arriving in Philadelphia 8th of October, 1683: five years later in 1688, the same time in the year our ancestor arrived by way of New York and Germantown. By such as these, in the language of Prof. Seidensticker, "was opened the door, through which poured a continuous and widening stream, which created the industries and shaped the destinies of the new Province."

The first settlement of the Mennonites on the Delaware from Amsterdam was in 1662.

The Dutch name Dirck is derived from Theodoric which was a universal name, Anglo-Saxon and Visigothic, as well as Frank and German. In the "Nibelungenlied" there is a fictitious Theodric ("Theodoric of Bern"), and in history a real one, Theodoric, King of the Ostrogoths in Italy, from A. D. 475 to 527. Two saints made the name everywhere popular in the Middle Ages. It was abbrevi-

DIRCK KEYSER, THE FOUNDER OF THE FAMILY in America, was born in 1635; he was up to the time of his departure for Germantown engaged in the manufacture and sale of all kinds of silk and silk wares, on Printzen Graght opposite Reestraat in Amsterdam. His marriage with his first wife, Elizabet ter Himpel is recorded with the formalities belonging to a man of prominence; the banns were published at Amsterdam, in all the churches, and on the 22d of November, 1668, the marriage formally solemnized in the church at Buyckesloot, in the presence of the Lord and congregation. She died Monday, the 12th of May, 1681, aged forty-three years six months. By this marriage he had two sons Dirck, and Pieter Dirck Keyser; and one daughter Elizabet, who died June 23, 1681. He married a second time, Johanna Harperts Snoeck also in the church at Buyckesloot on the 22d of November, 1682. She lived only four years, and on Thursday, the 29th of August, 1686, was buried from his residence on the Printzen Graght in the Wester Kerk, in the thirty-eighth year of her age. By this marriage he had a daughter Johanna and one Cornelia who died 22 Oct. 1686. Two years after, in 1688, he emigrated with his little motherless family from Amsterdam, then being fifty-three years of age. He brought with him his sons, Pieter Dirck, and Dirck by the first wife; and his daughter Johanna by his second wife, the survivors of the family of five children. They arrived in New York in the fall of the year 1688; his daughter Johanna, a little girl five years old, died on their way to Germantown in September that year. He could not remember the day she was buried, but the place was on a plantation named Congenaue between that city and Philadelphia. He was a man of most excellent scholarship, of exceptional refinement and of great determination and endurance—qualities, some of which, as we have seen, were notably shown by the first bearers of our surname, of whom we have knowledge. He invested in land in Germantown, first a purchase from Cornelius Cieuviers on the 9th March, 1688, prior to his

ated and altered in English into Derrick; in French into Didier and Thierry; in Italian into Dieterico; in German into Diedrich and in Dutch into Dirck or Dirk. The Dutch still use it in its abbreviated form. The first Count of Holland who reigned from A. D. 900 to 925 was called Dirck and six of his successors bore that name. It means "People's Ruler." Peter comes from the Greek "Petros" (a stone) or "Petra" (a rock).

"Thou art Petros, and on this Petra I will build my church."—*A. Van Helden.*

coming here, twenty-five acres, and then fifty acres from Strieper in April 1689, and again twenty-five acres on the 12th September, 1689, from Herman up de Graff, attorney for Dirck Sipman.   He was one of the original possessors who cast lots April 4, 1689, and drew lot 22,* fifty acres as originally located October 29, 1687.   It lay on the east side of the Main Street toward the Bristol Turnpike.   He was naturalized March 7, 1691, taking the oath of allegiance to the British government and again by act of Assembly 1708.†   He was engaged in the ministration of the Gospel until his death, a venerated father of the family, and beloved follower of the Saviour.

We have been able to make certain the fact that he was exercising the duties of the ministry from 1708 to 1714 here in the old log meeting house —the First Mennonite Church of Germantown—and the first in the Province; the following record of a marriage is in the old family Bible of Jacob Kolp, "Married, Jacob Kolb and Sarah Van Sintern May 2nd 1710 by Dirck Keyser in the presence of the full congregation in the log meeting house in Germantown."   He was among the first promoters of the first school in Germantown—and its continuous supporter, his first subscription was made to it December 27, 1702.

He lived until the 30th of November, 1714, and died here aged seventy-nine years.   He carefully preserved the records of the marriages and deaths in his immediate family on the male and female sides and they are yet in the family's possession.   Among his effects was a copper plate which contains the arms of Holland, his monogram, place of business, the arms of the family, with silkworms and skeins of silk, which was used in his business, it has been an object of much interest to the family and is now in the possession of Hannah Nice, its oldest living descendant now (1889) ninety-four

* In the first tax-list for Philadelphia County passed in 1693 Dirck Keyser appears in the list of taxables of Germantown; this, then Borough contributed in all £12 14 sh., that for the whole county being £314 12 sh. 9 p.   The real-estate owners paid a penny on the pound, servants out of servitude for six months paid six shillings a head; out of the £12 14 sh., the real-estate owners paid £9 8 sh.; the servants £3 6 sh., and in fact more of the tax in proportion than two-thirds of the real-estate owners. The Proprietor and his Deputies, the largest of the real-estate owners, were let off altogether; all persons with numerous families and an estate of less value, beyond their indebtedness, than thirty pounds, also paid no taxes; as our ancestor had no numerous family, and his estate was worth more than thirty pounds, he paid his taxes along with the other more or less fortunate owners; the holdings of real estate at that time had an average of fifty pounds each, and were divided among forty holders, liable to taxes; Dirck Keyser's assessment was on sixty pounds.

† 3 mo. 7, 1691, Thomas Loyd Deputy-Governor granted naturalization to sixty-four of the first settlers of Germantown being foreigners, and so not freemen according to the law of England, for the better securing of their estates, real and personal—Francis Daniel Pastorius, Dirck and Pieter Dirck Keyser, Andreas Souplis, Gerhart Levering and Wigard Levering, with others, being High and Low German and inhabitants and owners of land, in Germantown.   Recorded Rolls office, Philada., Book A, page 275.

years of age; it was engraved over two hundred years ago, and is in perfect preservation. He was, if we may study his portraiture backward
from the general characteristics of the family, a tall man, erect, with

A REPRODUCTION FROM THE COPPER PLATE.

The plate contains: above an engraving of the arms of Amsterdam with the words
in scroll "Amsterdam dyed silk." Below the arms of the family, and his monogram
4 D DK, meaning Dirck Keyser the fourth generation from Dirck Keyser. The whole is
illuminated with the devices of his trade, cocoons, skeins of silk, and silkworms. The
general description designates his business place; above the words "in the Emperor" and
below the words "Dirck Keyser makes and sells all kinds of silk and silk goods lives on
the Printz Graght (Canal) opposite Ree (Deer) street at Amsterdam."

blue eyes and dark hair; these are probabilities. His dress was in the
style of the time, of which there are very numerous representations.*

* Traditionally, a coat he wore sometimes after his coming here, was of silk which for a long time
was a source of disquiet to some of his neighbors, which he lived down, and very probably the coat also.
Daniel K. Cassel, the author of the late history of the Mennonites says as to this coat, that some of the
brethren especially those at Skippack, complained of him, as to his extravagance and worldliness and
a committee was appointed to call upon him in relation to it, when the committee called he was working
in his garden, as they approached him he wiped his hands upon his coat, before extending to them the
grasp of a fraternal recognition, so showing them that he valued it no more than any other, and they
concluded to say no more about it.

He was buried here, the first notable burial in this ground in the midst of his congregation.

The signature of Dirck Keyser, Jr.

I. DIRCK KEYSER[3], JR.—His son Dirck, Jr., there being no silk to be made, or even worn if made, in those times, went back to a lower branch of his grandfather's occupation, and became a cordwainer. He married Deborah ———, who survived him. He settled at Manahatawny, in the County and now City of Philadelphia, survived his father only one year and died (probably in January) 1715. He signed his name to his will, Dirick Keyser, Junior. This will, the first of which we have mention in the family is dated one year before his death and as it exhibits the devotional spirit in which the family came hither, and remained, I will quote a portion in the words in which it is written: "In the name of God, Amen. The 16th day of Febryary, in the year of our Lord, seventeen hundred and fourteen. I, Dirick Keyser, Junior, of Manahatawny, in ye County of Philadelphia, cordwainer, being very sick and weak, in body, but of perfect mind and memory, thanks be to God therefore, calling to mind the mortality of my body and knowing that it is appointed for all men to die, do make and ordain this my last will and testament. That is to say, principally and first, that I recommend my soul into the hands of him that gave it, and for my body I recommend it to ye earth to be buried in a Christian like and decent manner at ye discretion of my executors, nothing doubting, but at the general resurrection, I shall receive the same again by ye mighty power of God."

The signature of Peter Dirck Keyser—the common ancestor of the family here.

PIETER DIRCK KEYSER[3].—Pieter Dirck Keyser the then surviving child of our first ancestor here, and the ancestor of the whole family now living, was born in Amsterdam, November 25th, 1676, and was twelve years of age on his arrival. He married when twenty-four years of age,

3

Margaret Souplis (Sieplie, afterward written), daughter of Andreas Souplis, a Burgher of New York, and lived twenty-four years thereafter; he died, leaving a widow and numerous family.* The first of these and the first of the family born in America, was a son Dirck Keyser, named after his grandfather and his uncle. He married Alice Neus. The second, Andries named after (Andreas) Keyser, his grandfather and his uncle, Andreas Souplis, married Hannah ——. The third, Pieter Dirck Keyser, named after himself, married Susanna Pennebacker. The fourth, Jacob Keyser, named after his uncle, Jacob Souplis, that is to say Jacob Keyser, married Margaret ——. The fifth, named after a cousin or nephew, Johannes Keyser. The sixth, named after a cousin or nephew, Abraham Keyser. The seventh, Elizabeth Keyser, after his mother, and her grandmother; married Peter Pennebacker. The eighth child, named after her grandmother and aunt, Anneke Keyser; married John Pennebacker. Two brothers, Peter and John Pennebacker, marrying these two sisters, of our family. His ninth child, a daughter, named after her aunt, Kathelina (Cateleynte); married Ludovick Horning. His tenth, Johannes Keyser, after his the son's uncle and deceased brother, married Barbara Funk. His eleventh child Margareth (Margaret) after her mother. She married Cornelius Conrads of Cresheim. Of these children Johannes the first died 23 Sept., 1711, and Abraham 30 Dec., 1717. From one or another of the remaining nine children living at the time of his death all the descendants of Dirck Keyser, the first emigrant, either in the male or female lines, have their origin. The will of Pieter Dirck Keyser for its kind consideration for his wife's mother and the confidence it shows in his wife's future care of his children,' merits mention here. He died in 1724, 12th of September; and his will devises and bequeaths his whole estate † to his wife during her life if she remains his

* In his father's Bible which descended to him, he made the following entry of his marriage (in the Dutch language).

"A°. 1700, Sep. 4. I was married to Margaret Souplis aged 18 years, the Lord grant us his blessing and all which will be necessary in this world and in the world to come and we will praise his holy name now and forever. Amen. PIETER DIRCK KEYSER."

† Peter Dirck Keyser inherited from his father the ground he bought of Cornelius Cicuvers (Sewers) —twenty-five acres and that he bought from Dirk Sipman—twenty-five acres—he also purchased during his life other estate from Cornelius Clausen; Claas Berents 31 May, 1705, three acres; and from Paul Engleson 20 May, 1717, fifty acres, both tracts in Germantown. He bought also of John Roelofs van den Werfe Sept. 4, 1716, one hundred acres on the Skippack, Co. of Philada. The prices he paid for the conveyancing of the last lots which was done by Francis Daniel Pastorius and the charge for which appears in his Debit and Credit Book, p. 371, were : John Roelofs' deed 24 Jan., 1716, £7, Paul Engle's deeds, each £7.

John Roelofs was a son of Berend Roelofs a Mennonite preacher in Hamburg who in 1659 joined the Society of the Friends ; he was agent for Penn for the sale of Pennsylvania lands.—*Seidensticker.*

widow, and if not then provides for his children, giving her still a large share of his estate. He wills further then, that his wife shall take all possible care of his old mother-in-law, Elizabeth; if she be helpless or in want of some attendance, that then his wife if she shall be living shall assist her, with all necessaries for her livelihood, and if his said wife shall die before his said mother-in-law, that then his executors shall take the same care for his mother-in-law; that she should be so taken care of and maintained out of his estate. He was naturalized with his father 7th of March, 1691, and subsequently by act of Assembly 1708. He was a subscriber to the Pastorius school on the 19th May, 1708, £10.

One of the last acts of his life was to join in a subscription to build the front wall of the upper Germantown burial ground which was begun May, 1724, the year in which he died. He was a member of the Mennonite church when it was first built of logs, in 1708, and was very probably one of its builders.

There is in the Scriptures and in other ancient tomes a peculiar use and recurrence of the number seven and its multiples, with Peter Dirck Keyser the number four and its multiples were a part of his fatalities; he was twenty-four years of age when he married, he lived twenty-four years after his marriage, he was married on the 4th of September, he died on the 12th of September, the year of his birth was 1676, a multiple of four, and he died in 1724.

OUR FEMALE LINE.—It was our good-fortune and the cause of the survival of our qualities in a large measure, that there were intermarriages in our family with families of similar qualities, occurring and recurring, in the male and female line—the enduring stock of the Nices, the Leverings, the Pennypackers, the Conards, and the Foxes, Lynds, Knorrs, having very generally the same or very like characteristics of the Dutch and Teutonic races have kept our line whole and strong to this hour; it is with man as with the lower orders of creation, it is only with intermixture within like stocks that you can perpetuate qualities; too close you will injure, but outside of these lines, you will destroy. The German race endures, the most healthful and vigorous of all existing races cognate with ours because of its intermarriage with the German race. The families with which the Keysers intermarried are the Goverts family, Van Gestel, Van Singhel, Vortgens, Jacobs and ter Himpels in Holland; and in this country, the Souplis, de Neus (Nice), Wood, Rinter, Conrad, Levering, Duy, Ottinger, Knorr, Weaver, Lynd, Heislers, Hammer, Reese, Leibert, Clemens, Lehman, Backus, Eyre, Canedo, Gorgas, Fox, Engle, Snyder, Shearer, Baker, Henderson, Marselis, Magargee, Shaw, Pryor, Morris, King, Miller, Kirk, Thomas, Polk, Chenoweth, Hussey,

Fort, Wilson, Langstroth, Geyer, Steiner, Stouffer, Wyman, French, Makay, Inglis, Drayton, Boyd, Brunner, Davis, notices of these will appear in the genealogy.

THE SHEARER line intermarried with the Nices with whom the Keysers also intermarried; the Shearer family was, through the intercession of the States-General of the Netherlands, taken from the prison in Berne and sent with others to Holland under guard to be sent to Pennsylvania; they were Anabaptists; sixty of them lay in the winter of 1710, in that prison with their feet fast in iron shackles; they were twenty days on the Rhine, going to Minequen in great misery; the sick and old had been put off the vessel at Mannheim; they were cared for by the pastor at Minequen; Laurens Hendricks wrote in a letter Apr. 9, 1710, how they parted from them there, with weeping eyes and swelling hearts, separating with the kiss of peace; they were a rugged people and could endure great hardships; they wore long and unshaven beards, disordered clothing, great shoes, which were heavily hammered with iron and large nails; they were very zealous to serve God, with prayer and reading the Scriptures; very innocent in all their doings, as lambs and doves. They had lived far from cities and had little intercourse with other men; a number of them left Rotterdam March 20, 1717; some went to Lancaster County; 1727 there was a further emigration of other families from the same place; the family allied with our line settled in Moreland township, now part of Philadelphia. One of the grandsons of the first emigrant intermarried in the Levering family, and the daughter of another grandson in the Keyser family, they were members of the old Pennepack meeting; the most notable man of the family, was Jacob Shearer. (See *History of Moreland and Byberry*.)

THE CUNARDS.—Thones Kunders the ancestor of the Cunard and Conrad line of our family was one of the Burgesses, Corporators of Germantown. In his house in 1683 the first Mennonite meetings were held in Germantown.

THE NICES.—Jan Neus—Jan de Neus—John of Neus—a Holland town ancestor of the Baker and other lines of the family was a Mennonite and a silver-smith, some of his work is yet in the family, he was a member of the first Mennonite Church as was also Hans Nice (de Neus); one of the family was a printer in Amsterdam in 1686.

THE ENGLES.—Paul Engle's name—ancestor of the Engle line is on the oldest marked stone, in the Mennonite ground, on the Skippack, 1723. Jan Neus and Paul Engle were made citizens in 1698; Jan Neus received for the Mennonites the deed for three square perches of ground 1702–3, February 10th, from Arnold Van Fossen on which the log meeting-house was built in 1708, which preceded the present meeting-house in which we assemble; after its disuse as a meeting-house it was used as a school-house. Cornelius Engle and Teen his wife worshipped in the present meeting-house 1770–75.

THE FOXES.—Justus Fox ancestor of the Fox line was one of the early lot holders, on the Main Street Germantown, one of the first board of Trustees of the first Dunkard Church with Peter and Michael Keyser and others—in 1784—and one of the purchasers of the lot to enlarge the burial ground in 1804 with Peter and Michael Keyser and other trustees.

THE LEVERINGS are the descendants of "Rosier Levering, who probably left France during some of the religious persecutions which visited the Waldenses and Huguenots;" he married *circa* 1648 Elizabeth van de Walle of the city of Wesel in Westphalia, and left two children, Wigard and Gerhard Levering. Wigard married Magdalena Böker, a Dutch woman of Leyden. He lived in Gamen, and afterward in Mulheim. He left Holland and emigrated to Germantown with four children prior to August, 1685.

His brother Gerhard came about the same time. His granddaughter Hannah married (32) 'Peter Keyser', and was the mother of Peter Keyser[6], the preacher; the Levering connection with our family appears very fully in the genealogy of that family written by Horatio Gates Jones.

THE KNORRS are descended from John George Knorr. His son Matthias left a family of eleven children. Matthias the third son married Molly Keyser[6], the daughter (x) 'of Derick Keyser[5] and Rachel Ottinger. Molly Keyser was a woman of great energy and decision of character, very tall, with very small hands and feet, buoyant in spirits, fond of singing and dancing. Notwithstanding her height (she enjoys the distinction of being the tallest of our ancestral mothers, six feet high), she was a very graceful woman. The Ottinger stone house, still standing in Montgomery County, has the date 1713, with a pot of tulips in bloom cut in a large stone on its front, and the initials of their names.

Mary Slingluff[7] named after her mother is the immediate ancestor of the Slingluff line of this family, and is now living in her eightieth year.

John Keyser Knorr[7], the most distinguished man in the family bearing the name, was a graduate of the University of Pennsylvania and of the Jefferson Medical College. I have this written of him by a member of the family: "He was almost worshipped by the poor for his skill in his profession and his consideration of their condition;'' he was called "the Beloved Physician.'' He was one of the advocates for the consolidation of the city, and was one among the members of the family in the Councils of the city at that time to whom it owes very much in the reorganization of its Districts into one Municipality. In the Councils at this time were also those well remembered influential men Charles Magarge and Dr. Isaac N. Marselis, both connected with this family line, the latter a descendant of the Rosa, Janse and Vrooman families of the first Dutch emigration to New York. The Knorr family were Mennonites; Jacob, Hannah his wife and Susanna Knorr were members of the meeting in 1770, worshipping in this house—Dr. Knorr left representatives in his line in the profession—Nathan Keyser Knorr, a graduate of the University of Pennsylvania—Dr. Thos. Passmore, Dr. Joseph Berens, Dr. John Keyser Knorr.

THE PENNYPACKERS are descendants of Hendrick Pannebecker, who came to Germantown prior to 1699. The family are of Dutch origin. He was a man of liberal education, speaking and writing in Dutch, German and English—a fine penman, the first surveyor of this origin in the Province. He was among the largest land-owners here; his holding was three thousand four hundred and sixty-two acres. He died in 1754, aged eighty years, leaving eight children.

His third son, Peter, married (23) ⁷Elizabeth Keyser¹, from whom descended the Pennebakers of Montgomery, many of the Pennypackers of Montgomery and Chester, the Pennabackers of Lancaster and the Pannebakers of Juniata County.

His fourth son John married (21) ⁸Anneke Keyser¹; she lived to be ninety years of age, having as her descendants the Pennybackers, Samuels and Byrds of Virginia and many of the Pennypackers of Chester County. Susanna, one of the daughters married (19) ³Peter Dirk Keyser¹ of Worcester.

THE FUNK FAMILY LINE.—Heinrich Funk settled in Montgomery Co. in 1719. He was a minister, an author of high reputation, and long a Bishop of the Franconia Congregations. The family have exerted down to the present time a greater influence than any other for the Mennonites in America. Jacob Funk, Sr., his nephew, bought land of Jacob Keyser in 1774 and connected himself with this meeting and was its minister from 1774 to 1816—forty-two years. Christopher Funk his brother settled in Germantown in 1726. He had one son, Henry, and five daughters. Their Homestead, with fifty acres of ground, adjoined the Friends' meeting-house and Main Street. (26) ¹⁰Johannes Keyser⁴ married Barbara, one of the

daughters, and bought the Homestead of his brother-in-law, Henry Funk, for their residence (May 20, 1750). From her the line of the tenth child of our ancestor here descends. They were a long-lived family, literary, and of great religious devotion.

THE WORK OF THE FAMILY HERE.

EDUCATION.—Among the first things that were done by the family in Germantown after its settlement here was to promote the cause of education, and for their continuance in this work, the family have been notable to the present time; to the first school in Germantown, the first in the Province with a teacher conversant with the Classics (Francis Daniel Pastorius), our ancestor as I have already said was a contributor ; his first subscription being made Dec. 17, 1702. His son Pieter Dirck Keyser[3] * followed him commencing May 19, 1708, with a subscription to the school of ten pounds, and Jacob Keyser[4], one of his sons followed him, and so on down to the present time. And that sense they have shown of the value of education was their Holland inheritance. There were at the time of our ancestor's leaving five Universities in the United Provinces all instituted after the Reformation and all state institutions ; Leyden in 1575,† Utrecht, 1636; Franeker in Friesland, 1584; Groninghen in 1614; Harderwick, 1648, formerly a monastery ; each seminary had four divinity professors, as many of physic, two or three of law, history, *belles-lettres*, languages, eloquence, mathematics, philosophy, Greek and Roman antiquities, Hebrew and Oriental languages ; Latin was the basic language of their studies, and French and German professors were in all the universities. The professors were paid either by the state, or by the magistrates ; it was a picturesque sight to see the students in the streets, in loose gowns, with swords on, perukes, hats, brown slippers, and a book or two under their arms. The nobility and princes of Europe were educated here, and it was observed that the influence of the population on the strangers was very great ; the students were remarkable for frugality in expense, order, a composed behavior, attention to studies, and assiduity in all things ; no oaths were imposed on them ; all sects sent their children there. Besides the universities, there were academies in most of the cities of the Netherlands, in Amsterdam a very noble one in a house converted to this use from the monastery of St. Agnes in 1631.

* The figures following the family names denote the generation to which they belong, beginning with the father of Dirk Keyser (Dirk Gerritz Keyser) in Amsterdam as No. 1 in the line and Dirk Keyser, our ancestor in this country, being 2 and his son 3, or the third generation, and so down.

† This university now owns real estate (1889) in value $8,000,000, and is the richest institution of learning in the world.

From the Holland printing presses was first given to the world the literature of modern Europe, the literature of France and its philosophic schools—education begins in England with Erasmus—cheap literature which is the boast of this country began there—the art of printing was brought by its great navigators from India where it has its origin, and the city of Haarlem claimed that Tully's *Offices* was the first printed book in Europe ; it was in the library there in our ancestor's time, and a statue erected to Laurens Coster its printer with this inscription : "Memoriæ Sacrum Typographia Ars artium optima Conservatrix. Hic primum inventa Circa Annum—MCCCCXL.;" the book itself was kept in the town house in a silver case wrapped up in silk. The Dutch were beyond any question the best letter founders and best printers of Europe, and he who possesses an Elsevir, possesses a Stradivarius in the printer's art. The boldest thinkers, the founders of modern rationalism, as well as the restorers of primitive Christianity, were born, lived and died there—the English language itself has one of its numerous sources there.

The world's triumvirate of learning in their century were, Erasmus of Rotterdam—Lux in Tenebris; Grotius of Delft—Noblissimus Amplissimusque; and Boerhaave of Leyden—Simplex Sigillum Veri.

In Philadelphia two centuries later (1888) the best result in this line of education is our common-school system, for the whole population ; it embraces a High School for males, a Girls' Normal School, a Manual Training School, and Industrial Art School, Grammar, Secondary and Primary Schools and Kindergarten ; the city is divided for school purposes into thirty-one sections. There is also a system of night-schools, there is adequate provision made for both sexes and colors; they are strictly non-sectarian ; there are 460 buildings used for these schools ; 2425 teachers, and 110,258 pupils, with fifty-three night-schools occupying some of the same buildings and having 16,079 registered pupils with an average attendance of 10,361 and 341 teachers ; the annual cost of maintenance of the whole system is $2,000,000, of which $1,360,000 is (1888) paid in teachers' salaries, the average cost to the city being for each pupil $17.60. In the High School Latin and German languages are taught, and the Girls' Normal School educates in cookery, physiology, sewing, drawing, music, elocution, mathematics. Of the schools outside of this system, there are besides, the Divinity School of the Protestant Episcopal Church; a school for the education of the blind, and one for deaf-mutes, supported in part by the State, and both large institutions ; the Academy of the Protestant Episcopal Church ; of the Friends to instruct colored persons; the Friends' school; the Friends' Association for the instruction of poor children; two business colleges, with an attendance each of over

one thousand; a Friends' institute. The George, also a Friends' institute; the Law Academy; the Lutheran Theological Seminary; the Hebrew Educational Society; the Baptist Educational Society; the School of Design for Women; the Polytechnic College; 20 Medical colleges; the Wagner Free Institute of Science, the Academy of Natural Science, the Academy of Fine Arts, the Woman's Medical College; the Spring Garden Institute; the Northern School for Soldiers and Sailors' Orphans; besides a very large number of private schools and academies. The University is the chief institution of learning in the State with 169 Professors in the several departments, and 1222 students (1888-9). Its library, which is an official depository of the government for later publications, contains 140,000 pamphlets and bound volumes; it admits annually under an agreement with the city about twenty-five graduates of the High School to free scholarships. There are four historical societies and 30 public libraries, and the Young Men's Christian Association. Both in law and medicine, Philadelphia has maintained the first place in the country; in natural sciences has also the first institution;* in engineering has also been the foremost; the great national and municipal roads of the country have been for the most part the enterprises of her citizens. The part which the family have taken in the founding and direction of any of these institutions, and those from which they have received their education will appear in the genealogy. I may mention here the work of some names best known in the family.

After ([3]) [1]Dirck Keyser's[2] contribution to the Francis Daniel Pastorius School, the first school in Germantown, and ([12]) [3]Pieter Dirck Keyser's[3] contributions to the same school, ([20]) [1]Jacob Keyser[4], the grandson, ap-

* Of all this large work of education, the beginning not only for the province of Pennsylvania but for the whole nation, is with the emigration to Germantown. The Hollander William Rittinghuysen built on Paper Mill Run, near this German town, the first paper mill in America. Christopher Saur printed here the first Bible, English or German, in America—its third edition at the opening of the Revolution. In 1748 the *Martyr's Mirror* was printed in Ephrata, and was the greatest work in literature till that time in America. These immigrants were the first importers of books and printers of newspapers. The most highly educated man of the time was Francis Daniel Pastorius, a citizen of this German town, learned in the law, and using either in his writings or conversation, the Greek, Latin, German, French, Dutch, English and Italian languages. In 1712 the Mennonites had their Confession of Faith (reprinted in this volume) printed in English in Amsterdam in 1712, and reprinted by Andrew Bradford on paper made in Germantown in 1727. The study of astronomy in America begins also with David Rittenhouse, a descendant of that Ruttinghuysen of this town, *inheriting the knowledge* also from Holland, where the telescope was invented. And, as Haarlem claims the invention of printing, so without dispute the first types made in America were made (the moulds forged by Fleckenstein on an anvil) in this German town; and the first essay written and published in America on the subject of school tuition was printed in this same German town in 1770; it promulged the same views as to the disuse of force in tuition (solitary ones outside of the Mennonites of this German town at that time), which are now the fortunate property of the common schools of Pennsylvania, and of school instruction generally.

pears as one of the contributors to the fund to build the Germantown Academy, and one of the first managers of that school, which in its second century of existence has (1888) the highest character as a preparatory school for colleges and universities; and is one of the largest of these schools in the country ; many of the family, among them Samuel Stouffer Keyser[7], were educated there.

(19) [3]Peter Keyser[1] was one of the trustees of the first school of Worcester township (Montgomery Co.), the first school organized to teach the Dutch and English languages in the Province, and admitting children of all denominations.*

John Penebacker a yeoman of Providence, who married (21) [8]Anneke Keyser[1] in 1754, united with several other persons in a petition to the society for the education of Germans asking for the establishment of a school in the Lutheran House in Providence.

John Keyser was a contributor to the fund to build the Concord school, and was a trustee of that school in 1784-5 and from 1791 to 1799.

Jacob Keyser[6] was the first Auditor of its school board after its organization, was elected a trustee in 1805; in 1820 was appointed treasurer and remained so until 1838.

Rev. Peter Keyser[6] was one of the early advocates of and a director of the Public schools when the Common-school system was first adopted by the State. I notice under this head also that Margaret Keyser[7] was one of the first subscribers to the newspapers of Germantown in her time.

Isaac Samuels Pennybacker[7] (Anneke's great-grandson) was one of the regents of the Smithsonian Institution.

James Edmund Pennybacker in 1873 was superintendent of the Public Schools at Franklin, Pendleton Co., W. Va.; he was in 1875 editor of the Pendleton *Daily News*.

Samuel Keyser in 1834 took his father's place as trustee of the Concord Academy.

* Oct. 6, 1739, Henry Rittenhouse granted to Peter Keyser, *et al.*, trustees, " two lots of ground in Worcester township, Phila. Co., for the Dutch Anabaptist Society for a place of worship and burying-ground for their dead, and also for a school-house to teach the children of the said Anabaptists, *and others without exception* living in the neighborhood at a convenient and reasonable distance from the same ; an English school to be first taught in the said house for six months, and then a Dutch school for two years ; then an English school for two years, and so on in rotation for ever, unless the trustees shall judge it for the good of the neighborhood to order otherwise in future time." A deed of confirmation, after the erection of " the meeting-house," to the said Peter Keyser and George Baker, son of a former trustee, *et al.*, 8 Apr., 1771, recites that as " three of the former trustees were not of the Anabaptist persuasion, yet it is nevertheless agreed that their posterity may, from time to time, bring any godly Protestant minister into the meeting-house to preach at burials or other times, so as not to interfere with the meeting days of the Anabaptists." D. B. I., vol. 13, p. 119.

W. S. Baker

Susan Knorr[7] was a teacher in Germantown and taught the children of two successive generations.

Daniel L. Keyser was a member of the board of trustees of the Concord Academy in 1865 succeeding his father as his father had succeeded his, as the treasurer of the Board in 1865; he was also long identified with the Public Schools of the Ward where he lived. The last school-house built in (22d Sec.) Germantown under this system bears his honored name.

Julia A. Orum is a teacher of elocution in Philadelphia, the founder of a school of the science of voice culture. Thomas S. Keyser is an editor in Philadelphia. Mrs. S. K. Savage is remembered for her work in the night school for boys and girls at Harrowgate. Peter Dirck Keyser, M. D., was a director of the Public Schools 1859–60–65, is a trustee of Delaware College since 1880, and Professor of Ophthalmology in Medico-Chirurgical College. Romaine Keyser has been a trustee of the Concord School 1885 to 1887 and Secretary of the board, being the present representative in the board of our family, in whose hands it has remained in unbroken succession for over a century.

Roland S. Keyser is (1888) a teacher in Schoharie Co., N. Y., and an Alumnus of the Syracuse University.

Linneus Keyser is 1888 in Wilmington, Vt., editor of the Deerfield Valley *Times.*

Matilda Henderson, born 1803 in Phila., and a daughter of Charles Keyser, "The Teacher," was for fifty-two years connected with the Soulé school, Murfreesboro', Tenn., from its commencement until her death. She was an educator of the young for three generations—a woman of great capacity, energy and faithfulness. Wm. S. Baker[7] is a member of the Council of the Historical Society of Penna., of the American Philosophical Society, of the Board of Directors of the Athenæum of Philadelphia, member of the Numismatic and Antiquarian Society, and corresponding member of the American Numismatic and Archæological Society of New York.

William Keyser[5] of Baltimore, was an active member of the Mercantile Library of that city, and a director for several years; he is now a trustee of the Pratt Free Library, and the McDonough Free School, which have together endowments of two and a quarter million dollars.

Charles Keyser[6] was "The Teacher" of Philadelphia, with a great reputation for general scholarship, and "The Penman" of the city, *par excellence.*

He was a classic scholar as well as versed in modern languages. He gave instruction in German and English, the Latin and Greek classics, and higher mathematics. He was engaged in this work from 1793 to 1842, nearly half a century. Of his writings many books yet remain.

ART WORK IN THE FAMILY.—A characteristic of the family has been its love of art work with the needle, embroidery, painting and in penman-ship. Our ancestor wrote a strong artistic signature. Mr. Peter A. Keyser was a remarkable penman. Charles Keyser, "The Teacher," was for work with the pen by far the best in his time in Philadelphia. His sister Mary also a teacher was as admirable a penman and engrossed the resolutions of the City of Philadelphia in 1834 on the occasion of Lafayette's death. His brother, Ezra, was scarcely less notable in Texas, where he lived, for the elegance of his pen-work. Joseph Keyser[6] was a man of the most refined artistic taste and extreme excellence in this work with the pen. Benjamin Keyser Fox[7], pupil of C. G. Childs, was an engraver. Cornelius C. Widdis[8] is an accomplished penman. John A. Inglis[8] inherits in a remarkable degree the same artistic taste. In the hand of William H. Fry* the pen of our family transcribed messages in two administrations—the most import-ant in our government. Out of 17,000 applicants for a clerkship in the Treasury Department in 1861 his extraordinary facility with the pen gained him immediately on the filing of his application a place which he filled through the latter part of Lincoln's and the whole of Johnson's administra-tions. Silvester Keyser showed this taste in his love of flowers; he kept extensive hot-houses blooming like an oasis in the wilderness of his indif-ference to the conventionalities of his surroundings. William Keyser[8] of Baltimore was one of the managers of the Maryland Institute and School of Design; John Fox, an artist; Algernon S. Keyser, grandson of John Keyser, amateur inlayer of woods. Charles S. Keyser[7] has been a member of the Academy of Fine Arts from 1856, and after its reorganization, from 1884, was also one of the reorganizers of the Artists' Fund Society of Phila-delphia, and author of the plan through which the statuary commemorative of the Revolution was erected in the Centennial Grounds, Philadelphia, in 1876. William S. Baker[7] is Vice-President of the Academy of the Fine Arts and a member of the Board since 1876, and of the Board of the Phila-delphia School of Design for Women from 1874 to 1886.†

---

* [1]William H. Fry[9] was clerk in the loan division of the Treasury Department from 1861, one of the signers of the first demand notes, and the coupons of the 5-20 bonds; and all the messages sent to Congress in the latter part of Lincoln's, all of Johnson's, and the first year of Grant's administration, were transmitted in his handwriting. He was disbursing agent of the Government under the act of July 23, 1866, and clerk of pardons in the Executive Department.

† His works are an essay on the origin and antiquity of engraving (Philadelphia, 1872; Boston, 1875); American Engravers and their Works (1875); William Sharp, Engraver, and his Works (1875); and engraved portraits of Washington (1880), medallic portraits of Washington (1885), character portraits of Washington (1887), Bibliotheca Washingtoniana, a list of the biographies of George Washington.

Miller Bullard

This art taste comes, along with the rest, as a Holland inheritance. Flowers were eagerly sought for of all varieties—and tulips were a mania at one time in which great fortunes were made and lost on a single flower. Painting reached its highest possibilities; engraving, very great excellence, in Holland, and art-works of high character were a common property in that country. There was not an ordinary Burgher's house that was not plentifully furnished with such pictures as would adorn the houses of the noblemen of other countries; flowers and fruits, and ships and storms, night-pieces and buildings; in the spin-house as well as in the Stadt-house were valuable paintings. Their books were illustrated with admirable engravings, many books printed merely to illustrate engravings, and a great wealth of art was in the dissenting churches; curious books fairly written and flourished and adorned with golden letters; there was, in fact, no such country to train the eye by the constant exhibition of the best works of the engraver or the painter, as Holland in our ancestor's time. They possessed great advantages over ourselves in this matter. We must remember John of Bruges, was the inventor of oil painting, and all the pictures in oil of all the galleries of the world, owe their existence to him. Our ancestor was a young man when Paul Potter—also a young man—died there; Rembrandt was his contemporary, and our ancestor it may be, as the city very generally followed what was mortal of him, who was very probably Art's highest name, from his humble home in the Rozengraght, to his last resting-place in the Wester Church, where so many of our family were buried.

TRADES AND OCCUPATIONS.—I find in one line of the family Peter Keyser[6], the preacher, Elhanan W. Keyser, Peter A. Keyser, Nathan L. Keyser[7], John Keyser, Silvester Keyser, George Fox Keyser and Francis Keyser were dealers in lumber; and there was one marriage in this line into a family of notable shipbuilders, the Eyre family; the lumber business beginning with the family in the third generation, and continuing down to the present time; Peter[8] and Peter A. Keyser were engaged in it for 70 years, from 1793 to 1863. This was in the line of the work in Amsterdam; in no country of Europe was so much and so many uses for lumber as Holland; on the land its cities were built upon it, on the sea it floated the greater part of the commerce of the world; the yards of Amsterdam had at the time our ancestor left there a capacity for building and completely equipping one ship a day; and a centu·y before he came 2000 ships were built there annually; so in the leather manufacture the first two boys were cordwainers and tanners; Peter Keyser[9] was a tanner, and the trade in the manufacture of leather I find was still in one instance in the family in the last generation; Peter ter Himpel was a morocco-leather manufacturer, and the leather trade in the Netherlands was a vast trade with very diverse uses, for curtains for wall covers, for books, for clothing, for shoes, and, with its gold and silver embossing, the better sorts were fit for palaces and used on the walls of palaces. And so it was in Germantown, while our ancestor was reading the word of God his sons were making the leather for the backs of the Bible, and the shoes the good people wore who were listening to it for their souls' preservation. And in another line Samuel Keyser[6] of Baltimore, who died* 1839, and Derick Keyser[6] were large dealers in queensware; Charles Maris Keyser[7] succeeded his father in the same business; that also came from there; the town of Delft gave its first name to the chinaware of Europe.

I have mentioned these among the many occupations of the family, because I clearly trace their origin to Holland antecedents; but to mention every trade and business in which the family have been engaged would reach beyond the limits of this occasion. They embrace nearly every variety of employment; as legislators there have been many; of judges we have had eight; together with a large number of executive, municipal and State officers; we have had many bankers,† farmers and members of the three professions; some railroad and canal constructors; one mariner, William E. Keyser[7] of Philadelphia; some telegraph superintendents—Miller Bullard[9] and Samuel K. Bullard of Sedalia; there have been many also in mercantile and some in literary work. George Keyser[7] of Baltimore was an engineer; William Keyser[8] of Baltimore, among his many occupations, a town-builder. Keyser bears our family name as a reminder of his railroad services;‡ but he was the builder (1873) of the town of "Garret," in the centre of the mile-square De Kalb County, Indiana, which he, with two or three others, bought for that purpose, the citizens of which, now a

* Samuel Keyser[6] was ninth child of ([37],[9] Michael Keyser of Germantown; his very considerable estate, as is the case with other members of the family, in Germantown and Philadelphia, still remains with his descendants. He was allied by marriage with the Garrets, Kings, and Kimmels, among the most prominent railroad and business-men of the country. He was the representative man of the family South in his generation, of distinguished presence and engaging manners.

† In Germantown Samuel Keyser[7] was a Director from 1851 for twenty-one years of the Bank there; his brother William a member of the Board in 1833-4 and '39, and Naaman[8] from 1841 to 1843. In Norristown the family have representatives as bankers in the Slingluffs for a long period of years; in Philadelphia and in Baltimore, a very considerable list of names. Nathan Keyser Knorr[7] was a practitioner of medicine until his death (1851). Dr. Thos. S. Passmore, who died of disease contracted in the duties of this profession. Dr. Joseph Berens[9] was a physician of much prominence who died from blood-poisoning contracted while operating. Dr. Bernard Berens[9], Dr. Conrad Berens[9], and Dr. Thos. Passmore Berens[9] of the Knorr line are all of this profession.

‡ Keyser, county-seat of Mineral County, situated on the Potomac River, at the head of New Creek Valley, West Virginia; population, 2000. The traffic of the B. and O. R. R. is concentrated here and made into trains for all parts of the system.

large and thriving municipality, have given the township in which it is built our family name. Of the family who went into Maryland and Virginia from Germantown, many engaged in metal mining, sale and manufacture. John H. Keyser[7] was engaged in the manufacture of iron work in New York.

Dirck Penebacker[5], Anneke Keyser's son, in 1778 moved to Maryland, leased a furnace near Antietam, was ruined there financially by a freshet, and went into the ·Shenandoah Valley and built Pine Forge, near New Market, in 1781; later erected a furnace called Redville, near Luray. Benj. Penebacker, Anneke Keyser's grandson, carried on the iron business at Pine Forge, died in 1820, and left a large estate, including six men, four women, four girls and three boys; value, $6250. His son, George M. Penebacker[7], living in 1877 near New Market, was before the war an ironmaster largely engaged with numerous slaves. Benj. P. Newman of Woodstock, Va., was an iron-manufacturer; Joel Pennypacker[7] was an iron-manufacturer.

Samuel Stouffer Keyser[7] of Baltimore began his business career as a clerk in an iron-store; formed the firm of Samuel S. Keyser & Co., later Keyser Bros. & Co., retired with a handsome fortune 1860, having been in business for thirty-six years. William Keyser of Baltimore was from 1857 to 1883 engaged in the iron business; was one of the incorporators of the Abbott Iron Company, and a member of its board and executive from 1865 to 1881, during which time it was one of the largest iron concerns in the country, employing at times over nine hundred men. In 1884 he organized the Baltimore Copper Smelting and Rolling Co. with a few friends, contributing a capital of half a million dollars. He also organized the Old Dominion Copper Company—of which he is president—with a cash capital of half a million dollars, employing a large number of men, and have an output the present year (1889) of four to five million dollars.

[1]Robert Brent Keyser[6] is the treasurer of the Baltimore Copper Works, of the Old Dominion Copper Co. and the South Baltimore Car Works, and president of the Baltimore Land and Improvement Company.

PUBLIC EMPLOYMENT.—The family, from the tenets of their religion, were not only averse to warfare, but also to taking any part in the government of the country in which they lived. They would not accept public office or serve in the Courts for conscience' sake in Germantown.* The first instance of a departure from this was Dirck Keyser, one of the grand-

---

* It was hard for them to conceive how they could be judges over others, it might be, even less censurable than they themselves were, to their own consciences, or what need for oaths there was for them who dwelt in truth's simple verities, or what use there was for government for those who were a law unto themselves.

sons of our ancestor, who was commissioned a judge of the Orphans' Court and Common Pleas and Quarter Sessions of this city, April 4, 1741.

Charles Maris Keyser[7] was a representative in 1848 in the Maryland Senate, and in 1860 nominated for the Mayor of Baltimore, but declined the nomination.

Elhanan Winchester Keyser[7], a member of the Select Council of Philadelphia, in 1827, President of the Board of Commissioners to build the Almshouse, in 1837, Candidate for Mayor of Philadelphia in 1844; Warden of the Port in 1854; member of the Board of Managers of the Almshouse the same year; and its President until his death. Peter A. Keyser[7], a commissioner of the district of the Northern Liberties of Philadelphia, a member of the Board of Guardians of the Poor from 1837 to 1847, member of Select Council from 1854 to 1856; Chairman of the Railroad Committee of Councils, the city having at that time invested in the various railroads in the State $8,275,000. He was in the Almshouse Board at the time of his death.

Robert T. Conrad[7] was Mayor of Philadelphia in 1854, prior to this time Recorder of the City, then commissioned judge of the Court of Criminal Sessions and March 20, 1840, of the General Session, and of the Common Pleas November 30, 1856. During his term of office as Mayor he raised the city from a condition of great disorder; at its close it was said that the Sabbath, for many years given over to rioting, was during his administration kept a sacred day.

John Keyser Knorr, M. D.[7], was a member of the Select Council in 1854–55 to 1856, and was selected for the committees of health, poor, prisons, markets and water, showing the reputation he had brought there for this character of work. He introduced, as chairman of the committee on health, the resolution to remove the City Hospital from the built-up portion of the city, which he carried through. He introduced the supplementary ordinance organizing the health department, and a bill for the cleansing of the city. The city is largely indebted to him for the small-pox hospital.

Nathan L. Keyser[7] was a member of the same body 1854–55, and a leading member of the committee which passed the resolution for the first purchase of ground for park purposes, under the act of Consolidation.*

* The administration of Mayor Conrad was the most earnest endeavor of the municipality to bring about the same condition which Amsterdam had brought about two centuries before to avert the evils of the debasing immigration which still continue here, and which under its free and liberal institutions finally flooded that city; that is, by imposing compulsory labor on its vagrancy, which has resulted in our House of Correction, by an earnest endeavor to crush out its intemperance by almost

James Lynd[4] was a member of the Select Council of Philadelphia and its president in 1863, City Solicitor in 1866, afterward elected a judge of the Common Pleas, and continued in this office until his death.

Daniel L. Keyser[4] was in the Borough Council of Germantown from 1835 to 1840, and a Town Commissioner in 1844.

Benjamin U. Keyser, National Bank Examiner, Washington, D. C.

George G. Pieric[3] is at the present time Recorder of Deeds in the City of Philadelphia.

George Fox Keyser[3] was in the Water Department, and a Director of the Public Schools, and James D. Keyser (deceased since the reunion) Assessor in the Real Estate Department of the Tax Office of the city.

Dr. P. D. Keyser[4] is Chancellor-in-Chief of the Order of the Loyal Legion of the United States.

John S. Keyser[3] was lieutenant of the consolidated police force of the Spring Garden district, and 1850 chief marshal of the police of Philadelphia, and the creator of the office.

Dr. Harry N. Marselis[7], Surgeon in the U. S. service, died at a post on the frontier.

John Slingluff[8], president of the Montgomery National Bank, Norristown. Wm. Fry Slingluff[8] is its cashier and Wm. H. Slingluff[7] was an officer of it for 50 years. Harry Marselis[9] and Charles Marselis are in the U. S. Navy.

Samuel W. Lynd, D. D., was president of the Baptist Theological College, Covington, Kentucky, and one of his sons a judge of one of the Courts of Cincinnati, Ohio.

Charles S. Keyser[7] was one of the first promoters of the purchase of Fairmount Park, the great common and pleasure ground for the people of Philadelphia; Master of Ceremonies of the celebration in the Centennial Grounds, July 5, 1875, of the Congress of Authors, in Independence Hall, July 2, 1876, and member of the advisory board of the President of the United States Centennial Commission for the ceremonies of July 4, 1876, in Independence Square, of the plan for which ceremonies he was the author.

---

prohibitory license laws, by requiring and exacting, as he did, the most strict preservation of the Sabbath day from disorder, and finally by an appeal to the reputable and considerate citizens by whom he was elected to put forth every effort, so that in a community as affluent and humane as ours (I quote his language) there should not be a single case of mendicancy in our streets to reproach our humanity—results which we have, in a large measure, now attained. The family had a very considerable share in this work—E. W. Keyser, as President of the Almshouse Board, Dr. John K. Knorr, Peter A. Keyser, Nathan L. Keyser, and Dr. I. N. Marselis and Charles Megarge, both closely allied with the family, and all members of the most important committees of Councils at that time, and John S. Keyser as marshal and high constable of the city.

4

William Keyser[8] of Baltimore is a member and a vice-president of the Civil Service Reform Association of Maryland, and, in connection with Robert T. Baldwin, organized, in 1882, the great independent movement in the politics of Baltimore, making the opening address at Concordia Hall, the result of which was to lift the politics of that city out of the almost hopeless condition into which it had sunk at that time; was one of the committee of five, that year, whose labor with their fellow-citizens gave a judiciary to Baltimore second to no other in the country.

Philip Walter Keyser[8], son of George Keyser[7] of Baltimore, was judge of the County Court of Sutter Co., Cal., by appointment, 1860, and the following year was elected to the same office; in 1867 again elected, and held the same office until 1870; elected 1869 judge of the District Court of the Tenth Judicial District, comprising four counties, and remained in that office ten years, under the new Constitution 1879, which established a Superior Court, with not less than one judge, for each county of the State, except in Yuba and Sutter counties, where the same judge should preside. To this judicial position he was elected in 1879, which he still (1889) occupies—a continuous judicial service (except from 1864 to 1868) since 1860, five years in the county court and twenty years in the highest Nisi Prius Court.

John H. Keyser[7] was one of the seven men who cast the first ballot in New York City in 1844, for the first national candidate for the abolition of slavery, James G. Birney.

Benjamin Samuels, great-grandson of Anneke Keyser, was a member of the Iowa Legislature, and was the Democratic nominee for governor and United States Senator, and one of the most prominent men of the State during the war.

Benjamin Pennybacker[6], Anneke's grandson, was a justice of the peace; died in 1820. His grandson, Benjamin P. Douglas, was a judge of the Circuit Court of Indiana and member of the State Senate 1877.

Joel Pennybacker[7], Anneke's great-grandson, was district attorney for Shenandoah County and member of the House of Delegates and Virginia Senate 1836.

Isaac Samuels Pennybacker[7] (Anneke's great-grandson) was judge of the United States District Court for Western Virginia, United States Senator 1845 from Virginia, and was the youngest member of the Senate at his death, in 1847. "He died," as was said on the floor of the House of Representatives in the ceremonies of the occasion, "without a solitary reproach to follow him or a solitary enemy."

John Dyer Pennybacker was a member of the Virginia Senate 1858; United States examiner of public surveys June 25, 1885.

James Edmund Pennybacker was in 1875 State's attorney for Pendleton County, West Virginia, and in 1877 member of the West Virginia House of Delegates and judge of the Circuit Court.

John Strayer Pennybacker in the Treasury Department, Washington.

Henry Jeff. Samuels was a member of the Legislature of Virginia 1855-56, and judge of the Circuit Court, and was the only member of this line of the family in that State who adhered to the Union side.

Green Berry Samuels, great-grandson of Anneke Keyser, was member of the Twenty-sixth Congress 1839, and 1850 a judge of the Circuit Court; 1851 judge of the Court of Appeals of Virginia, and occupied during his life a position of the highest distinction in the State.

Benjamin Rush Pennybacker was a member of the Virginia Senate in 1861, and commissioner of Wood County, West Virginia, 1877.

Nathan Pennypacker of Chester County, Pennsylvania, was a member of the Assembly 1812, 1814 and 1830; his son Jacob was president of the Medical Society of Chester County.*

COMMERCE THERE AND HERE.—While in many things which develop a civilization we have made great advances, in commerce, on the sea or land, our nation may never control so large an area of the world as the country of our ancestor; and, as far as our family here is concerned, what has been done in ocean commerce, has been done in the New Amsterdam, the metropolis of New York, by the Cunards, descendants of Margaret Keyser. For the rest, Peter A. Keyser was the owner of a line of vessels in the coasting trade; William Keyser of Philadelphia was an officer in the Cope line of packets, and was master of the brig Independence at the time of his death; Elhanan W. Keyser was one of the first promoters of the first railroad in Philadelphia; Miller Bullard⁷ was superintendent of the telegraph lines of the Missouri Pacific Railroad at Sedalia; of the Eastern Division of the Missouri Pacific Railroad; and on the consolidation of the Missouri Pacific and K. T. Roads superintendent of the combination, and Samuel K. Bullard is now (1889) superintendent telegraph Missouri, Kansas and Texas Railway.

Charles Maris Keyser of Baltimore was one of the early directors of the Baltimore and Ohio Railroad.

William Keyser' of Baltimore is the representative man of the family in this line; he was a director in the Western Maryland Railroad, and the representative of the City of Baltimore in that road; he was also a director in the Susquehanna and Tidewater Canal, and the representative of the

* These notices of the Pennebacker line are from Hon. Samuel W. Pennypacker's MS. biographies and genealogy of that family.

State of Maryland in that corporation. He was for ten years second vice-president of the Baltimore and Ohio Railroad Company; president of the Pittsburgh and Connellsville Railroad Company, the Parkersburgh branch Railroad Company, the Valley Railroad Company of Virginia, and of the Washington County Railroad Company. He is at present a director in the Baltimore and Ohio Railroad Company, and has been a director in several other prominent railroad enterprises, both on the seaboard and in the West. These represent a large part of our Eastern Railway system.

It will be interesting to such men as these, and to those who may follow us in these commercial lines, to know something more than is generally known of the vast commerce of the country of our ancestor at the time he left there, in 1688. At that time, the cities, and citizens of Holland, Amsterdam having the controlling share,* were in fact the owners and masters of the whole East Indies; in Banda and Amboina they had Governors ; they had a great trade with Macassar, where they had a garrison, and with Timor, Siam, Bengal, and Japan, where they had a right of trade exclusive of other nations; they traded with China, where they had at that time sent an Ambassador, getting from that country silver, iron, and copper, rubies, pearls, silks, diamonds and sapphires; they carried on a great trade with Bengal in spices, copper, tin, lead and quicksilver, and in the territories of the grand Seigneur a very extensive trade; they brought bales of silk from Syria; they traded with Genoa, Leghorn, Venice, Naples and Messina; the Register of the Custom House in Amsterdam in 1659, showed that they imported from France alone fifty-one million guilders in merchandise; and employed from five hundred to six hundred vessels in that trade annually. The same Register shows in 1683 that they brought from the Coromandel coast, where they had a Governor, calicoes to the value of two million four hundred thousand guilders; they carried on a trade with Arabia, Eygpt, and Persia, where they had Ambassadors. The trade between China and Japan in 1650 was worth annually to them one million five hundred thousand livres; from Ceylon they brought of cinnamon, some years half a million pounds; they had a Governor also there; their trade further extended along the coast of Africa from the Tropic of Cancer to the Cape of Good Hope, where they established colonies, which yet remain; and along the eastern coast of America from the Straits of Magellan to Newfoundland, where they established colonies and a city, which yet remains the chief city of

---

* The Holland idea of a combination of the Cities and States as partners in these great works, as " the east and west India companies," has been followed very generally in this country, and it is interesting to observe, that a member of our Holland family has been the representative chosen by his City and State, as the custodian of their interest, in similar corporations.

our nation; from 1633 to 1636 they put to sea in that trade eight hundred vessels, took in battle five hundred and forty-five vessels with sixty millions of dollars of treasure; in 1625 brought home the Peru fleet with one million in silver bars with merchandise and precious stones amounting to twelve million florins. In the year 1640 they destroyed ninety-two men-of-war of the enemies to their trade. The Governors General of the two companies, carrying on this trade for the city and cities of the Netherlands, were more imperial in their retinue than kings; fifty horse guards preceded their carriages, a company of foot guards followed them, and twelve pages magnificently attired walked on either side; the most distinguished personages sought the honor of the service of these companies; the Count of Nassau was representative of the West India Company in Brazil, and the ruler over seven of its provinces. They employed twelve hundred ships on the Baltic sea, and in 1609 three thousand of their ships were in the herring fisheries on the English coast; out of this trade they sold seventy-five million livres annually; there remained in fact little of value in the world which was not in the hold of their commerce. Of those connected with their trade, in our ancestor's time, the names of Spielman, Champtesse, Sieur de Hamel, De Bases, Bullestrat, and Braems survive; these men were far greater in the power they wielded and the wealth they controlled than any of the descendants of the Dutch emigration here, although some of these have been the largest owners of land, and one of them to-day is the wealthiest man of our country and among the wealthiest in the world.

Spielman—the first of these men, was not only as William Keyser the representative of his City and State in its greatest corporation, but could make war and peace when he pleased for and in the name of the cities and States of which he was the representative and partner. Champtesse the second, not only, as this country's Van der Bildt could give a war vessel to his government, but was the Admiral of one hundred and twenty of such war vessels and twenty-five thousand men, and had under his absolute control one hundred thousand men capable of bearing arms, could and did send Ambassadors to Kings, and controlled the labor of sixty thousand slaves in the India mines. The three next, not only like our dutch Patroons in New York, held the title of great tracts of land, but they had under their control the whole east coast of America and its islands and in the same manner the whole west coast of Africa; and the last one of these world representatives of commerce was on his voyage to anchorage in Amsterdam when our ancestor left there and brought there from the East Indies amid the ringing of the bells in the churches and the chimes in the Stadthouse tower, and the booming of cannons, "the greatest and richest return that ever came from the Indies" or to any other city of the world.

MUSIC.—We have always had as a family a great fondness for music, song and instruments; the flute had many notable players in the earlier generation; there have been sweet singers, from the third generation down to the present living one, of whom we still treasure the memory; the Dutch delighted in singing, the violin was heard in Amsterdam all night long in our ancestor's time, the grandest organs were in their churches, the sweetest chimes of bells in their towers. In the fifteenth century the best musicians of France and Italy were Flanders born; John Tinctor was the earliest theoretician whose name survives; his treatise at the close of the fifteenth century, was the first ever printed in Italy, and he was the founder in Naples of its first musical conservatory; Claud Goudimel was the founder of the first musical conservatory in Rome, and Willaert, of the first musical conservatory in Venice; John Ochenhein of Flanders, was the first composer of music in parts; Orlando di Lasso, born at Mons 1520, first made music the expression of words, and he and Cipriano Rore, were the first two masters of harmony; they were the first to venture upon Chromatic passages and accidental flats and sharps. Keyser, a Hollander of our name, was the first musician, who gave the German theatre celebrity.

Among the many who illustrate this characteristic of our family I will mention here, Molly Keyser[6], a hundred years before our time, the sweet singer singing in the evenings with her husband and children, and El- hanan Winchester Keyser[7], in the last generation, who interested himself so much and was of such great service to the musical progress of our City as one of the Board of Officers of the Musical Fund Society from 1841 and the Vice President of that Society from 1853 until his death; Joseph Key- ser, William Keyser of Philadelphia, Silvester Keyser of the Rising Sun, flutists; Frank Keyser, Sallie K. Savage, with her sweet voice and never to be forgotten ballads; Roxana Conrad for her sweet voice so well re- membered.

DOMESTIC ECONOMIES.—Those of us who remember the Dutch house- keeping in our families years ago, and its afflictive cleanliness;* the sand cleaned tins and table tops, and wooden floors, and snow white linen bleaching in the grass, will have a pleasure in knowing that this was also an Amsterdam inheritance; as it is with a ship, so it is with Holland, the

---

* This influence is still felt in Philadelphia. The following description of the work of the Dutch housewives in Holland in 1866 is as applicable to this City as the Cities of Holland : "Fortunately the weather was cold enough to put a stop to the usual street flooding and window washing or we might have been drenched. Sweeping, mopping and scrubbing form a passion with them." See also Sir Wm. Temple's account of what befel a pompous magistrate visiting a lady in Amsterdam.

Mary Slinghuff

first requisite there is cleanliness; it is a life and death matter on the sea, and Holland itself is but a ship moored to the fast land of the continent, and beat about continually by the winds and waves; you must even take off your shoes when you enter some of its village houses, not that they are holier, but that they are cleaner than ours.

Comfortableness, was perhaps the best word to express their living—they had brought over the custom of setting out wine upon their sideboards—which was always there and formed part of the inevitable chatter about the weather, and mishaps of the time—delicate cordials long since passed into complete disuse—"perfect love" and "anisette"—"currant wine"—and port—and madeira—much mahogany in chairs and tables—parties for sleighing—continual visiting—regular church attendance—sitting in high-backed pews, standing in prayer—on their tables heavy linen, much old silver—no plated ware; pewter dishes, silver spoons and brass candlesticks—clothes for the summer and winter carefully put away from season to season; shapes and qualities of goods as little known to their descendants as the language in which they customarily conversed in their homes;* unostentatious and always seclusive—quiet—laborious men and women—saving, and very particular in their marriages—Christmas, a day of great observance—Dutch cake and wine on all the tables in the morning—Christmas trees, rabbits of gingerbread, and mince pies redolent with the stilled vintages of Alsace and Lorraine, and the cider presses of Berks and Lancaster—all for the most part with much sedateness and undemonstrableness in the men—and gentleness and thoroughness in the women—the straight, long, buttoned coat of the one, and the book muslin handkerchief folded across the breasts of the other, were the external evidences of their disposition and behavior.

Their amusements were largely out of doors; all the men of the family were skaters, fond of athletic sports summer and winter, swimming, ball playing, riding, driving. Elhanan W. Keyser was one of the early mem-

---

* Wardrobes.—In the address of S. W. Pennypacker he gave us the wardrobe of Anneke Keyser*, who lived a little less than 200 years ago, as follows : A shawl, a silk shawl, a cloak, a beaver hat, six pairs of cotton stockings ; two worsted, four linen, five linsey, and five cotton petticoats ; three lawn and ten check han lkerchiefs, four table cloths, seven short gowns, twelve pillow cases, sixteen check aprons, sixteen towels, twenty sheets and forty-eight shifts. I here add Ann (Nice) Keyser's, who lived a little less than 100 years ago : 1 cloth cloak, 1 levanteen coat ; 1 lead colored silk gown, 1 black crape do., 1 black bombazine do., and 1 black silk do.; 1 black levanteen dress, 2 plaid gingham do., 1 green calico do., 1 brown do., 1 plaid gingham do.; 1 black levanteen shawl, 1 figured cotton do., 1 beaver do., 1 lead colored silk do., 1 lead colored crape do., 1 lead colored silk do.; 1 marten tippet, 3 book muslin hdkfs., 1 calico short gown, 1 silver bladed knife, 2 pair black woollen stockings, 3 linen and 3 muslin shifts, 4 pair of pockets, 2 petticoats, 2 pocket handkerchiefs, linen ; 3 flannel petticoats, 5 book muslin neck hdkfs., 11 caps, 1 muslin shawl. Plain and adequate enough for those dear old ladies, the last of whom was my grandmother.

bers of the Archery Club of Philadelphia, an elegant pastime pursued in the Netherlands with great splendor of appointments, but requiring more strength of arm than was general among the student youth of Philadelphia until the great revival of athletic sports in the closing years of the present century.

ENDURANCE AND STATURE.—Dirck Keyser[2], our ancestor, died at the age of 79. Tobias Govertsz[1] was still a preacher at 80. Anneke Keyser[4] died in her 91st year. Molly Keyser[6] celebrated her birthday in her 86th year among her children, grandchildren and great-grandchildren.

John Keyser[5] died at 91. Dirck Keyser[5] at 73. John Keyser[5] (in 1813), aged 83. Michael Keyser[5] died 1825, aged 80. Samuel Pennebaker[5] died at 80. Hannah Keyser[6] died at 72. Jacob Keyser[6] at 92. Dirck Keyser[6] at 78. Ann (Keyser) Baker at 75.

Charles Keyser[6] died at 82. Mary Heisler[6] at 78. Peter Keyser[5] at 86. William Keyser[6] at 84. Peter Keyser[6], "the preacher," died 1849 at 83. Enoch Keyser[6] died in his 90th year.

His niece Hannah Nice[7] survives him (1889), now 94 years of age.

Samuel[7] died 1868, aged 84. Margaret Keyser[7], 1864, aged 84. Hannah K. Knorr d. 81. Hannah Knorr Lang 73.

Mary Slingluff[7], daughter of Molly Keyser, is now (1889) 88 years old. Ann Hagy (Ann Weaver) died Feb., 1870, aged 86. Susannah K. Weaver[6] at 81. Mary Knorr, in the same generation, is now 80 years old.

Silvester Keyser was (1889) over 82 years of age, without indications of great length of years.*

Sarah Kirk d. at 77. Nathan L. Keyser at 74. Mary Langstroth[7] d. at 77. Clementine Lynd still living, 86. Elizabeth Keyser d. 1878 at 80 years. Elizabeth Urner[7] at 80 years. Gideon d. (1888) at 82.

In addition to length of years they were tall men generally. Michael Keyser[5] was 6 feet, Silvester 6 feet, Rev. Peter Keyser[6] 6 feet 3 inches and very erect, as most of the family were and are. Joseph Keyser[6] was 6 feet in height, a man of great strength and vigor. His three sons were each 6 feet. Harry Keyser (E. W. K.'s son) 6 feet 4 inches. George Keyser 6 feet 1 inch. Joseph, son of Jacob Keyser[6], was 6 feet. Elhanan W. Keyser[7] was 6 feet 2 in. in height and weighed 200 pounds. His sons were all 6 feet or over. Peter Keyser was 6 feet 3 in. Enoch Keyser was 6 feet 2 in. Charles and Gustavus Engle[7] are 6 feet. John R. Savage's children are beyond the family average, and one son is 6 feet 4 inches high.

Peter A. Keyser was 6 feet 3 in. in height and weighed 250 pounds at one period; later in life 285. His sons were 6 feet.

Dirck Pennybacker[6], Anneke's grandson, weighed 300 pounds. Nathan

* Fatally injured while driving Feb. 10, and died Feb. 11, 1889.

Daniel K. Kleyser,

L. Keyser was 6 feet 1½ inches high, spare build and of great endurance. His sons living are tall men. John S. Keyser, 250 pounds, height 6 feet 2 inches. Sylvester Keyser is probably the strongest man of the family now living.

Daniel L. Keyser was a man of great strength as well as activity. It was his good fortune through this to have rescued persons from drowning.

So there have been notably tall women—as it was in Amsterdam, some exceeding the stature of the men. Molly Keyser[6] was 6 feet high, but magnificently proportioned, a very graceful woman—with very small hands and feet. This peculiarity reappeared in the most remarkable woman in many respects of the family—Keturah Keyser Benson—who was very tall —weighed 240 pounds—intellectually as abnormal and with the same little hands and feet which were in the family a century before.

Jacob, brother of Gideon, was 6 feet high. Naaman was a man of great stature; but without multiplying instances we may say that generation after generation their height and endurance distinguish the men and women as a family. In their strength they have been as remarkable.

I have given the story of Sylvester Keyser's endurance in the war, let me add here this statement about the most notable men of the family in strength; the first from my own remembrance.

John S. Keyser was stronger than any other man in public life in Philadelphia until the close of his marshalship, which was tested on two occasions, one of these, the arrest of Greer and Sowers, two men who had long defied the authorities of Spring Garden; both carried away by him at one time, to which many now living will bear testimony.

Another, Enoch Keyser[6], had a far greater strength in the earlier part of his life, as I have upon the testimony of many, than any one living about Philadelphia. The millstone he lifted on a well-remembered occasion is still in Germantown, and cannot well be lifted, it is said, by three ordinary men. The stone (recently measured by Romaine Keyser), 5 feet 7¾ inches diameter, at the centre 8 inches thick, and at the circumference 7 inches thick, was raised bodily by him. It weighs about 2000 pounds.

Abraham Keyser, in his 91st year, walked from Main Street, opposite the Friends' Meeting House, Germantown, to Second and Market Street, and back again, a distance of 12 miles. Jacob Keyser, who died at 93, would customarily walk his three miles for exercise. Peter Keyser, the preacher, memorized the whole New Testament and the greater part of the Old.

As this is the most remarkable instance of mental toil long continued in the family, I have taken pains to verify it. It rests among many others on the testimony of the Rev. Dr. Mayer, in the memoir of his life, to which I here add another statement as unquestionable as it is exact :

I was well acquainted with the Rev. Peter Keyser. He told me some of his early life; that his father had been a tanner, and that he was early put at the bark mill for grinding it. Above it he made a shelf, on which he kept an open Bible, and as the grinding went on he would read a passage in it, memorize it—and so he would take up verse after verse and chapter after chapter, until he had completely memorized the whole of the New Testament—of the Old Testament he memorized the whole of the Psalms and the Prophets, and the five books of Moses ; the whole of the New and the greater part of the Old Testament.

ABRM. H. CASSEL.

FEB. 5, 1889.

Mr. Cassel adds also that he never failed to repeat any verse or chapter from those portions of the Bible on any of the numerous occasions made to test this extraordinary and wellnigh incredible labor of the brain.

William H. Fry while in the Treasury Department in Washington in 1861 wrote his signature 4000 times daily for several months in succession.

Another illustration of strength and endurance is Charles Keyser's[6] last work with a pen. It is without an error or evidence of age, and consists of two volumes, together 1838 pages, 8½ inches long by 6½ inches wide; these two volumes contain every reference to the New Testament taken from Cruden's general Concordance. He commenced the first volume of this work 15 day 1st Mo., 1849, and the second volume on the 30 day 8th Mo., 1849, at 12 o'clock—finished the whole work on the 23 day of the 6th Mo., 1850, and was engaged upon it continuously—1 y. 3 mo. 8 da. He was then 80 years of age. He died 1st Mo., 1852, aged 82. The work is entitled a Complete Concordance of the New Testament. It contains, by careful computation, two million (2,000,000) letters and figures, each of which is as carefully and completely formed as if by a graver's tool; the old remembrance and disposition to continue to do this work which had been indurated into the brain and veins of his long gone ancestor in some monastery where he worked, had transmitted themselves to him, and for seventy-two years fastened down his hand to a pen year after year—until his two under fingers became crooked and immovable under it, and so he taught on and wrote on until the day he died. No other labor would he do, even his shoestrings his children or servants tied.

In nothing is this family more remarkable than for these physical qualities, traceable far back over three centuries ago, of mental and physical endurance, and two centuries ago of length of years; a century and a half ago of a remarkable height; in this last century, of great strength—qualities, some of which, height, longevity and endurance, are as remarkable in them to-day as at any earlier period in the long years of the family's history.

B. M. Prentiss

THE WAR RECORD OF THE FAMILY.—John Keyser[5] was engaged in caring for the wounded and burying the dead of both armies after the battle of Germantown; and John Pennybacker[6], grandson of Elizabeth Keyser[1], was one of the Committee appointed by the Council of Safety to distribute food to the soldiers in Berks County during the Revolution, but outside of this work the family, with one exception, have no war record during the Revolution—they adhered to the tenets of their creed, paid the fines imposed upon them, endured the suffering and loss the war entailed, and held the faith that some time these cruel instrumentalities in the change of human conditions would cease.*

Samuel Pannebecker[5], Elizabeth Keyser's[1] son, was fined at various times during the Revolution for non-attendance on the militia—£9 15s., £37 10s., £2 10s., £3 5s., £9 15s., and £9 15s. He was the owner of Pannebecker's Mill in 1777. Jacob Pennebacker, who married a descendant of Abraham op den Graeff, one of the signers of the first petition for the manumission of our slaves, was fined during the Revolution for non-attendance on the militia £39 12s. 10d., and the soldiers of our army also devoured his substance and carried away the accumulations of many years.

Dirck Pennybacker[5] (Anneke Keyser's son), named for his grandfather, our ancestor here, a Berks County farmer, was the one exception who took part in the struggle. He rose to the rank of captain in the Army of the Colonies.

In the War of 1812 the family broke away from the strict tenets of the Mennonites. Elhanan W. Keyser was in the Washington Blues. Joseph Keyser[6], grandson of Jacob Souplis Keyser, at Fort Dupont. John Samuels, g. g. s. of Anneke Keyser, a private. George Keyser[7], major of the 36th Reg. U. S. Infantry, was in the battle of Bladensburg, and later, in the same year (Sept. 12, 1814), participated in the defence of Baltimore. Charles Maris Keyser, of Baltimore, was commander of the Eutaw Infantry, and Daniel Penebacker[6], grandson of Elizabeth Keyser, was an ensign in the 7th Co., 1st Regiment Berks Co. Militia. Benjamin Keyser[7], g. g. son of Jacob Souplis Keyser, a private in the war with Mexico, with Col. Moorhead's regiment; was wounded in the battle of Cerro Gordo and died at Puebla. Benjamin Mayberry Prentiss[3], a captain, and Joseph Samuels, a lieutenant, in the same war, both g. g. g. sons of Anneke Keyser.

In 1861, Daniel Keyser was with the Pennsylvania Reserves, Co. G,

---

* " They did not find freedom of conscience, as they said, to take up arms—they had dedicated themselves to serve all men in everything helpful to the preservation of men's lives, but found no freedom in giving, doing, or assisting in anything by which men's lives were destroyed ; they were ready to pay the tribute according to Christ's command, and so were willing to pay the taxes, but not at liberty to conquer their enemies, but rather to pray to God for themselves and them."—*Excerpt from the Anabaptists' and Mennonites' Declaration to the Assembly of Pennsylvania, 1775.*

8th Reg. Dr. Peter D. Keyser entered the service of the government as Captain in the 91st Pennsylvania Regiment, served in the Army of the Potomac in the Chickahominy Campaign until after the battle of Fair Oaks, when his health being impaired by wounds and sickness he resigned his commission. In 1864, again entered the service of the government as Assistant Surgeon at the Cuyler Hospital in Germantown. Charles S. Keyser[7] was a private in the First City Troop, attached to the 2d U. S. Cavalry under Col. Geo. H. Thomas, at the opening of the war; served through the first campaign in the valley of Virginia; resigned Feb. 5, '63. William F. Keyser was in the Commissary Department at City Point during the Grant Campaign. Joseph B. Keyser was in the Western Department with Captain Joseph R. Paxton, 15th U. S. Infantry, of the Regular Army, under then General Geo. H. Thomas. Mathias K. Knorr was Ass. Surgeon for Hospital Service at the McClellan Hospital, and Andrew Keyser Knorr in the service at Carlisle at the time of the invasion of the State. Samuel Keyser, mustered in Aug. 19, 1862, corporal, killed at Gettysburg, July 1, 1863. Henry C. Keyser enlisted in Co. G, 8th Regiment Pa. Vols., Sept. 12, 1862; re-enlisted July 18, 1864, Co. H, 197th, and 3d Assistant Engineer in U. S. Navy on U. S. Steamer "Massasoit." Charles P. Keyser enlisted in Co. A, 150th Reg. Pa. Vols., Aug. 19, 1862, as Sergeant; promoted to Sgt. Major Sept. 19, 1862; promoted to 2d Lieut. Co. B, Nov. 14, 1862; killed at Gettysburg. Harry Riehle, son of Hannah Keyser Riehle, private with the 3 mos. men, Washington Grays. Eyre Keyser, Lieut. 183d Pa. Vols.; wounded at Cold Harbor and the Wilderness.

Cornelius C. Widdis enlisted private 22d Pa. Infantry, April 23, 1861; mustered out Aug. 6, '61; re-enlisted Aug. 23, 1862, as Captain Co. A, 150th Pa. Vols.; was in the battle of Chancellorsville, and wounded and captured at Gettysburg evening of July 1, 1863; was a prisoner of war in Libby Prison, Richmond, Va.; at Danville, Va., Charlotte, N. C., and Macon, Ga.; was one of the 600 ranking officers placed under fire in Charleston to prevent firing on the city (ineffective) by our army; removed to Columbia, S. C.; escaped, recaptured, paroled, and exchanged Feb., 1865. The following promotions were received by him while in these prisons: Commissioned Major March 6, '64, and Lt. Col. March 18, 1864. After his exchange he remained on duty at Military Prison, Annapolis, until mustered out May 16, 1865. Francis Keyser, 1861, Capt. of Co. H, 23d Reg. Pa. Vols., and continued in service until the close of the war; he was stationed at Fortress Monroe; was at the siege of Yorktown, at Williamsburg, Chancellorsville, Fair Oaks and Gettysburg.

Albert Keyser enlisted with the Washington Grays (3 mos. men), Gen.

Patterson's Division in the Valley of Virginia. Byron Keyser[3] enlisted with the 3 months' men, and then with the 3 years' men, 23d Reg. Pa. Vols., Co. B, in 1861, under Col. Birney; died in camp near Bladensburg. James Keyser was a Major of Pa. Militia, Emergency men. Paul Keyser, Co. G, 8th Reg., enlisted Sept. 12, 1862. Jacob Keyser, Co. A, 150th Reg. Pa. Vols., mustered in Aug. 19, 1862; wounded at Gettysburg July 3, 1863; transferred to Vet. Reserve Corps May 1, 1864.

Sylvester Keyser enlisted Co. E, 2d Reg. Mich. Vols. April 18, 1861, for 3 months; May 25, 1861, re-enlisted for 2 years; promoted to 1st Lieut. July 7, 1864; promoted to Captain Sept. 30, 1864, and "for gallant and meritorious service, before Petersburg," June 17 and 18, 1864, promoted to Brevet Major, April 2, 1865. He was in the battle at Blackburn's Ford, Va., wounded slightly, July 18, 1861; Bull Run, Va., wounded severely, July 21, 1861; Siege of Yorktown, Va., April 4 to May 4, 1862; Fair Oaks, Va., May 21, June 1, 1862; near Richmond, Va., June 18, '62; Glendale, Va., July 1, '62; Malvern Hill, Va., July 1, '62; 2d Bull Run, Va., Aug. 28, 29; Chantilly, Va., Sept. 1, '62; Fredericksburg, Va., Dec. 12, 13, 14, '62; Siege of Vicksburg, Miss., June 22 to July 4, '63; Jackson, Miss., July 11 to 18, '63; Blue Springs, Tenn., Oct. 10, '63; Campbell Station, Tenn. (here wounded severely), Nov. 16, '63; Petersburg, Va., June 17, 18, '64; The Crater, Va., July 30, '64; Weldon R. R., Va., Aug. 19, 21, '64; Pegram's Farm, Va., Oct. 2, '64; Hatcher's Run, Va., Oct. 27 and 28, '64; Fort Steadman, Va., March 25, 1865; Capture of Petersburg, Va., April 3, 1865; Lee's Surrender, April 14, 1865.

Philip Weaver, g. s. of Julia Anna Keyser, enlisted with the Bucktail Regiment, 150th Pa. Vols.; taken prisoner in Gettysburg, in the 1st day's fight, under Gen. Reynolds, and died in Libby Prison, Richmond.

Henry Jefferson Samuels, g. g. g. s. of Anneke Keyser, mentioned as having adhered to the North during the war, was the last Adjutant General of the undivided State of Virginia.

Benjamin Mayberry Prentiss[3], the most distinguished military character of the family and one of very high distinction in the nation, having first served in the war with Mexico as Captain, re-entered the service in 1861 as Col. of the 7th Ill. Vols. (April, 1861); was made Brigadier General of the 3 mos. men at Cairo, Ill., and Brig. Gen. of the U. S. Vols. May 7, 1861. Dec. 28, 1861, he fought the battle of Mt. Zion. In April, 1862, joined Gen. Grant, and was taken prisoner at Shiloh, in the Sunday morning battle, and released in October. He was then made Maj. Gen. (Nov. 29, 1862), and defeated Price and Holmes at Helena, Ark., in the battle of the 4th of July, 1863.

On the Confederate side, the five sons of Derrick Pennybacker, g. g.

son of Anneke Keyser, were all in the service. John Strayer Pennybacker entered the Quartermaster's Department at the beginning of the war; Thomas Jefferson Pennybacker was 1st Lieut. Brook's Gap Rifles (Cavalry); Adjt. 10th Va. Inf.; Capt. Co. H, 10th Va. Cav.; killed in action at Flint Hill, Fauquier Co., Va., by a shell.

Dirrick de Haven Pennybacker entered the service as Corp. Co. B, 7th Va. Cav.; then 2d Lieut.; served during the whole war with 7th Va. Cavalry.

Albert Dallas Pennybacker was a private in Brook's Gap Rifles and 7th Va. Cavalry. Joseph Samuels Pennybacker entered the service as 1st Serg. Brook's Gap Rifles (7th Va. Cavalry), and on the reorganization of the company elected 2d Lieut. Co. B, 7th Va. Cav., under Ashby; their brothers-in-law—Charles Brock was in Lieut. Thos. Jeff. Pennybacker's Co., the Valley Rangers, and H. K. Devier was Orderly Serg. in Joseph Samuels Pennybacker's Co. B.

Joseph Samuels Pennybacker was in command of the Confederate right at Bolivar Heights, Harper's Ferry; was in the rear guard of the army in the Valley, fighting for twenty-six out of thirty days; was in the battles in Orange and Spotsylvania, where Rosser's Brigade fought Hancock's 16th Corps; in the fight at Stony Creek, and made his record in the Valley at the time of Sheridan's famous ride; three times wounded; in one engagement shot through the body and disabled for the rest of the war. Dirrick had several horses shot under him—a blooded horse at Brandy Station, and was in the battle of Manasses.

Genl. Rosser says of this Cavalry: "It was never defeated and never surrendered." It was first under Genl. Ashby, until he was killed, and then under Genl. Rosser until the close of the war.

Benjamin Pennybacker, Geo. Mayberry Pennybacker's (g. g. son of Anneke Keyser) only son, was a private in Rice's Artillery Co., Stonewall Jackson's command.

Isaac S. Pennybacker's three sons (Anneke Keyser's g. g. g. sons) were also in the service. John Dyer Pennybacker entered the service as private Co. G, 10th Va. Infantry; was Col. of Cavalry on the staff of Governor Letcher until 1863; in 1864 joined Woodson's Co., Partisan Rangers, which, with McNeil's Co., captured Genls. Crook and Kelly at Cumberland, Md.; 90 men taking these officers from their command of 4000; paroled at Harrisonburg, Va. Isaac Samuels Pennybacker entered the service as private Co. G, 10th Va. Infty., afterward Co. H, 7th Va. Cav.; desperately wounded at Greenland Gap in Rosser's raid to West Virginia; served during the whole war, a brave and distinguished officer; and James Edmund Pennybacker entered the army at the beginning of the war, then 16 years of age;

joined the 10th Va. Infantry, Co. B.; afterwards Capt. of the Va. Reserves; was in the battles at Cross Keys and Port Republic, and with the 7th Va. Cav. at the surrender. Judge Green Berry Samuels' sister's sons, Abraham Samuels Byrd and Perry and Erasmus Byrd, were in the service; Perry was Quartermaster 10th Va. Inf., and Erasmus with the Texas troops. Alexander H. Samuels was a Captain; killed in action Jan. 3, 1864. Four of Mark Pennybacker's[7] five sons (Jonesville, Tenn.), Anneke Keyser's g. g. g. sons, George, Benjamin, Isaac and Alfred, were all killed in action or died from wounds received during the war. Henry Mayberry, Genl. Mayberry Prentiss's[8] cousin, was in West Virginia, Jackson's command. Joel Pennybacker's[7] three sons, Anneke Keyser's[4] g. g. g. sons, were in the service; Francis Stribling Pennybacker was a private in the 10th Va. Inf. and 6th Va. Cav. Joel Pennebacker joined Genl. Price in Missouri; was at Vicksburg, Jackson, Miss., and Mobile; served during the war, and Geo. Mayberry Pennybacker was a surgeon; his grandson, Joel Pennybacker, was in the Confederate Infantry in Missouri. John Mark Mitchell was in the 8th Va. Cav.; three times wounded and once a prisoner. Joseph Mitchell was in Stonewall Jackson's command in the Valley. Sylvanus Samuels, g. g. g. son of Anneke Keyser, was in the Commissary Department, and Lafayette Samuels 1st Lieut. Co. A, 16th Va. Cav. William and Hiram Pennybacker, Maurice and Benj. R. Pennybacker, the sons of Benj. Pennybacker, were all in Stonewall Jackson's command.

Derrick Byrd, Jesse, Samuel and Lamar Walton served during the war in the 33d Va. Inf., under Stonewall Jackson. Of Judge Green Berry Samuels' sons: Green B. Samuels was 1st Lieut. in the Muhlenberg Rifles, and Samuel Samuels was killed in the Wilderness.

The principal battles in which those in the Cavalry were engaged were New Creek, Romney, West Va., and Kernstown.

Some of the family South were severe sufferers by that war. Margaret M. Pennybacker[3], g. g. g. d. of Anneke Keyser, in the Shenandoah Valley, went through the same experience as Samuel Pannebecker of the Pennybacker Mill the century before, and met it with the same steadfast endurance, but whether with the resignation of that old Mennonite I have no mention. She was twice " in the burning " in the Valley—and saw the Northern Army, " 32 times in advance or retreat," continue its desolation around her. Her barn was the only one left in that Valley of Desolation at the war's close—saved by her " constancy and courage."

Derrick Pennebacker, Anneke's g. g. son (his grandfather the nephew of the Samuel Pannebecker of the Pennybacker Mill), was the wealthiest of the family there, and suffered more than any other of the wealthy slave-owners in the Valley in his losses of barns and houses, and in horses and cattle and slaves. When Sheridan passed through, in the last burning, he saw at one time four of his great mills—a plaster, an oil, a grist and saw mill—and three barns, with four thousand bushels of wheat, burning together.

Samuel Pannebecker, Elizabeth Keyser's son, was the first sufferer of our family by this departure of our State from the "peace and mercy" which were the first principles of its foundation. I will conclude this record with a memorandum he made for, among others, ourselves.

The Army of the Revolution had camped at his mill, the Pennypacker Mill, and were there 12 days. They came at 4 o'clock one afternoon, the 26th of September, 1777, and by night the fences, the grain stored there, the wheat, the straw, the whole supply of the family for the winter, was gone—destroyed or carried away by the soldiers. Twice Washington set his camp there in those 12 days, and the second time his army completed its peaceable work of destruction, and went away—this time forever.

Then this ancestor of ours, who could not reach up out of his simple Christianities—to separate one cause from another cause when men were destroying each other's lives—to whom war was no other thing than war, and desolation no other thing than desolation—looked out toward the Perkiomen and saw his fields bare and his barns empty, and the winter before him; and in the great sorrow of his heart—for the suffering coming and come to him and so many others dear to him—took down his large Bible, which was his solace under every affliction, unclasped its great leathern lids and wrote there:

On the 26th day of September, 1777, an Army of thirty thousand men encamped in Skippack township burned all the fences, carried away all the fodder, hay, oats and wheat, and took their departure the 8th day of October, 1777.
Written for those who come after me by

SAMUEL PANNEBECKER.

And so left all, as I do here, to the more considerate judgment of those who come after *us*—with the sincere desire that so far at least as war is concerned, among ourselves, we may for all future time adhere to the creed of our Mennonite ancestors.

THE CHARITABLE WORK OF THE FAMILY.—There were two distinct characteristics of the population of Holland, and these appear in its emigration to other countries; on its material side, were its manufactures and its East and West India trade; on its spiritual side, was its charitable work, its religious tolerance and its reliance on God's providence, which was the ultimate strength of the State. On its material side, were its wars for trade, and on its spiritual side its defenses for conscience' sake; on the one

side, the ostentatious retinue of the Governor General of the Indies; and on the other, the plain clothes and character of the Burgomaster; on the one side, the Stadthouse and its wealth of gold and silver, and on the other the Gasthouse and its humanities. From its material side, it sent out the Founders of what is now the foremost State in wealth and numbers of our nation—the prolongation in this age, and on these shores, of its grandeur, force and wealth of commerce; from its spiritual side, it sent out the Mennonites, the followers of the Saviour, to this province of Pennsylvania; two diverging streams, the one to bear on its bosom the trade of the nations, the other to refresh the weary and overladen on their journey to the better inheritance beyond the grave; the one has given us its highest illustration in the ocean steamship lines and streets of palaces, the Printzengraghts and Heerengraghts of the metropolis—New York; the other in the Common schools, the common grounds for the people, and the charities of the city of homes—Philadelphia.

In this charitable work our family has been most remarkable; a long list of names widening and lengthening from the first, down to the present generation, well attests these words I have written ; and it will therefore interest us to know its condition in Holland when our ancestor left there. The 12 great hospitals and other useful and charitable foundations of Amsterdam at that time (1688) served as models for the rest of Europe. There were the Weeshouses or Homes for the Orphans; the Old Men's and Old Women's Homes, where for a moderate sum first paid, they lived for life; the Gasthouse for the sick; the hospital where travellers were fed for three days; the Dollhouse for the insane; the Rasphouse or house of correction for men, and the Spinhouse for women; there was provision for 20,000 poor in the city at that time, and great care was taken of poor children, especially the children of poor citizens, but the stranger as well had his share; there were houses also where young ladies whose fortunes were not equal to their birth were educated; the provision was for life, or if the young ladies chose to marry a sum of money was given them. There were in addition to these houses a final house or penitentiary for the worst offenders; the profits of the labor of its inmates went to support themselves and after that the State. All these houses were kept in the best of order with even, as a traveller described them, inconveniable cleanliness. In some of these almshouses were 1400 to 1500 inmates; in the Weeshouses from 3000 to 4000 children were fed and clothed and taught trades; for the widows and children of seaman they made the most adequate provisions, and this with a pension for decayed sailors in the service, and the care of bankrupts relieved the State from the conditions of poverty which generally accompany vast accumulations of individual wealth such

5

as were there. To the Dutch Committee on Foreign Needs, which from the
beginning of the 18th century for 80 years continued the work of assisting
foreign emigration, is mainly due the settlements in Pennsylvania from the
the Palatinate. The beneficial society which was the last outgrowth of
this system of beneficence I will mention here was established in 1818, and
every reputable person in the kingdom could become a member by paying
4 shillings and twopence annually. This began with a membership of
16,000; its object was to provide a home and land for each subscriber. In
1822 it had 20,000 members, and provided homes and land for part and
took care of others to the amount of 8000 with a capital at that time of
400,000 pounds. The Belgian society began in 1822, with like results.
It was said that at the time our ancestor left there, and which was the case
for a century and more after, no beggar was ever seen in the streets of
Amsterdam; there was no unalleviated poverty which was not the result
of idleness and worthlessness; and these last were punishable as crimes.
But to effect this the charity of the individual continually contributed to
the work of the State; this charity born out of the incredible former sufferings of its population for freedom and conscience' sake was beyond example and above comparison; they were continually giving to the poor;
to the church contributions every one, servants and children, were contributors; the velvet purse used in their churches, similar ones were kept
a long while in the Baptist churches of this city, was narrow but very long,
long enough for the deepest pocket and narrow enough for the giver in the
most straitened circumstances; it was not made of open network but
velvet, that the neighbor's left eye might not see what his neighbor's right
hand was doing. In our churches here they got shorter and broader in
time, and the open basket with its display of dimes and dollars at last
superseded the other altogether. This old purse of Amsterdam was fastened to a long stick, and to this a little bell was attached which tinkled
as it was passed along the aisles, it may be to waken the sleepers at the
end of the long sermon, to prove their faith by their works.* In Philadelphia this charitable work is continued; we have asylums here for widows
and single women, for children, for orphans, for the aged and infirm, a
benevolent society composed of French citizens, one of English, one German, one Hebrew, one Hibernian, one Italian, one Polish, one Scandina-
vian, one Scotch, one Welsh, one Swiss, and one Belgian, 32 of these
altogether; of charities in fuel, clothing and so forth, 20 societies; we have
nurseries for children 5, one of them supplied 30,000 meals to children;

* Few nations have equalled Holland in important discoveries and inventions, none has excelled
it in commerce, navigation, learning and science or set as noble examples in the promotion of education and public charities.—*Dodge*, 1866.

6 diet kitchens for food and clothing for the invalid poor, 1 supplied last year daily 150 persons; flower missions for the sick; 8 dispensaries for the gratuitous treatment of disease, in one last year 13,000 were treated (the Northern, the oldest in Philadelphia); we have societies for employing and providing temporary lodgings for the poor, 8, one of these served 17,000 dinners in 11 months; a Baptist Home; the Hayes Mechanics' Home; one for merchants; a home in the summer for women and children; a home for aged couples; an old colored persons' home; one for the Homeless; one for Consumptives; one for Incurables; an indigent Widows' Home; an Old Ladies'; an Odd Fellows'; an asylum and a working Home for the Blind; an Invalids' Home; 2 Wayfarers' Lodges; Soldiers' Home; a Newsboys' Home; 4 Young Women's Homes; the Women's Christian Association; an Actors' (the Forrest) Home; a Home for Friends, for Masons, for Odd Fellows; two Old Man's Homes; a Chinese Home; 17 Children's Homes; 4 Maternity Charities; 7 Nurse Societies; the Mary J. Drexel Home, and 16 Orphanages; the greatest in the whole Country is here—the Girard; the Williamson Institution for Education in Trades now being organized; 12 Reformatory Homes; a Home for Discharged Prisoners; the Workingmen's Association; Relief Societies for Females in Reduced Circumstances; and for the Relief of Firemen; for Clergymen's Widows and Daughters, for the education of their sons; the Prot. Epis. City Mission, its sick-diet kitchen furnished, 1887–8, 38,000 meals; a society to erect fountains for the public use; and a Hospital (the Ryers) for Aged and Injured Animals; a Society to Visit the Prisoners; to Relieve Mariners; to Rescue from Drowning; to Relieve Pilots; for the care of Indian youth; a Society to distribute reading for the sick in hospitals; an Institution for the Deaf Mutes, and one for the Imbeciles; a Society to Colonize the Negroes; a Society to Educate and Employ Black and Indian Children; the Union Benevolent, which since its incorporation has relieved 400,000 persons and distributed $1,000,000 in money and materials; the Penn Widows' Asylum; the Old Ladies' Home, Howard Institution, Rosine Association, Sheltering Arms for Infants, Union Home, Western Home for Poor Children, House of Mercy, House of Industry, Southern Home for Destitute Children, Northern Home for Friendless Children, The Pennsylvania Society to Protect Children from Cruelty. The city is further divided into 31 districts under the Mayor, to systematize the relief of all persons in the city in necessitous circumstances; 30 hospitals for the blind, lame, and special organs and diseases; among them the Episcopal Hospital, the Presbyterian, the Pennsylvania, the Wills Eye Hospital, the St. Mary's and St. Joseph's (Catholic), the Medico-Chirurgical Hospital, the Medical Dept. of the German Society, the

Philadelphia Hospital, the University Hospital, the Jefferson College Hospital, the German, the Children's, the Germantown Hospital, and Small-pox Hospital. All these societies, over 400, are independent of the great institutions provided by the city for the poor—the Almshouse; for the reformation and employment of children—the House of Refuge; and the employment of persons committed for minor offences—the House of Correction. Our family, from its remote beginning in the houses of the first members in Germantown down to the present time, has done its share towards making Philadelphia in this regard a worthy successor of Amsterdam in the New World and justify its name as a City of Charities.

Its work in this line, as far as we have record, began with Michael Keyser⁵. He gave three feasts a year to the poor, and all strangers coming to the town were sent to his house, where he gave them a supper, their lodging and breakfast, and then bade them Godspeed on their journey. It was he who took off and gave his hat and coat to Christopher Saur while in prison during the Revolution.

Peter Keyser⁵ was among the incorporators of the German Society in Philadelphia. Rev. Peter Keyser was a member, Peter A. Keyser was also, and Dr. Peter Dirck Keyser is now—four generations.

Rev. Peter Keyser⁶ was for many years secretary of the Board of Health, and a member of the Society for Alleviating the Miseries of the Public Prisons.

Joseph Keyser⁶ is remembered by one of the oldest members of the family for his very active work on the committee to relieve the sufferers by fire in Wilmington, N. C., Dec. 29, 1819.

Hannah Keyser⁶ kept her house open to the poor, and to strangers coming to the town, and left a legacy towards supporting the poor after her death.

George Keyser⁷, of Baltimore, a member of the Masonic Order, of which he was Grand Marshal in 1809 until his death in 1837, at which time he was Eminent Commander Knights Templar and Grand Sire and presiding officer of the Grand Lodge of Odd Fellows of the United States.

Charles Maris Keyser⁷, in connection with other Baltimoreans, organized and incorporated the House of Refuge of the State of Maryland. He was made its first Vice President, and on the death of its first President succeeded to his office, which he filled until his death in 1874, 20 years.

John Keyser Knorr, M. D., was greatly revered by the poor among whom he practised for his goodness to them.

Amos Pennebacker⁷ was another one of the beloved physicians of Philadelphia, full of sympathy for the poor, a great many of whom he attended in sickness, making little or no charge for his services; and Charles Clin-

ton Keyser, of Baltimore, when the yellow fever desolated that city, volunteered his services and so lost his life. In his obituary, written by Prof. J. H. Butler of the University of Maryland, May 19, 1867, it was said: " Baltimore mourns the loss of one of its best physicians and most noble men; as President of the City Council he will be missed by his colleagues —by whom he was held in just respect and honor—as well by us the more; so has passed away a good man who, to save the lives of many poor, helpless people, risked and thereby lost his own. If you seek for his monument you will find it in the hearts and in the prayers of the poor."

Elhanan W. Keyser was a member of the Masonic Order and a member of the Board of the Philadelphia Hospital, and it was said of him by his fellow-members of the board officially, "that the poor had in him a friend whose ear was ever open to their complaints, and the sick and insane an almoner always ready with open hand and heart to minister to their sufferings." Peter A. Keyser was a member of the Masonic Order and a member of its Finance Committee during the building of its present Temple on Broad street in Philadelphia; member of the Board of Guardians of the Poor and of the Philadelphia Hospital.

Samuel Keyser, as the rule of his whole life, gave bread to the hungry, and brought the outcast to his house, giving not rashly but considerately.

Daniel L. Keyser was a member of the Masonic Order, and for many years connected with the management of the Germantown Almshouse.

Caroline Keyser Inglis is the first Vice President and one of the organizers of the Home for Incurables, and succeeded Susan Keyser as one of the Board of Managers of the Old Man's Home; has been for 19 years connected with the Women's Christian Association, and a member of its Board of Managers from 1872 till 1884, and one of the organizers of the Wayfarers' Lodge. Charles S. Keyser was of the Board of Councils for the first two of these institutions, and honorary member of the Workingmen's Association (1889).

Peter Dirck Keyser, M. D., was acting assistant surgeon in the hospital at Germantown in 1864, and surgeon in charge of the Philadelphia Eye and Ear Infirmary, of which institution he was the founder in 1869; surgeon to the Medical Department of the German Society in 1870, and one of the physicians of the Women's Christian Association from 1871; one of the surgeons to the Wills Eye Hospital from 1872 to this time, 1889; ophthalmic surgeon in Medico-Chirurgical Hospital.

Mrs. Sallie Keyser Savage was one of the organizers of the Episcopal Hospital; up to 1865 was daily there attending to its sick and wounded brought from the battlefields during the war.

Cipriano Canedo practised medicine among the poor of Ameca, Mexico, without money and without price. Three thousand poor people were there, under his gratuitous care, during the years 1887 and 1888.

A. P. Keyser is trustee of the new Almshouse, Germantown.

Romaine Keyser has been associated with work of the St. Clement's Hospital and Dispensary and the Guild of the Iron Cross. Keturah Keyser Benson was the head of much leading charitable work in Baltimore.

John H. Keyser[7] in 1879 began a school for boys discharged from prisons in Connecticut, and subsequently aided in the formation of the New York Prison Association and "the Strangers' Rest," in Pearl street, New York, which fed, cleansed, and often clothed, 10,000 homeless persons annually; in 1871 he built "the Strangers' Hospital," Avenue D and Tenth street, in that city, at a cost for the buildings of $90,000 and $25,000 per annum for its maintainance for the following years, 1871–74.

Mrs. Geo. Jones, d. of Charles Keyser, the teacher, and her daughter, Sarah F. Jones, are both connected with the Pennsylvania Hospital for the Insane, an institution of the greatest distinction in the country.

Wm. Keyser of Baltimore, who, as appears in this paper, has devoted so large a share of his time to the various movements and institutions which have contributed to the religious, educational, commercial and political advancement of his native city, will be remembered in connection with this work of the family, as one of the organizers of the Hospital for the Women of Maryland, of which institution he is at this time one of the governors, and treasurer since its foundation; of the Samuel Ready Institution for Orphan Girls, of which he is also a trustee, and which has an endowment of $650,000; the Mary Byrd Wyman Memorial for the Education of Girls, with an endowment of $250,000; the Church Home and Infirmary of the Protestant Episcopal Church of the Diocese of Maryland, and the Hannah More Academy—the Diocesan School for Girls.

RELIGION.—Our family have been for two centuries a religious family, and, although divided into many sects, have remained all these years very steadily in the Protestant line; they have kept to the spirit though not to the creed of their Mennonite inheritance.* When our ancestor left Amsterdam there were 13 churches there, three large ones all belonging to the Calvinist or Reformed Dutch Presbyterians, two French churches, and one English church. There was a High Dutch church and two synagogues; the Catholics had four score and five chapels; of the Mennonites themselves we have no classification. The members of all these churches were treated with the same consideration by the State, except that the Anabaptists,

* The first request of the Mennonites of Germantown, Sept. 3, 1708, of their friends in Amsterdam was a "loving and friendly" one for some catechisms for the children and little Testaments for the young.

Mennonites and Quakers were in no public employment,* and the Catholics had not the privilege of ringing their bells either in the streets or in their chapels, and all the religious houses of that sect were subject to the inspection of the authorities; and no religieuse or other person could be secluded in these houses; and monks and nuns must always have the privilege to go out and in at their pleasure, and lawfully marry whomsoever and whenever they chose; but what is of the most interest to us here is the present condition of that church to which he devoted some of the early and all of the last years of his life. In this country, I may add that it now greatly exceeds the limit it reached in the century, after it began its mission in Germantown.†

In the Netherlands they number 40,000, less than one-fifth the membership on this side of the Atlantic, which had its first foothold in this Germantown, and among its first ministers our ancestor; but this sect expresses only a minor portion of the result of that regrowth of Christianity on the earth which began as early as the tenth century, and which was fed with human blood for so many following centuries; under one form or another, the substance being the same, its sincere spirit permeates the

* The Mennonites would accept none.

† At the close of the 18th century, 1793, the Mennonites had communities in Schiebach (Skippack), Germantown, Matuchen, Indian Creek, Blen (Plain), Soltford (Salford), Rakkill (Rockhill), Schwanen, Deep Room (Deep Run), Birkosen (Perkasie), Anfrieds, Grotens Swamp (Great Swamp), Sackheim (Saucon), Lower Milford, with two meeting houses, Hosensak, Lehay (Lehigh), Term, Schuylkill, and 40 in the neighborhood of Kunestogis (Conestoga). In 1786, a community in Virginia. In 1793 the whole number of communities, distinct from Baptists, was from 200 to 300, of which 23 were in the Districts of Lancaster and Kunestogis (Conestoga), Pa. The minutes of the Ohio Conference show a membership in the entire community of North America in 1860 of 128,000.—*Pa. Mag. of Hi t., Vol. 4, No. 2.*

At the close of the 19th century, 1888, there are in Lancaster County, Pa., 43 Mennonite places of worship, and including Omish and Herrites, 65; in Berks, 6; Lehigh, 4; Montgomery, 15; Northampton, 2; Chester, 6; Philadelphia, 2; Lebanon, 4; Bucks, 14; Dauphin, 4; Snyder, 2; Adams, 2; Juniata, 5; Franklin, 12; Cumberland, 7; York, 10; Perry, 2. There are also churches in Westmoreland and other western counties. In Washington County, Md., 4; Rockingham Co., Va., Frederick, 3; Augusta, 5. In Knoxville, Tenn., 1. In the State of New York, 5 churches, known. Colorado, 2; Missouri, 6; Ohio, 8, including Omish, 30; Michigan, 1; Indiana, 11; Dakota, 4; Iowa, 12; Minnesota, 4; Kansas, 30; Nebraska, 10; Illinois, 10.

In Manitoba, there are according to the statement of Mr. Shantz, agent of emigration, 1300 Russian Mennonite families. In Canada, Waterloo Co., 17 churches; Oxford, 2; York, 6; Lincoln, 2; Haldeman, 2; Perth, 2; Huron, 2; Bruce, 2; Wellington, 1; Welland, 3; Elgin, 2; Stevensville, 2; Black Creek, 2. (Statistics furnished by Daniel H. Cassel and Bishop N. B. Grubb.)

The whole number of Mennonites in the United States and Canada is estimated at 250,000, and including Omish and other cognate sects in North America, fully 100,000 more.

The old places of worship about Philadelphia established in the early part of the last century still continue. In Skippack, they have five ministers; in Plain, 3; in Salford, 4; in Rockhill, 4; in Deep Run, 5; in Perkasie, 6; in Swamp, 1; in Saucon, 2; in East and West Schwamm, 4; Germantown, 1.

family, its religious life makes one continuous biography—of which I will give these illustrations:

Rev. Peter Keyser[6] was brought up in his father's tannery, where he constructed a shelf above the hopper of the mill, and set his Bible, and from it while there began his lifelong study of the Scriptures. In 1785 was called to the ministry; in 1802 was installed as Bishop or Elder, and for 63 years thereafter was pastor of the Germantown and Philadelphia churches, 47 years of which he was Bishop. In his latter life he became totally blind, but continued reading the Scriptures from memory and still continuing his ministrations until his death.

Albert Duy[5], called the child born of God, began reading the Scriptures at 6 years of age, and from his fifteenth year was so consistent a Christian that the Rev. Samuel A. Clark, into whose church he was received, said there was no one hour rather than another in which it could be said that from that time he dedicated himself to God. Very far back also, I may say, that Michael Keyser[5] was a living witness of the Word, visiting the poor in prison—it was he who gave his own hat and coat to Christopher Sauer in his misery—and he had a place set at his table for the poor and the stranger passing through the town. And so Robert T. Conrad, in 1854, as the Chief Magistrate of Philadelphia, set before himself the task to have the Sabbath-day once more a day of sacred observance by every one, and closed the saloons of the city for the first time on Sunday in this century. Nor must the influence on the family be forgotten of Susan Keyser, of whom it was said after her death by the Board of the Old Man's Home, with which she was long associated, she spent her days in doing good, her motto being, " Be kindly affectioned one to another with brotherly love; in honor preferring one another, not slothful in business, fervent in spirit, serving the Lord," and who lived up to that sublime rule. Sally Keyser Savage, the family illustration of goodness and gentleness, patience and charity, so gratefully remembered for her work in St. Mark's Church, Frankford, in the Sunday-school. Ann (Keyser) Baker[6], for 56 years a member of the Baptist Church, Philadelphia, illustrated the Christian life of so many of the family.

Silvester Keyser, not a church member, always read after each meal a chapter of the Bible, selected by him for himself and family.

Samuel Stouffer Keyser[7], the merchant of Baltimore, who for a quarter of a century contending with a disease that must end fatally, never lost his faith in a kind and overruling Providence or his unquestioning belief that all was wisely ordered for his good, until his life's close; and Ann Childs' gentle influence in her home, the spirit of whose life is written on the tablet in the chapel at Chestnut Hill to her memory, and last that strong

woman of our family, Keturah Keyser Benson, who was fifty years superintendent of the Sabbath-school of the Baptist Church, Baltimore, and
devoted all her great gifts to religion and humanity; undeterred by their
surroundings and sometimes danger, she went into the haunts of
wretchedness and crime and by the bedside of the sick and dying passed
her life in these ministrations. The Rev. Samuel W. Lynd[7], D. D. (grandson of Michael Keyser[5]), who at the age of 22 devoted his life to God's service, married, as our ancestor's father had done, the daughter of an eminent
divine (William Staughton, D. D.), and passed twenty years as pastor of
the Baptist Church, Cincinnati, and then as an instructor in theology, and
completed his days in that service.

I may fitly close this record with the thanksgiving to God found
among the private papers of Daniel L. Keyser after his death. It was
written in his 60th year and is signed with his clear plain signature:

BIRTH DAY.

Blessed be God for my creation and birth; for giving me a being from honest parents,
fearing God; and in a Christian and Protestant country; for the means of grace, the assistance of the Holy Spirit and for the hope of glory; for all the known or unobserved favors,
providences and deliverances, by which my life has hitherto been preserved; most humbly
beseeching Thee my God and Father, to pardon my neglect or abuse of any of Thy favors,
and that I have so much forgotten Thee, in whom I live, and move and have my being,
Good Lord forgive me the great waste of my precious time; the many days and years of
health, and the many opportunities of doing good which I have lost; and give me grace that
for the time to come I may be truly wise that I may consider my latter end and work out my
salvation with fear and trembling, ever remembering the night cometh when no man can
work and that the day of my death may be better to me than the day of my birth. O gracious God, grant that before Thou takest from me that breath which Thou gavest me I may
truly repent of the errors of my past life; that my sins may be forgiven and my pardon
sealed in heaven when the Good Lord shall vouchsafe me a better and an everlasting life
through Jesus Christ. Amen.   DANIEL L. KEYSER.

Born Feb. 21, 1819.

THE LAW OF INHERITANCE.—From what is written here, we may see
very plainly, that while we have grown into and become a part of the larger
development of this country since our ancestor came here, yet in all that
we are and in all that we may hope to be; in our business lives, in our sense
of the value of free institutions, in our devotion to education, and what we
have done for the poor and the prisoner, the aged and the sufferer, according to the measure of our abilities, we are but the result of the compelling
force of that blood of those ancestors in our veins. Our qualities have been
only a continuing growth of their qualities; their same habitudes remain
in our fingers and brains. That Dutch race into which our family merged,

originating as far as we have historic knowledge in the northwest portion
of Europe—land and sea together, absorbed and recreated the best blood
from France as it absorbed our German blood and that of other parts of
Europe, and developed as we have seen the highest civilization of our later
centuries; its influence still endures there and here, the piles on which its
vast structure of tolerance in religion and manual and general education
were built, do not decay, are not beaten back and forth by every wind and
wave, are solid throughout and wholesome; and let us hope our country
with its ever increasing populations and domain may hold and acquire yet
more of the population and with it more of the greatness of that country,
the disposition for a broader intercourse with the world in commerce which
was and yet is in the Netherlands, the more conscientious work in manufactures that was there, and the higher official character which was there;
that it may reach the immeasurably higher plane in the arts which was
there, the broader education which was there, the yet more effective charities that were there, and what is farther away from us than any of these,
and yet more valuable than any, the more profound sense of the meaning
of the doctrine of the Saviour in which the Mennonites lived; in a word,
the higher plane of civilization which our ancestor left in "the United
States of the Netherlands," when he came to this Province of Pennsylvania.

EDUCATION BENDS THE TWIG, AND SO INCLINES THE TREE, IT LEAVES
THE FRUIT THE SAME; two centuries have not lessened from or added one
inch to the statures which we received from our ancestors nor in any degree the attributes they gave us; it is so with all families and nationalities. From this should come to us a broader lesson, that not through
education alone, and not by constitutions alone, depends our progress as a
nation; but mainly on the preservation and development of the races here
which have the largest leaning towards order, liberty and humanity, and
the exclusion of those who bring with themselves, and in themselves, as
part of the tendencies of their existence, want, disorder, and servility; for
should these constitutions and every bond and ligament with which society
is bound together here be destroyed, the stocks which developed them, as
that pious ancestor of ours could have done with the Scriptures, would
replace them again. OUR CONSTITUTIONS EXIST ONLY BECAUSE THE RACES
EXIST, WHICH CREATED THEM, AND THEY WILL PERISH WITH THEM. It
is a witless thing to see a people whose earlier instruction was to light the
fires of economy and to raise children, expending great sums of money on
better breeds of cattle, and preserving with the greatest care the pedigrees
of its horses, while at the same time neglecting the preservation of its own
families, and degrading the earlier emigration with its broad free spirit

and higher conscience by allowing and inviting the inflowing here of the most degenerate races of the earth.

Brothers, sisters, fathers, mothers, children, we have met together, many for the first, and many others it may be, the last time; let me hope it will strengthen the family feeling, one to the other; not only for its pleasures, and advantage to ourselves, but by our example as far as it goes to the community. Single lines of families die out. The broad family strain survives. If among us there shall be any to die childless, wifeless, fatherless and motherless, it must be a pleasant thing to know, that to some one at least, nearer than the State, his accumulations greater or smaller will go. That he may not in this isolation which may come to any of us, wholly die, but yet remain a part of this living lineage, which like a broad and centuries enduring river, will still flow on, when the little stream which was ourselves, is hidden and lost under the grasses and flowers, in the valley and shadow of death.*

THE HOMES, MEETING-HOUSES, AND BURIAL-GROUNDS, BY PETER D. KEYSER, M. D.

KINSMEN AND KINSWOMEN: As the morning hours are passing and you have had so much to interest you in the excellent address of my predecessor, I do not desire to detain you with any lengthy dissertation, as we have more to follow, as you see by the programme, but to continue the history of the family by giving you a short description of the homes occupied by our ancestors, the meeting-houses in which they worshiped and the burial-grounds in which they have found the last and long rest from the cares, troubles, and pleasures of this earth.

When the first immigrants came here with Francis Daniel Pastorius in 1683 to settle this place, they were obliged to live temporarily in caves until there was some division of the lands, so that what habitations they put up could be permanent. The plot of land for this place, containing over five thousand acres, was originally taken up by a company formed in Frankfort, Germany, called the Frankfort Land Company. Francis Daniel Pastorius was appointed the agent of the company to come here. He visited the lower Rhine and Holland to solicit the Mennonites and Quakers to come with him to form a settlement where they could be free in their religious worship and not suffer the persecutions they had been subjected to for so many years; so when some concluded to come and purchase land it was necessary to know from whom to buy and receive title, as the company did not have the stock franchise as at the present day, but each sub-

---

* A general summary only of this paper was read at the reunion. C. S. K.

scribed for so many acres of land, and it was necessary to divide the land in lots for the members in sizes according to their subscriptions. This division was first done in April, 1684, in the cave of Francis Daniel Pastorius, and each subscriber received his number of acres, personally to those subscribers who came over here, and others through their agents appointed for that purpose, and then each disposed of his portion as he desired. After this division some settlements were made, but really nothing permanent was done until 1689 as the Patent for the land was not issued until early in that year.

Many more settlers having arrived in the meantime in the colony, and

RESIDENCE OF DIRCK KEYSER[2], BUILT BY HIM 1689.

wishing to carry out the methods of the mother-country to live in close communication, it was decided to form a town, and so much of the land for that purpose was laid out in town lots, and to remove any feelings relative to the situation of the lots, it was considered best that they should be chosen by lot, that is, distributed by a drawing as in a lottery. This took place on the 4th of April, 1689. The arrangement of the lots was that there should be twenty-three on each side of the main road, to contain with certain side lands fifty acres each. In this drawing Dirck Keyser who had arrived here in the autumn of 1688 (just two hundred years ago), drew lot No. 22 on the east side of the road. The southern line of this lot is about one hundred to one hundred and fifty feet above this church line.

Upon this lot he built his domicile, fronting on the line of the public road, and like all Dutchmen who were accustomed to strong, stone houses, he erected a solid mansion in such manner, strength, and form, that in case of necessity it would afford protection from the Indians or other external influences; and with such solidity that it stands in fine order to this day. It has passed down in the line of the family in excellent preservation; and is No. 5149, just a short distance above here. It is occupied by Mr. John Channon, a gentleman now 82 years old, and who came into possession of it by his wife who is a descendant of Dirck Keyser.

The custom in Holland of cutting the initials or full name on a stone in the front wall was carried out by him, for on a stone alongside of the front door frame is still to be seen, although somewhat worn by time, the letters D. K. This is about the height of the bell-pull of the present day, and no doubt answered the same as the present doorplate to designate the owner and resident.

As the whole region of Germantown is stony, there was no difficulty in getting building materials. Stone was presumably cheaper and easier to handle than timber. The house is built of surface stones as can be clearly seen on examination, especially the ends, for the front has since been fixed up and lined with plaster to look like large, dressed stones. Lime was easily made as there was and is plenty of limestone in this region.

It is natural to suppose that the first few settlers in 1683–84 and 85 had gone over the whole country and knew the resources of the place, so that when the incomers of 1686–87 and 88 arrived it was a much easier matter to provide houses. The walls of the house are very thick, and on the gable ends still show the lines of the size of the original house. It seems to have been composed of two rooms front with a kitchen containing a bake-oven and smoke-house on the rear end (Mr. Channon says that this bake-oven was very large and when he tore it out, contained stone enough for him to build a good sized back kitchen to the house) on the first floor, with some sleeping-rooms above in the second story. The pent roof extending over the door and windows is still there, but on account of the necessity of changing the steps in the alteration of the street grade, the original steps and portico have been removed.

This house was a large one in its day, and appeared to be large enough for Dirck Keyser and his son Pieter, a boy of 12 years of age, and no doubt a housekeeper. As the boy grew up and married, and his family increased it seems that additions were made thereto, and also by Pieter's son Dirck, who lived therein after his father's death.

A curious arrangement is that there are three cellars under the house without any communication with each other. With only one is there any direct communication to the upper floor, and this is by a set of solid stone steps going down from the entry or hall under the stairs leading to the second story. To go into one of the cellars it is necessary to go outside and enter from the street, while with the other, which is under one of the additions in the back, a trap-door is cut in the floor of the room above, down which a pair of wooden steps run. Alongside of this cellar the old

JOHN KEYSER'S HOUSE WITH THE ADDITION BY THE REV. C. RODNEY DUVAL.

well is found and is in most excellent order. It serves not only to give good water but to keep this part so cold that everything is preserved in summer without ice. Thus they provided a refrigerator for warm weather.

Dirck Keyser, the judge and grandson of the original Hollander, purchased during his lifetime many properties, one of which is the second house on the west side of this street above Washington avenue, then called Keyser's lane. This house is a fine, large, double, stone mansion, built I think by either Paul Engel or Ludwig Engelhardt. Dirck Keyser's son Peter purchased it on the division of the estate and lived and died there. His son the Rev. Peter Keyser, the Dunker bishop, was born, lived and died there. After his death his daughter Mrs. Lynd took it in her division of the estate and soon after sold it to Mr. Ellwood Johnson, who now occupies it. Mr. Johnson has remodeled it by putting a mansard roof on it.

John Keyser built a stone house further up on this side of the street, opposite now Duval street. The Rev. C. Rodney Duval purchased it and added thereto. The original part is the upper end of the present house. Michael Keyser's large house stood below here, but long since torn down in the march of modern improvements. All of the original houses had what is called a pent roof projecting over the door and windows of the first floor, and small balconies in front of the door with a seat on either side, where the residents would sit pleasant summer afternoons and evenings. A few of such are still to be seen on some of the old houses standing up the road toward Mt. Airy or Chestnut Hill.

All of these houses were well and strongly built, and many must have been the days of solid comfort and pleasure enjoyed therein, but at times crossed and subdued by hours of sorrow. There were strong hearts and sturdy bodies, as may still be seen running through the descendants. God in his mercy blessed them with prosperity of worldly goods as well as with large families. So much with the latter, that in almost every State in this Union as well as in Nova Scotia, Mexico and Europe, the descendants of the pious, solid old Dutchman Dirck Keyser are to be found.

The first meeting of the Mennonite settlers was held in the house of Tunis Kunders in 1683, and for some years worship was held regularly in the houses of the members, and under the shade of the trees in the open air in fair, pleasant weather. But in 1702, a few years after the arrival of William Rittinghuysen, who was the first regularly-ordained minister, the lot occupied by this church and graveyard was received from Arnold von Flossen, and in 1708 a log house was built, which was used to worship in, and at the same time as a school-house for the children.

Bishop Rittinghuysen died in 1708, and his son Claus Rittinghuysen and Dirck Keyser were chosen as the preachers. Dirck Keyser officiated here until his death, in 1714. In 1770 the stone house now occupied—and in which we, the descendants of Dirck Keyser, are this day assembled—was erected.

Prior to the building of the first church it is impossible to say where the dead were buried—presumably, on the lands of the possessors. But after the land and church were in possession of the trustees, then the burials took place in the churchyard. Our ancestor Dirck Keyser died in 1714, some time after the log church was erected, and, having preached therein from 1708 to 1714, it is presumed that he is buried in the graveyard. His son Pieter, who died in 1725, was interred there, for his head-stone—which had fallen and had become covered with earth—was turned up some years ago while digging a grave. Instead of replacing it in its original position, it was removed and stood against the south wall, where it remained for some years, but eventually became lost. Dirck, Pieter's son who died in 1756, lies therein, as seen by his tombstone now standing; and so on many members of the family have found their last resting place here.

Dirck Keyser the first here has no mark of any kind raised to his memory—nothing to show that he was one of the earliest settlers of this place, nothing to indicate that he was a follower of the Lord and a dispenser of his divine word in this religious community, nothing to designate that here lies the remains of our common ancestor. Is it not fitting, as well as incumbent, upon us his descendants to erect such a monument in this little God's acre? It will show our respect for his memory—one who left home and fortune, who braved the rolling sea, to preach the gospel in this then wilderness, and now lies resting forever with his family in sacred ground. A plain, inexpensive, but massive, stone would be most proper, and a small contribution from all of us who are of his blood would soon accomplish it.

In 1719, Alexander Mack, Jr., came from Holland and introduced the Dunker ideas, it being a split or deviation from the Mennonites on the question and form of baptism as established by his father, Alexander Mack, Sr., in 1708. Many of the members of our family accepted these ideas and joined with him, thus really carrying the greater part of the family into the community, one of whom, Peter Keyser, became a very prominent preacher and bishop of the church.

The Dunkers purchased a log house and lot on the main street a little way above here, in 1731, and held worship there until 1740, when the present house was built. In this graveyard the majority of the family are inhumed and continue to be interred until this day—so much so that it is almost a Keyser-family cemetery. It is a beautiful little spot, and will well repay a visit to its sacred region. It is on the right side of the main street, above Sharpnack street.*

---

* The first Dunkard church was built, of logs, in 1731, on ground originally purchased by Alexander Mack, Christopher Saur, Peter Leibert and George S. Schrieber, they making a declaration of trust of the ground for the society. In 1784, Alexander Mack and Peter Leibert, surviving trustees, conveyed the property to the new board of trustees, Christian Lashet, Justus Fox, John Weaver, William Leibert, Thomas Langstroth, Peter Keyser, Michael Keyser, Adam Weaver, and Garret Clemens. The burial-ground was enlarged in 1804 by the purchase of a lot in the rear from Philip Weaver by Michael Keyser, William Leibert, Jacob Bowman, William Bowman, Peter Keyser, Justus Fox, William Keyser, Benjamin Lehman, and John Weaver, trustees. The stone house now standing was built in 1740.

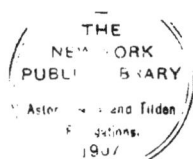

Julia A. Orum.

For some years all the graveyards belonged to some religious denomination; so that there was no place for the interment of those of different faith or for strangers, until 1724, when Paul Wulff gave land on the east side of the main street, above Keyser's lane—now Washington avenue—for a free ground. Any one of any faith or sect could purchase a grave or lot and be buried there. This ground was designated as "The Upper Germantown Burying-Ground," called, improperly, "Ax's Burying-Ground," after the first superintendent. It was also called "The Concord Graveyard," from the Concord schoolhouse, alongside of it. This ground was given to the borough of Germantown, and a committee of overseers appointed to take charge of it. The citizens contributed funds to build a stone wall around it. Peter Keyser and his first wife, who lived opposite to it, are buried therein. There are others of the family also interred there, but none of the name. Some of the officers of the American army killed at the battle of Germantown are lying there.

These three grounds where rest our forefathers are historic and interesting, and well worthy a visit.

I must ask pardon for detaining you so long, when there is so much to come after me; but I have been as brief as possible, to be interesting.

I have now the pleasure of introducing Miss Julia A. Orum, a descendant of Dirck Keyser, who will read to you an account of the Mennonites and the martyrdom of Leonhard Keyser.

THE MENNONITES.*

READ BY JULIA A. ORUM.

After Christianity had become a state power, the religious houses accumulated great stores of wealth from the living and the dying; but these accumulations were contrary to the letter of the Scriptures on which their power rested, and it was necessary, therefore, for them to keep these Scriptures to themselves. This was the more easily done since the writings were in languages unintelligible to the people at large, and could only be duplicated at the cost of much time and labor, and so the book remained in their keeping for many centuries. Of the fact that it required an intelligent acceptance by the believer—that the evidence of that acceptance was the believer's walk and conversation—the world remained in ignorance for long centuries; and so it would have remained for longer centuries if the vassalage of that church had remained with the races with whom it then, and yet conserves its power; but when the religious houses seated themselves in France they were among a people

* Written for the occasion by Charles S. Keyser.

6

with whom there could be no, centuries long, endurance; and when they reached the Low Countries and our race, they could only inaugurate a struggle, which must finally end in their overthrow. It was in effect an effort by the masters of the inferior races to dominate races to which all that is free and sincere belongs, to continue the malarial growth of the marshes of Rome along the sunny fields of France, the wholesome seas of Holland and God's enduring rock the German fatherland. In France in the early part of the 12th century this definite dogma against them was asserted: that the Scriptures were not written for unconsciousness and ignorance but for that condition of intelligence which could accept its ordinances, which is the first foundation stone of the great structure of the Mennonite doctrine; and Peter Bruis in 1126 laid down these propositions, first—that children could not be saved by baptism; that there was no part of the body or blood of Christ in the wafer that the priests were eating; that the churches inlaid with gold and silver and jewels were without warrant in Christianity; that meat was to appease hunger and should be eaten on one day as well as another; and that it was senseless to pray for the dead; and further that the writings of the fathers were without the authority of the Scriptures; that the priests should marry and that the vices of the monasteries were unendurable; these facts he made so clear that every one could see that the power of Rome with its then unspeakable iniquities should in one way or another be destroyed; he was followed as he went from place to place through France by many people, and was at last burned, but for three hundred years after, the remembrance of what he had said, lived. Henry of Toulouse his disciple continued his work, going about reading the Scriptures to the people in their own language.

In 1160 Peter Waldo came upon the earth;[*] he was a citizen of Lyons and through him the power of Rome received another and severer blow. He was a very wealthy man and he found in the Scriptures that the Saviour had required the man with large possessions to sell all that he

---

[*] From his reducing himself to poverty his followers in France were called the Poor Men of Lyons and Chaignards, Dogs; beyond the Alps they were called after one of his disciples Josephists; in England, Lollards, after one of their preachers there, and after two others Henrichians and Esperonests—after another preacher Arnoldists; in Provence, Siccars; in Italy, Fratricelli—little brothers. As Sunday was their only holiday they were called Insabbates—Sabbath non-observers; Patarians because they were sufferers; Passagenes, because they were wanderers. In Germany, Cazares—the abominable. In Flanders, Turlilupini—dwellers with wolves, because they hid in the wildernesses; Lombards in Lombardy; Picards in Picardy; Bohemians in Bohemia; Runcari in Runcalia, Italy; Barrini from another district in Italy, and Cotterollos and Comists from other localities of Italy. In Germany also Grubenheimen, because they dwelt in caves. In Flanders Texterants, because many of them were weavers. Much the same order of people, and living in the same condition as the first followers of the Saviour, they were under these various names Waldenses, Anabaptists, Mennonites—believers in the Scriptures, as they were written, as a rule for their living and dying.

had and give to the poor and he began in this way, and having at last
freed himself from the cares of the world and the deceitfulness of riches,
as Henry of Toulouse had done, read the Scriptures to the people in their
own language, saying nothing, reading on continually; driven by persecution to other countries, he continued the work so long, and with such
force and power that the believers got a firm foothold on the earth.

The creed of his followers under their various names, was that the
church was not a system or building but a congregation of believers; that
the obeyal of orders of governments was no part of the same; that the
swearing of oaths was not allowable; that the rite of infant baptism was
without authority; that the water of baptism was no more than the water
of rivers; and that they must "love their enemies, do works of mercy,
shun idleness, possess their souls in patience and not avenge themselves;"
these precepts among others first written in the 13th century *remain* the
doctrine of these Mennonites, as was their later name. The lives of the
leaders of these Believers—Waldenses as was then their name, were a continual fast and prayer; they lived on bread and water, seven times a day
they engaged in prayer and labored as mechanics meanwhile with their
hands, content with the necessaries of life.

In the 15th century they again say, that while the story of the creation
in Genesis and the fall and punishment of man, the redemption of man
and his restoration were verities, yet that Adam's children were born
before his disfavor and were therefore not born to condemnation but in a
state of reconciliation with God; that when men have attained knowledge
and then are drawn away from a state of innocence they are justly condemned, but children not; they further allege that Adam did not sin by
the fore-ordination of God, but through his voluntary desire; and that the
saving grace of God extends through all humanity including everyone
living; and that since infants have neither knowledge, ability, inclination,
nor emotion, concerning such things as good or evil, neither faith nor
unbelief can be attributed to them; that they are simple and ignorant and
as such perfectly pleasing to God and deserving of our imitation; that
men were not made wholly evil by the fall of man, but yet retained good
principles; that the evidence of faith is works, without which it is dead;
that without faith attested by works neither circumcision nor uncircum-
cision, baptism nor supper were of any avail; that not only Christ's
humanity must be believed in but also his spirituality and eternity of
existence; that the church is not a house nor a creed but a body of believers drawn together by faith, through love, that it may be distinguished
from all others by the good works of its members, and by its unblamable
ministers, and finally by the universal love of its members towards

humanity and by its charitableness to everyone; that they believe in the Trinity as it is written and in the incarnation and death and resurrection of the Saviour, the resurrection of the dead, and the final judgment, and observe the ordinance of the supper, baptism and separation. That baptism is a sign without power to cleanse or save, that it exists as a symbol of the fact of faith, and repentance, and cannot therefore be applicable to infants without knowledge, responsibility or language; that the bread and wine used at the supper differs in no respect from any other bread; that it is in the mouth natural bread and wine through faith and in the spirit received as Christ's flesh and blood, of which the supper is the sign or representative; and that for the same reason and as a sign that they wash the feet of their brothers; and they finally say—they must use no weapons of warfare, that they must be charitable even to their enemies, though they destroy them; that they must have no poor among them, but must minister to them of their temporal possessions and for the rest that they must put away avarice, and abstain from drunkenness and revelling, that no oath must be taken for any cause whatever; and believers must not exercise the office of the magistracy for they are only sojourners on the earth with no abiding city; that they are without laws or rules and government and so it must remain.

And at the last day, which they say may at any time, come without warning, unexpectedly, the Saviour will appear again, revealing himself amid the clouds as King of Mighty Kings, with the power of the Almighty Father, a great retinue of angels around him, the trumpets pealing unutterable sounds, the mountains and isles of the sea moving, and the whole earth weeping and wailing for fear and expectation; and until that day the souls of believers and unbelievers must wait for reward or punishment; that the body shall be united with the soul which had become separated in death, and the pious shall be made like unto the angels of God and the living with the dead as one, be transfigured and glorified after the image of Christ, and that in that last day he will say to the believers, Come ye blessed of my Father inherit the kingdom prepared for you from the foundations of the world, and to the unbelievers will say, Depart from me ye cursed into everlasting fire prepared for the devil and his angels; and the sun shall lose its brightness and the stars fade away and all the light and glory of the world be changed to everlasting darkness; the water and streams shall be turned into pits and brimstone which shall burn for ever and ever; and seeing the earth is called hell in places of the Scriptures and no mention made of any other, that they regard it as the place of damnation, and in it the souls and bodies of the unbelievers then united shall burn for ever and ever; but the believers shall be received into the glorious kingdom prepared from the foundation of the world, a city filled with good things—the New Jerusalem coming down from heaven prepared for the Lord as a bride for her husband—the streets pure gold, the gates adorned with precious stones where the brightness and eternal light shall shine for ever and ever; there shall be no more sorrow there, no cold, nakedness, thirst, or hunger there, satisfying joy and consolation in place of these, and the souls of believers separated from their bodies by death, and kept in the hands of God until this hour, shall be caught up to meet the Lord in the air, and as a bride received by her husband through grace into the presence of God, and the heavenly host; their robes of mourning—their mortal covering of flesh shall be put off and the immortal put on; they shall be clothed in white and be fed by the Son of God with the hidden heavenly bread, eat of the tree of life, drink of the living water, sing the new songs, be priests and kings of God and reign with Christ forever.

So it was that when this Book of Books was first put into the hands of the great, toiling masses of Europe, and read to them for the first time in their own language by those surviving ministers of the Saviour after ten centuries of its burial in monasteries revealing once more in all its living glory and brightness those facts, their deliverance from death and that eternal light of glory that waited them, nothing—neither principalities nor powers nor chains nor drowning could subdue them. It could not have been otherwise—eternity was for them an ever present reality, while they were perishing, Christ's Kingdom was beginning, and death itself only kept their souls secure for that great day of the Lord—so that while the Catholic priests and the Protestant rulers themselves united to utterly extinguish them, men and women, their faith increased only the more and more and so Christianity was kept upon the earth.

Among the leaders and a part of this profound movement of the under strata of humanity which changed the structure of the spiritual world was Menno Simons.

Menno Simons was born probably in 1492, he was brought up a Catholic priest, but had never read the Scriptures until he had been two years engaged in this priestly office; from that time he began and continued to read them daily, he accepted the views of the believers as to their doctrines and the time for the administration of the rite of baptism; his brother lost his life with the Munsterites in 1535, and he left the Catholic church a year after; in 1536 he was baptised in the creed of the believers, in 1537 was ordained into the ministry and brought back many Munsterites to the non-combatant disposition of the believers, they being in other matters of faith and doctrine the same; he then became a Baptist minister of the old evangelicals who strongly denounced warfare; and he spread abroad their doctrine in the depths of the forests, went from place to place as a wood-chopper, lived in caves and gathered the believers together. Altogether outside of the State Alliance of the Reformation Menno Simons and his followers asserted and maintained the absolute right of private judgment in religious matters as against the civil power, in a word made the rights of all dissenters, from churches allied with states secure; MADE OUR CONSTITUTIONS IN THIS REGARD POSSIBLE AND MADE THE ASSERTION OF A HIGHER LAW THROUGH WHICH, IN DESPITE OF THOSE CONSTITUTIONS, HUMAN SLAVERY WAS DESTROYED HERE, ALSO POSSIBLE.*

But the cost at which this was done was very great. In Switzerland these Anabaptists were branded with the Arms of Canton of Berne, and sold to be chained to the seats of and work in the galleys, along the Mediterranean Sea; they were branded and sold to work in the fortresses at Malta, and to the Barbary pirates. In the city of Antwerp more of them, as Hon. W. Samuel Pennypacker has written, were burned than of those who were burned in the whole reign of the English Mary. In Suabia and in Bavaria, where he who glorifies our name suffered, three thousand of them perished by drowning and fire.

The pious chronicler Van Braght having written the history of the first fifteen hundred years of Martyrdoms, from the advent of Christianity and come down to this time of the Mennonite persecutions says, it is true that fifteen hundred years extend over a longer period of time than about one hundred and fifty of like years, and that the persecutions which occurred during that longer time when put in the balance would be heavier than this last one, as well as the number of persons who were persecuted, but, he continues, never in the preceding fifteen centuries did any persecution continue for so long a time without alleviation; never was there, in so short though actually long time, so much innocent blood shed, never were there in so small a space, so many dark prisons, deadly tribunals, scaffolds, fiery stakes, and other instruments of death erected and made use of as were at this time in Germany and the Netherlands.

* As the first protest against slavery in this country came from the Germantown Mennonites, meeting with the Friends—so the Baptists into which our family merged largely in later generations—and the same in their first origins together with the Friends, urged upon the Continental Congress (Oct., 1774), then sitting in Carpenters' Hall, Philadelphia, "the abolition of all laws touching the support of the Christian religion by general taxation, and to secure religious freedom for all persons;" the same Baptist Association which made the formal protest on that occasion, still existing and rejoicing in the success of its work, by its committee met in the same Hall (Oct. 8, 1874) and held a thanksgiving service for the State dissociation and the measure of toleration we enjoy. Among them was Horatio Gates Jones as a representative of the Baptists, Horace J. Smith of the work of the Friends' Society, and Charles S. Keyser of the work of the Mennonites.

I will now read you the Mennonite confession, as it was brought here by our ancestor in this old book of the Martyrs.

THE MENNONITE CONFESSION.

ARTICLE 1. Sets out a belief in one God, the Father, Son and Holy Ghost, and in none more, nor in any other, who was before any other, and after whom was none other, and that he made the heavens in six days, that he created Adam the first man, and placed him

THE SUFFERINGS OF THE MENNONITES.

in a pleasure garden, took a rib from him and made Eve to be his wife, and that they were the parents of all living.

ART. 2. That they were seduced by the serpent, and the enemy the devil, for disobedience to God, that through the disobedience, sin came into the world and death by sin which thus passed to all men so that no other nor themselves, no man or any other creature in heaven or earth could reconcile them to God, and they would have been eternally lost.

ART. 3. But that God called them to him again, and showed them that it had been fore-ordained before the foundation of the world that the immaculate Lamb the Son of God would come and that he had been promised here to them while they were yet in paradise for salvation.

ART. 4. That he came and was made flesh and blood and was Mary's first-born son and laid in a manger at Bethlehem. But of how the body was prepared and how the word came flesh and he himself a man we content ourselves with the statement which the worthy evangelists have left us. We furthermore believe that he was when he finished his course, crucified, dead and buried, and on the third day arose from the dead, and sits beside God and will come again to judge the quick and the dead.

ART. 5. That he instituted his New Testament and sealed it with his blood and that neither angel nor man may alter it nor add to it nor take from it away.

ART. 6. That since the imagination of man's heart is prone to evil the first lesson is to bring forth generous proofs of repentance and desist from wrong, and that neither baptism, supper nor any ceremony can without faith and repentance avail anything to please God.

ART. 7. That baptism may be by water in the name of the Father, Son and Holy Ghost to penitent believers only.

ART. 8. We believe in a visible church, namely those who truly repent and believe.

ART. 9. That every city, church and place should have Bishops, Pastors and Elders to worthily administer God's ordinance baptism and supper and they should appoint Elders, ordaining them by laying on of hands and provide deacons to look after the poor and receive alms and dispense them to the needy saints and also aged deaconesses who should be widows, to visit the sick and comfort the sorrowing and needy, as also widows and orphans, that the deacons should assist the Elders and labor in the work.

ART. 10. We observe the Supper, breaking of bread and wine in remembrance of him that his body was broken and his blood spilled.

ART. 11. We also confess a washing of the feet as a sign of humility, following the Lord and Master who did the same, and to remember through it we are washed with his blood.

ART. 12. We confess to a state of matrimony of two free believing persons instituted by God in Paradise, and that the believers have no choice but to marry among their own spiritual kindred the chosen generation of Christ such and no others who first become united with the church and receive one baptism and stand in our communion faith and practice, before they shall unite with one another by marriage.

ART. 13. We believe that God has ordained power and authority to govern the world and that we therefore may not despise, revile, or resist the same, that we must be obedient to them, and ready for all good works especially in those not contrary to the commandments of God and to pay tribute and taxes, and pray for their welfare and for the prosperity of the country.

ART. 14. As regards revenge the Lord God has forbid it and we must beat the swords into plowshares. We must not inflict pain and sorrow, but flee if need be from city to city and suffer the spoiling of our goods, when smitten we must rather turn the other cheek and pray for our enemies and refresh them when hungry and thirsty and overcome so all ignorance, finally we must do good, do unto no one that which we would not have done to us.

ART. 15. We must not swear at all, all oaths high and low are forbidden to us, all our declarations must be yea for that that is yea, and nay for that that is nay, but that we must in all matters fulfil the same as by our oath.

ART. 16. We believe in a ban or separation from the church to keep the church pure; we must admonish with meekness.

ART. 17. If any one has so far fallen that he is separated from God and separated from the church, the same must be shunned without distinction by all his fellow-members in eating, drinking, and other similar intercourse, but not to the destruction but for the reformation of the same, and if he is hungry, sick, thirsty, or in any distress, we must render to him aid and assistance, not counting him as an enemy but admonishing him as a brother.

ART. 18. Finally, we believe in the resurrection of the dead, and the separation of the good from the evil, that the one shall sit at God's right hand and the other be cast into the everlasting pains of hell with no more hope.

This confession is signed by all the districts and cities of Holland; and for the city of Amsterdam, by Tobias Goverts van den Wyngaert, the grandfather of our ancestor, with four others; it is dated 21st of April, 1632—to teach it, and to illustrate it by his life was the work of our ancestor's remaining days upon the earth. I will now read the story of Leonhard Keyser's death, and with that conclude the paper.

LEONHARD KEYSER.

Leonhard Keyser died 3 days before Laurentii, Aug., 1527.

Leonhard Keyser, the story reads,* was a mass priest in Bavaria in the early part of the sixteenth century, a man of learning or what passed for such, in the monasteries to which "the Church" consigns such lives; he had already perished while Menno Simons was still remaining in their dark shadow. He earlier recognized the tendencies, and became himself a part of the movement of that age. He accepted the writings of Zwingli and Luther† and went to Wittenberg, and there held converse with the doctors; partook with them, the Lord's Supper, joined himself to the separated, cross-bearing church of the Anabaptists‡ in 1525; he returned to Bavaria spreading the work of the gospel with great zeal and power; the end, however, came as it does to all, in one form or another, in whom a higher truth of the advancing age, has its first manifestation. He denied the power, he refused obedience to the church of which he was a priest duly

* Translated by Charles S. Keyser 1862, from Van Braght's "Het Bloedigh Tooneel der Doops Gesinde." The copy from which the translation was made was brought from Amsterdam in 1688 by our ancestor. It has descended in Dr. Peter Dirk Keyser's line and is now in his possession.

† Luther at this time taught the Anabaptist doctrine of adult immersion, see his sermon 1519, and still argued that the rite should be by immersion, while he yielded to the importunities of his co-laborers for infant baptism.

‡ He was one of the Waldenses.— *Ten Cate.*

LEONHARD KEYSER, 1527.

accredited, he put aside the mystery and obscurity of the Latin tongue,
and went among the people telling them in their own language—the common language of the country, what they should do to be saved. The
power of the church was yet very great, and its answers to such leaders
of the future time was beating, drowning, burning, quartering, strang-
ling, flaying—modes of argument suitable to the ignorance and evil inten-
tion of the Masters of that age—but he did not therefore cease from his
labors, and so surely came to his end; he was taken at Scharding in
Bavaria, by the Bishop of Passau, and by the other Priests and Capitulars
of the church, and condemned to be burned alive. On his trial he repeatedly refused to speak in the language of the tyranny of the time—the
Romish language, he would answer them only in the German language—
the people's tongue. Three days before Laurentii, in August, 1527, he
was taken to his execution; it was midsummer, the trundle on which he
lay with its broad wheels, crushed down the flowers in the meadow along
which it was passing, as the church was crushing out his hopes and desires
for the future time; and while he was answering the monks following the
wain, they addressing him in the Latin, and he always answering in the
people's tongue, these flowers struck his eye; and reaching down he
plucked one and held it in his hand; beyond him the fire was burning;
on a distant hill, a group was standing, his friends or his enemies, watch-
ing the event; over him was the clear sunshine of the heavens. It was
his last hour on earth. And here this incident occurred. He said to the
judge riding near him, "I have plucked this flower, I hold it in my hand,
if you burn this flower with me, you have justly condemned me, but if
otherwise, if it shall not be burned in this hand, then consider what you
have done, repent and be saved." Of what follows there are two relations; Sebastian Frank in his chronicles of the Romish church says, that
he was taken to the fire by three executioners, bound crosswise on a ladder
and thrust into it; that he called on the name of Christ, that the ropes
burned and fell from his body, that he still alive fell from the fire on one
side, that the executioners thrust him back into the fire with their poles,
that he again fell out on the other side; that they then cut his body in
pieces but that the body was not burned.

His chief servant, who went afterward into the Netherlands, and
became a brother and lived and died there, gave the following account at
the time. That the judge and the three executioners first threw in a large
quantity of wood, which burned to ashes, but that the body was not
injured by the fire, that the three executioners and their assistants built
another great fire, but the body was still uninjured, his hair and nails
burnt only, *and that the flower remained unwithered in his hand.* They

both agree that the body was finally cut to pieces, he still alive, and cast into the fire, but yet was unconsumed—his servant's account further says, the pieces were cast into the River Inn. So it is written, that when the strong fibres holding the material framework of his undying soul together, were cut and hacked away, *the flower remained*, as he had said, *unwithered in his hand*—that, when like the prophet of the earlier times, his spirit was ascending to the heavens by a chariot of fire, there might still remain for his followers this assurance of his prescience for their consolation, and for the strengthening of the faith of future generations. And so this story having the undoubting acceptance of the believers of the time has been transmitted to us, as a precious legacy, of his nearness to the God he served so steadily to the end; and whatever in the clearer light of our increasing knowledge, be the veracity of its details, so much is certainly true, he perished by the hand of his executioners for conscience' sake; and beyond any interest in the assurance of the fact of that prescience which this relation of his death evinces, fair and gentle and strong as it is, and unforgetable, of far greater significance to us, is the high faith it illustrates; the long after ages have proven to us, that against such men's pure purpose and enduring courage, the gates of hell cannot at last prevail. Such men as these cannot be burned to death; the fire built for their destruction, lights only their immortality; their dissevered limbs, their perishing bodies only pass away along the stream of time, the truth they grasp, and living or dying will not let go, frail and perishable as it seems at the time to everyone but themselves, does not wither or decay, is indestructible.

THE HYMN JUBILATE DEO PSALM C. WAS THEN SUNG BY THE CHOIR.

Dr. Peter Dirk Keyser then introduced Hon. Horatio Gates Jones.*

REMARKS OF HON. HORATIO GATES JONES.

MR. CHAIRMAN AND FRIENDS: To have been invited to participate in the exercises of this Keyser Reunion, is regarded by me as a high honor,

* Horatio Gates Jones, descendant of the Levering line of the family, was a State Senator in 1876-'77-'78-'79-'80 and '82 and the most distinguished advocate in Pennsylvania of the rights of Seventh-day worshippers, Hebrews and Baptists, to an immunity from the penalties of the Sunday law of 1794. He has been President for 22 years of the Board of Trustees of the Philadelphia Baptist Association, President of the Welsh Society for 27 years, member of the New England Genealogical Society, the American Antiquarian Society, and the Historical Societies of Rhode Island, New York, Florida, Delaware, Wisconsin, and Minnesota; and a fellow of the Royal Historical Society of Great Britain; he is the author of the history of the Levering family, and of many of the Baptist churches; he has been a member for over 40 years, corresponding secretary for 17 years, and for 24 years vice president of the Historical Society of Pennsylvania, 1889. He is the descendant of a Holland family.

for I meet to-day the descendants of those early men and women who
were persecuted for conscience' sake in the Fatherland—one of whom was
burned to death at the stake, and it is a matter upon which the members
of our Levering family may felicitate themselves that one of them was so
wise as to do himself the honor of giving one of his daughters in marriage
to Peter Keyser, in the year 1752. She was a sister of my grandfather
Nathan Levering of Roxborough, so that your pious and celebrated
preacher, Rev. Peter Keyser of the Dunkard church, was first cousin of
my mother who was a daughter of said Levering. You thus see that I am
as closely connected as I can be, unless, like my great-aunt Hannah Levering, I had married a Keyser. This *might* have happened had I then
been living, as report says all the young ladies of the Keyser family were
remarkably handsome. All present on this occasion can see that the
report is true even now.

My maternal ancestor was a Hollander, named Wigard Levering. He
came to Germantown in August, 1685, and with his brother Gerhard and
Willem Rittinghuysen and Claus his son, the latter being the first paper
makers in America, were naturalized in 1691. My ancestor then went to
Roxborough and there bought 500 acres of land extending from the
Schuylkill to the line of "the German Township," on part of which I
now reside. He was well acquainted with the famous Hermits of the
Ridge, such as John Kelpius and John Selig. The latter lived and died
in a cave on the farm of my great grandfather William Levering.

It is needless for me, after the able addresses of Charles S. Keyser, Dr.
P. D. Keyser, and the paper so admirably read by Miss Orum, and in the
presence of such historians as Dr. Seidensticker and Mr. Pennypacker, to
attempt to enlighten you as to the early life here of those Mennonites, the
Keysers and the Rittenhouses; but I have with me documents signed by
William Rittinghuysen, the first Bishop of the Mennonites in America,
his son Claus Rittinghuysen, a minister of the church, and Jan Gorgas,
another minister, and Abraham op de Graf, one of the first Mennonite
settlers. Here they are open to your inspection. (Mr. Jones then dis-
played the documents and they were examined by many visitors.)

They all lived upright, honorable lives, and their posterity fill positions of honor and trust in nearly every department of society. This
gathering to-day only shows how highly our worthy progenitors are
esteemed. We reverence them for their devotion to the great cause
of Truth and Religious Liberty. They were far in advance of their
age. Rather than yield a single truth for which many of their asso-
ciates and brethren suffered death, they sought the wilds of Pennsylvania, where they knew the noble Quaker lawgiver William Penn,

would grant them full protection, none daring to molest or make them afraid. Nor do I say too much, when I assert as I now do in this presence, that should an attempt ever be made, which may God forbid, in this day to persecute any for their religious belief, every person who has in him any of the blood of that old hero Leonhard Keyser, faithful and true to the principles of Religious Liberty, would resist it—here to the end. We have now lived in this land of the free for two centuries and have formed various religious beliefs differing in the outward form but spiritually holding the same glorious truth which supported our ancestors in their years of tribulation, suffering and death.

But Mr. President, I have spoken long enough, and I am in the midst of very distinguished men here to-day who can interest you more than I can. In closing let me say that we are living in a wonderful time and none can conjecture what will be the condition of this city of Philadelphia when two more centuries will have been completed. If we are faithful and true to the principles which sustained our ancestors, we need have no fear.

> " Who'll press for gold the crowded street
>   Two hundred years to come ?
> Who'll tread this aisle with pious feet
>   Two hundred years to come ?
> Pale, trembling age and fiery youth,
> And childhood with its brow of truth,
> The rich and poor, on land, on sea,
> Where will the countless millions be
>   Two hundred years to come ?
> We all within our graves shall sleep
>   Two hundred years to come ;
> No living soul for us will weep
>   Two hundred years to come.
> But others then our lands will till,
> And others then these seats will fill,
> And others here will preach and pray,
> But, the same Gospel as to-day,
>   Two hundred years to come."

THE PANNEBECKER LINE.*

By Hon. Samuel W. Pennypacker, LL. D.†

LADIES AND GENTLEMEN: When I accepted the kind invitation to say a few words to you at this celebration it was upon the express condition that it should not be expected of me to write an address, and I am the better satisfied that my remarks are informal because of the very thorough study and presentation of your family history which have been made by some of those who have preceded me. Among the very early emigrants to Pennsylvania was Hendrick Pannebecker, a man of Dutch lineage who was here in 1699 and who probably arrived some years prior to that time. He understood and spoke three languages, Dutch, German, and English; he wrote an unusually dainty script; he had a library of books; he understood enough of mathematics to be a surveyor of lands and laid out for the Penns many of the roads and townships of Philadelphia county; so that his education must have been superior to that of the ordinary colonist. His association with the Keysers was close and intimate. Two of his sons married daughters of Peter Dirck Keyser; your family memoranda show the marriage of one of his daughters to a son of Peter Dirck Keyser; about one half of all his descendants have Keyser blood in their veins and I take it that about the same proportion of the descendants of Dirck Keyser trace their ancestry to him. Elizabeth Keyser married Peter Pannebecker and they lived on the Perkiomen creek where is now the village of Schwenksville, a place noted in the history of the Revolutionary war as "Pennybacker's mills," where the Continental army was encamped for about two weeks in the fall of 1777, from which Washington advanced to make the attack at Germantown and to which he retreated after the battle had been fought. At these mills the victory over Burgoyne was announced to the army and a salute of fourteen guns was fired in recognition of the event. There is connected with this military occupation a fact of family history which has always had for me a peculiar interest. The records of the Reformed

* The details of this address, of which only a synopsis is given, will be found in the preceding family history.—C. S. K.

† Hon. Samuel W. Pennypacker, judge of Common Pleas, No. 2, Philadelphia (1889), the genealogist of our Pennypacker line, was a private in Co. F, 26th Pa. Emergency Regiment, at Gettysburg, 1863; was graduated Bachelor of Laws at the University of Pennsylvania in 1868; 1868 President of the Law Academy; 1869 school director of the Eighth Ward, member of the Academy of Natural Sciences, of the Archive Committee of the Deutche Gesellschaft, one of the Council and Vice President of the Hist. Society, a vestryman and secretary of the Church of the Merciful Saviour (Epis.), author of the Annals of Phœnixville and one of the Cong. of Authors 1876; member of the Philadelphia Board of Public Education 1885-9, and the successor of the Hon. John Welsh as trustee of the University of Pennsylvania; conversant with the Greek, Latin, French, Dutch, Spanish, and German languages, and one of the most distinguished and eminent scholars of Philadelphia.

church at Goshenhoppen contain the following entry: "Born June 9, 1771, Susanna daughter of Wilhelm Pannebecker. Was burned to death when the soldiers left October 3, 1777."

I know nothing more than is contained in this record, but it points to a tragedy now long forgotten which rent the hearts of those near to her and suggests a bitter sacrifice made by them in the fateful struggle going on about them.

Anneke Keyser married John Pannebecker and they lived at the Trappe. She reached a great old age and was a busy housewife and a skilled needle-woman as the list of her wardrobe shows.* So far as I know among her descendants are to be found those of the Keyser lineage who have reached the highest political and social distinction. Her son Dirck about the close of the Revolutionary war went to the Valley of Virginia. Two of his grandsons read law together in the office of St. George Tucker in Winchester. One of them, Green B. Samuels after serving a term in Congress became a Justice of the Virginia Court of Appeals, the highest judicial tribunal in the State. The other, Isaac S. Pennybacker after having been a member of Congress, and a judge of the United States District Court, died at the early age of forty-two years the representative of that proud Commonwealth in the Senate of the United States. He was a regent of the Smithsonian Institute and declined the attorney generalship of the United States offered to him by President Polk. It has been jocularly suggested here to-day that some one of the descendants of Dirck Keyser ought to be President of the United States. If he had lived it is possible that this suggestion would have been realized. He was in the prime of life, an accomplished lawyer and judge, the leading citizen of a State which at that time had great prestige and wielded much political power, and the confident belief has been expressed to me by many citizens of the Shenandoah Valley that had it not been for his untimely death Franklin Pierce would never have reached the office of President.

Another of her descendants, Major General Benjamin M. Prentiss won great military renown, in the recent war. I have not the time to narrate the details of his career, and you can find them in any history of his country. His division held the advance at Shiloh and he afterward disastrously defeated Sterling Price at Helena. He was one of the court martial which tried and convicted Fitz John Porter.

The descendants of Anneke Keyser are allied with many of the best families in Virginia, and among them are persons who have attained to more than local reputation in the fields of war, politics, and the professions.

---

* The list cited by Judge Pennypacker will be found on p. 55.

Of the descendants of Peter Keyser and Susanna Pannebecker I have not so much knowledge, but if Charles S. Keyser, and William S. Baker so widely celebrated for his study of Washington and his monographs upon American engraving, are fairly representative of this branch of the family they may well claim to have won their share of success and achievement.

(Mr. Pennypacker in the course of his remarks showed the assemblage the family Bible of John Pannebecker and Anneke Keyser, in which at the time of the capture of Quebec they put a plan of that city and a portrait of Gen. Wolfe that have remained amid its leaves ever since.)

OSWALD SEIDENSTICKER'S PAPER.

Oswald Seidensticker, Prof. of the German Language and Literature in the University of Pennsylvania, was then introduced to the family by Dr. Peter Dirck Keyser, and said:

Such a meeting as this has a value and a significance reaching far beyond the personal gratification of those directly concerned. It reminds us that every individual has through his line of ancestry a share in the history of by-gone days and that his own record may hereafter be scrutinized by his descendants. Every one that lives in this world leaves a trace, acts upon the times, as the times act upon him. Reflections like these, which are brought home to us to-day, cannot but quicken our impulses for good. And thus the observance of the commandment, "Honor thy father and thy mother," if made to extend to our progenitors, as far as we can gain any knowledge of them, will not be without a fitting reward.

It is true, not everybody has the good fortune to keep track of his ancestry beyond his grand-parents. We must, therefore, congratulate the descendants of Dirk Keyser, that, thanks to the pains taken by some of them, they can to-day assemble and, casting a glance at their far branching *Stammbaum*, of which they may well be proud, do honor to their sire, old Dirk Keyser who arrived in Pennsylvania and settled in Germantown 200 years ago.

Up to 1683 the spot where Germantown was planted had been an unbroken wilderness, trodden only by the beasts of the forest and Indians of the Lenni Lenape tribe. A few years later about fifty families, hailing from the Palatinate, from cities of the lower Rhine (Crefeld, Mühlheim) and from Holland, had dotted the place with houses, gardens, and farms. Though coming from different quarters they were like one large family, bent upon prospering by thrift and industry, united by strong religious convictions. They did not belong to any of the dominant churches in their fatherland and many of them had bitterly suffered through intolerance. And even those who, like the Crefelders and Hollanders, had, at that period, not exactly to dread persecution, preferred to live in a country where their religion and mode of worship were not merely tolerated but recognized as entitled to the same respect and protection as that of all others. Moreover William Penn had visited Holland and Germany repeatedly; not a few of the Germantown settlers had known him, when as a simple Quaker missionary he had labored to spread his testimony over the continent. Now, that he had become the proprietor of a domain, as large as a kingdom, where religious liberty was proclaimed as the law of the land, they were glad to flock to so blessed a spot.

You know in 1683 a company was formed at Frankfort, that bought 25,000 acres of Pennsylvania land and about the same time five individuals of Crefeld bought 18,000 acres. Francis Daniel Pastorius was appointed by the Frankfort Company as agent and representative; this eminent scholar, whose comprehensive learning has probably never been equalled by another Pennsylvanian, became the leader of the little colony. Through him 5700 acres of land were bought west of the Schuylkill, and it was intended to lay out 4 places, Germantown, Crisheim, Sommershausen, and Crefeld. The area of Germantown proper was 2750 acres, belonging in equal parts to Crefelders and the Frankfort Company, divided into 55 lots of 50 acres each. Such a lot served for homestead, garden, and farm. It was one of these that Dirck Keyser had acquired before 1689.

The name chosen for the new settlement was "the German Town" (Pastorius sometimes called it Germanopolis), and this was quite natural, as by far the largest number of the settlers were Germans. But it would be a great mistake to believe that the inhabitants were Germans exclusively. And as this celebration concerns a pioneer of Germantown, who came from Amsterdam, I wish to emphasize the fact that Germantown harbored many other Dutchmen, I mean genuine Dutchmen, not only those called so by courtesy.

There was Jacob Telner of Amsterdam, a merchant whose prominence and active life has been so efficiently set forth by Mr. Pennypacker. From Amsterdam came also Reynier Jansen, first (1698 and 1699) a resident of Germantown, then a printer in Philadelphia, succeeding Wm. Bradford. And it is reasonable to suppose, that the other Jansens, known to have lived in Germantown at the beginning of the last century, Conrad, Claas, Peter, and William were likewise natives of Holland. The Rittenhouses (Rittinghuysen), the pioneers of paper-making in America, came from Arnheim (in the province of Geldern), where the manufacture of paper had long time been flourishing. Then we have two Dutch bakers, Cornelis Böm, the same who published 1694 an account of Philadelphia in Dutch, and Jan Duplowys, who married in 1687 Wyntie van Sanen.

That Cornelis Claesen was a Dutchman we learn from his will, written in 1708; so was very likely his son-in-law Claas Berents. I next mention Jan Gorgas, whose descendants still continue in Germantown, Cornelis Van der Geach, Williamse Bockenogen, Isaac Petersen, Jacob Gerritz Holthoven. On the strength of their names we also may claim as Hollanders the numerous Vans of Germantown, Paulus Van Vlecq, Gottschalk, Herman and Jan Jacobs Van der Seggen, Arnold Van Vossen, Jan and Richard Van der Werf, Herman Van Bon. Reinier Vandersluys, called by the Germans Van der Schleuss and anglicized Vanderslice, probably lived in Philadelphia. Others with Dutch names like Van Bebbern, Op de Graef, and Op de Kolck, if not coming directly from Holland, were unquestionably of Dutch stock. There can be no doubt that James Delaplaine was a Hollander, for when in 1698 he succeeded Pastorius as clerk of the court, he kept the minutes in Dutch. The same has to be said of his successor James Laply; otherwise the official language of the court was German. Not quite so strong but worth considering is the evidence as to Dutch nationality in the case of Cornelis Tisen, whose tombstone in Axe's burying-ground I think is older than any other in Germantown. The inscription, which makes the year of his death 1716, is almost effaced, but what remains of it is evidently in Dutch. Others that probably came from Holland were Jan Woostyne, also called John Wilderness, Herman Tuynen (Teunen), Cornelis Süers, perhaps also Aret Klincken, one of the pioneers of 1683. The latter, as well as James Delaplaine and Cornelis Süers was called several times to the highest office of the town, that of Bailiff; a proof, if we had no other, that Germans and Dutchmen were in best accord and fully amalgamated. As it was evidently inconvenient to keep up the languages of both nationalities in addition to the English, which could not be entirely neglected, the Dutch appears to have been abandoned by the next generation.

It cannot be a matter of surprise that so many Hollanders came to Pennsylvania and mingled with their brethren in faith, the German Mennonites. William Penn, who was himself the son of a Dutch woman, frequently went to Holland to do service in the cause of religion. The close affinity of the Quaker and the Mennonite in all matters of practical Christianity has been often dwelled upon. In 1677 William Penn travelled extensively in Holland and organized in Amsterdam a Yearly Meeting for the Friends in various cities of Holland and Germany. Harlem, Utrecht, Rotterdam, Hague, and many towns of Friesland he likewise visited. His offer, as proprietor of Pennsylvania, to give shelter and protection to all who suffered for conscience' sake, was therefore gladly accepted both by Germans and Hollanders. Among those who came from

Amsterdam, the famous centre of wealth and culture, was Dirck Keyser, in whose honor so many of his descendants have assembled to-day. About him and his posterity, living representatives of the line have discoursed and their comments are the most appropriate memorial offering upon this occasion. What could a stranger, though much interested in the history of early Germantown, add? Well, I will give you all I have, that is my only excuse for coming with such a bagatelle. Running over the tattered pages of the old Germantown Court-book, I happened to notice under the year 1691 the name of Dirck Keyser—father or son—just think of it, arrayed as a defendant. The charge against him was that he had not properly attended to his fence. He was fined 6 shillings and told if he did not put his fence in proper repair he would be fined again. These fences play a remarkable part in the court proceedings of Germantown. Sometimes, it seems, there would have been a most disgraceful lack of cases, if the offender against the fence statute had not come to the rescue. The court held one session every six weeks and then had often to adjourn for want of business. So it was always a happy relief, if a fence case turned up. And they went systematically about it. Every year a standing committee of fence-Beaufsichtiger (fence-inspectors) was appointed, numbering from 2 to 6, and among them we find most prominent citizens.

Dirck Keyser appears to have given thorough satisfaction after his first failing, for the very next year and frequently thereafter he was put on this important committee of fence-Beaufsichtiger.

In quite another connection his name appears in one of Pastorius' manuscripts. This industrious scholar undertook since 1702 to conduct a day and an evening school in Germantown, and among those who covered the expenses of the latter by voluntary subscription regularly was Dirck Keyser.

Our minds have to-day been transported back to the olden times of Germantown, the Arcadian home of Germans and Hollanders, the abode of peace and good will, where Pastorius, the sage, wrote poetry in German, English and Dutch, where Rittenhouse made the first paper, where Christopher Sauer printed the first Bible, where—but no, I must not at the close begin a new strain. We stand at the old spot. But how have the times changed it! Who would be more surprised, we, if we could see face to face the old sires, to whom our thoughts have been flitting, or they, if they could cast a glance on the present Germantown, Pennsylvania, America? And what would Dirck Keyser say, if he looked on this host, that has assembled to commemorate his arrival in America, on his numerous progeny, who have not forgotten him!

LARS WESTERGAARD'S WORDS TO US.

MR. LARS WESTERGAARD* was introduced to the family by Dr. Peter Dirck Keyser, and has kindly written the substance of the remarks he made on the occasion in the following communication in reply to the request of the committee:

CONSULATE OF THE NETHERLANDS,
FOR PENNSYLVANIA AND DELAWARE,
Philadelphia, October 17, 1888.

Synopsis of remarks made by the undersigned at the DIRCK KEYSER *Reunion*, at Germantown, on the 10th of October, A. D. 1888.

LADIES AND GENTLEMEN: It seems superfluous for me to speak on this occasion, after having listened, as I have done, with deepest interest, to the very interesting addresses made by the gentlemen that have spoken before me here to-day.

I come before you as a " *cosmopolitan* " truly, being a native of *Norway*, and for about twenty-two years having had the honor to be the *Netherlands-Consul* at this port, besides which I am a naturalized citizen of the *United States*, under whose protection I have resided as such, in the United States, chiefly here in *Philadelphia*, for about thirty years.

The *Reunion* here to-day of the descendants of *Dirck Keyser* is certainly a very happy event, and all of you who are fortunate enough to be present have had the history of the *Dirck Keyser* descendants placed before you, from generation to generation, in a very able manner, and certainly also in a most interesting way. You have indeed every reason to be justly proud of your *pedigree*, and in making a few brief remarks I will address myself more immediately to the *young people* among the *Dirck Keyser* descendants assembled here to-day.

Allow me to say to you young men, and young ladies, and also to the school-boys and the school-girls, that I was present a few summers ago, at Swedesboro, near Bridgeport in Pennsylvania, at an assemblage of the descendants of the Swedes who had settled there and founded *Swedesboro* more than two centuries ago, and that said *Swedes* and their descendants, from generation to generation, did, like the *Puritans*, and also like the *Mennonites*—the *Dirck Keysers*—carry the fear of God with them in their hearts, and the Word of God, the Bible, with them in their families, in

---

* It may be proper to state here in view of the preservation of this record for future generations that no official has so much endeared himself to the people of Philadelphia in our time as this representative of the government of our earlier and ever gratefully remembered country. In his long term of service among us he has become part of ourselves.

their homes, at their firesides. The three kinds of *emigrants* that I have named to you were all of them *God-fearing people.* Wherever they located, wherever they settled down *permanently* they built school-houses, meeting-houses, *and* churches.

Referring you back to the *Dirck Keyser* descendants for generations, permit me to point out to you the general thriftiness, the industry, the plain habits, and frugality of your worthy ancestors, and say to you in all sincerity, but with great earnestness: *Imitate your forefathers and their families* in ALL these matters, and you will *never* go astray, nor make any *serious* mistakes. We are assembled here to-day in the plain, old *Meeting-house* of the original *Dirck Keysers*, they were, as before stated, people who feared God and loved His Word, and I hope that all of us assembled under this roof to-day are imbued with settled religious convictions, for in the present day of rapid progress, and civilization, and of dangers that *especially* beset the *young people* of our time, there is no other safeguard against the many and varied temptations placed before you, than the main *sheet-anchor*, that namely of a *pure*, *simple*, and *confiding* love of *God and His Word.* That such may be your selection, my young friends; that it may be your *guiding star*, is a sincere and friendly wish, that comes from the bottom of my heart, and having nothing more to add I close by thanking all of you, ladies and gentlemen, young and old, for your kind patience in listening to me, for it is not given to me to speak to you with the fluency and the eloquence of a *native American;* the *latter* are, as we all know, *generally* very good *extempore* speakers.

LARS WESTERGAARD.

ADRIAN VAN HELDEN'S PAPER.

Adrian van Helden* was then introduced to the family by Dr. Peter Dirck Keyser, and read from a MS. whose admirable writing we regret may not be transcribed as well as the well-chosen words and sentences which so greatly interested the audience, and contributed so much to the pleasure of the occasion.

LADIES AND GENTLEMEN: It is an honor and a pleasure to me, and it does my Dutch heart good, to be present at this remarkable Reunion commemorating the arrival in Germantown, two centuries ago, of a pioneer Hollander whose posterity—though not as numerous as the stars of heaven or the sands on the seashore—is largely represented here. Having been

---

* In the preparation of this compilation I have been so much indebted to Mr. van Helden for his scholarship and thorough knowledge of Holland and its history, as well as for the interest he has taken in obtaining information of great service to the committee, that I must again express to him for the remembrance of the family the thanks of the committee in this note.—C. S. K.

requested to briefly address this meeting, I willingly comply with the request; regretting, however, that I cannot do so in an off-hand speech in my strong and terse mother tongue.

Your venerable ancestor *Dirck Keyser* belonged to that time-honored Christian denomination, the members of which derived their name from its noble founder, Menno Simons, who commenced his great work of church purification and reformation on the Dutch classical soil of religious freedom, where, after the cruel Spanish yoke was thrown off, every man could worship God according to the dictates of his own conscience. It is not necessary to tell you that the distinguishing characteristics of the Mennonites were not only their opinions about baptism, but also the prohibition of bearing weapons, swearing oaths, accepting civil offices, etc.

In the year 1688 King Louis XIV. of France declared war against the Dutch Republic, and the valiant William III., afterward King of England, a worthy great-grandson of the immortal founder of Holland's religious and civil liberty, William the Silent, whose picture is upon the wall in Dr. P. D. Keyser's parlor, was then Stadtholder or President of the Dutch Republic (for the Stadtholdership was no royal or princely dignity, as is oftentimes supposed, but a kind of hereditary Presidency, vested in the house of Orange-Nassau, which lasted to the year 1795 when the last Stadtholder, Prince William V., left his country and went to England, and his office was abolished by the rulers of the so-called Batavian Republic, to make place for a sovereign kingship in 1813). The said war, known in Dutch history as the Nine-years-war, in which William III. showed himself a match for the brilliant French King, cost the Republic 350 millions of florins, or 140 millions of dollars, and thousands of precious human lives. It came to an end in the year 1697 when a treaty of peace was made, known as the Peace of Ryswyk. During that war a great number of Mennonites, faithful to their religious convictions which forbade them the bearing of weapons, left the country for conscience sake, and it was possibly for this reason that Dirck Keyser emigrated to America. Be this as it may, the name of Keyser* did not then disappear from the old country. In the annals of Dutch art the names of Hendrik de Keyser and Theodor de Keyser are mentioned with honor. The former was a celebrated architect and sculptor, and the latter a painter of great merit, probably a pupil of Rembrandt, in whose broad style he painted some magnificent panels, which may be seen in the museums at Amsterdam and The Hague.

I think it proper to say here a few words about the denomination of

---

* It is spelt differently: *Keyzer* and *Keizer*, *Keiser* and *Keyser*, sometimes prefixed by *de* (de Keyser, etc.).

which Dirck Keyser was a member. The name of its founder belongs to history and is beyond human praise. Though weak in the body he was strong in the spirit, fearless and indefatigable, and neither Spanish persecutions nor outlawry could quench the fire of his religious zeal. His followers did and do distinguish themselves by the purity of their lives, their honesty and simplicity. There is in Holland no denomination which is held in greater honor and esteem than the "Mennonieten" or "Doopsgezinden" (that is, Baptists). "Oprecht als een Mennist" (*i. e.* "true as a Mennonite") has become a by-word. They are the smallest sect but one in the country, numbering less than a hundred thousand, with 126 congregations and as many ministers, and their Theological Seminary is at Amsterdam, where eminent scholars like Hoekstra and de Hoop Scheffer occupy professorial chairs. One of their primitive characteristics, that of refusing to accept public office, has been done away with, and society has been greatly benefited thereby. In both of the Chambers of the States-General (the Dutch Congress) Mennonites occupy seats; among the members of the Dutch Cabinet is a Mennonite; a late Chief Justice of the Dutch Supreme Court was one, and it is (if I am not wholly mistaken) to a Mennonite Minister of Justice, or Attorney General, that Holland owes since 1886 a penal code which is considered by domestic and foreign jurists as a model of legislation. A series of celebrated Mennonite names, excelling in almost every branch of science and art, could be mentioned, but I will not overstep the limit of my time. I will give but one name, and this one resounds in both hemispheres, that of Laurens Alma Tadema, the great painter and marvellous colorist, born at Drouryp in Friesland, of Mennonite parents, but since 1873 by naturalization a subject to the Queen of Great Britain.

In conclusion: the respected name of Keyser lives in Holland still. Three of those who bear it I have known: the first a professor at Leyden, author, among other scientific works, of a book on Mohammedan law which has made him famous at home and abroad; the second a prominent lawyer who received a royal appointment as recorder of deeds in one of the principal Dutch cities; and the third a highly esteemed minister in the Dutch Reformed church who was not only an earnest and eloquent preacher, but also a bright scholar, a promoter of that which is true, beautiful, and good, who "being dead yet speaketh," and to whose memory I bring a well-deserved tribute in the midst of those whose name he bore, and to which name he gave honor, lustre, and fame.

ADRIAN VAN HELDEN.

PHILADELPHIA, October 10, 1888.

THE CORRESPONDENCE.

The secretary of the committee then announced that in consequence of the lateness of the hour the reading of the correspondence would be omitted from the programme. A selection from it follows:

OFFICE OF THE MAYOR,

PHILADELPHIA,

October 8, 1888.

PETER D. KEYSER, M. D., 1832 Arch Street—

DEAR SIR: His Honor the Mayor directs me to state he sincerely regrets his inability to accept the kind invitation of the Committee to the Bi-centennial Reunion of the descendants of Dirck Keyser in Germantown, 10th October, owing to absence from the city on that date.

I am, yours respectfully,

LEWIS E. BEITLER, Sec.

CONSULATE OF THE NETHERLANDS,

FOR PENNSYLVANIA AND DELAWARE,

Philadelphia, October 8, 1888.

MY DEAR SIR: *Mr. Van Helden* and I will (Providence permitting) take the 9.12 TRAIN from BROAD STREET STATION on Wednesday morning, due at *Tulpehocken Station* at 9.35, but he and I *both* beg you to put yourself to no trouble *whatever* in any way to meet us at the *station* as I am a good *Democrat* able to pick my way to the place of *Reunion.*

Yours truly,

LARS WESTERGAARD, Consul.

CHAS. S. KEYSER, ESQ., 524 Walnut street.

FROM J. R. PLANTEN, CONSUL GENERAL OF THE NETHERLANDS.

NEW YORK, October 8, 1888.

P. D. KEYSER, M. D., Philadelphia.

DEAR SIR: I am very sorry that I have to forego the pleasure of accepting the invitation for the Keyser family gathering on Wednesday next, but business engagements which cannot be delayed compel such.

Will you accept and express to the gathering to be held my sympathy with same and great appreciation of desiring me to be with them?

Very truly,

J. R. PLANTEN.

FROM PROF. OSWALD SEIDENSTICKER, UNIVERSITY OF PENNA.

PHILADELPHIA, August 25, 1888.

DR. P. D. KEYSER.

MY DEAR DOCTOR: The invitation you tender me to be present at the Bi-centennial Reunion of the Keyser family on the 10th of October is acknowledged with sincere thanks and with the assurance that I appreciate it as a particular honor, since I do not belong to the distinguished "gens," which has been convoked for this interesting celebration. Whether I can be present will mainly depend on the arrangement of the college roster, *i. e.* the allotment of hours during which my services will be required. If no obstacle shall arise on this score, or if I can be relieved of my duties on that day, I shall be very happy to appear and also say a few words as you seem to desire.

I wish such memorial celebrations were oftener observed. As things go, one generation crowds upon its predecessor and those who have been supplanted and buried are soon forgotten. Only bodies of a public character, cities, states, churches, and other institutions appear to recognize a history, that links the present with the past, while in private life retrospective memory rarely goes beyond personal recollection. Let me congratulate you on the privileged position which your tribe—may it long increase—occupies in this respect. May also the honor you do to your ancestors and kin redound to your own.

Very truly yours,

OSWALD SEIDENSTICKER.

FROM JAS. D. KEYSER,* OF PHILADELPHIA.

PHILADELPHIA, October 8, 1888.

CHARLES S. KEYSER, PETER DIRCK KEYSER, M. D., Committee.

GENTLEMEN: It is with extreme regret that I am compelled by sickness to forego the anticipated pleasure of participating in the family reunion; with my best wishes for the Health, Wealth, and Prosperity of the Family, I am　　　　　　　　Yours truly,

JAMES D. KEYSER,

236 South Twentieth street, Philadelphia.

EXTRACTS FROM LETTER FROM CIPRIANO CANEDO.

AMECA, Mexico, August 30, 1888.

PETER D. KEYSER, M. D.

DEAR COUSIN: Yesterday I received the invitation for the union of the family to celebrate the bi-centennial anniversary of the arrival in North

---

* Died February, 1889.

America of Dirck Keyser. I am extremely thankful for the favor and sorry not to be able to be present, for this would give me the greatest pleasure to be in union with probably the greatest part of our relations, but only in thought I will accompany you all, wishing that there may exist an everlasting harmony and good will among all the relatives. praying to God to help us in all the vicissitudes that may come. * * * *

I hope you will give me the full particulars of the occasion. * *

For the last year and a half I have been living in this town of Ameca, and what do you think I have been doing? I have been practising medicine and with very good fortune, in the curing part, in pay matter no, for my pleasure is only to attend to the poor. My sister lives in Guadalajara. Arnulfo will probably go as secretary to the commission to settle the boundary between the United States and Mexico.

Believe me as ever your affectionate cousin,

CIPRIANO CANEDO.

FROM BENJ. URNER KEYSER.

WASHINGTON, D. C., Sept. 5, 1888.

DEAR DOCTOR: I have received through my brother George the circulars in reference to proposed Bi-centennial of the Keyser family to be held in Germantown, October 10 next.

I shall make my arrangements to attend this reunion, and hope to be with you; it may be my last chance of attending just such another. We are growing old, and who can tell where he will be 200 years hence.

Unfortunately I can bring nothing to the meeting but a profound reverence for the men whose advent we are to celebrate. Will our descendants do as much for us? Love to all.   Yours,

B. U. KEYSER.

FROM THE VENERABLE WILLIAM R. GORGAS.

904 N. THIRD STREET, HARRISBURG, PA., Sept. 24, 1888.

P. D. KEYSER, M. D.—

DEAR FRIEND: Your letter of the 13th inst. was duly received by my son and handed to me by him. He thought it would certainly be a great pleasure to me to meet the Keyser family and relatives on that occasion to celebrate the Bi-centennial celebration of the 200th year of his arrival. The probabilities are that my great-grandfather came with him. Dirck Keyser, Peter his son, and Johannes Gorgas, my great-grandfather, were naturalized in 1708-9. It would be gratifying to meet the Keyser families and their relatives on such a pleasant occasion and to visit the old church building in which I heard your father preach many years ago. He cer-

tainly was a very remarkable man and a good Christian. I would like to
visit the graves of our old friends, particularly those of my great-grand-
parents, but I am now going on my 83d year since the 8th of last May, and
while as able to go about as well as some of only 70 years, I fear that it might
not be at my age safe for me to go so far from home. I have had a great
desire for some years to once more visit Germantown and Philadelphia,
but I fear I will not get it accomplished. Give my love to all my friends
present, and my prayer and best wish is that you may all have an enjoy-
able time. I remain, Yours very respectfully,

WM. R. GORGAS.

FROM MRS. KATE KEYSER FRACKER.
An extract from a letter to Francis Keyser, Philadelphia:

ZANESVILLE, Ohio, October 2, 1888.

I am Kate Keyser Fracker and was reared by my father's sister Keturah
Keyser Benson. Do you remember her? She was a woman of "heavy
weight," brilliant intellect, and so strong a will that she longed to rule
the world, and if she had been in power every one would have been obliged
to maintain the same religious belief as she did, albeit her grandfather of
blessed memory left the Fatherland that he might enjoy religious liberty.

I do not speak of this to her discredit—far from it—I only meant to
insinuate that she was possessed of a powerful mind and will, and if she
had been of the gender masculine—there might have been among us a
President of the United States.

I often went with her to Philadelphia—I remember the days long gone
for ever, and the dear faces of years ago dead I can call them up and their
eyes look love into mine, as if they spoke again.

Frank, I remember your beautiful mother—I must have been a mere
child—I remember the old Dunkard Church—I can see now your venerable grandfather Peter Keyser in the pulpit, and his sweet-faced wife
looking up to him with holy awe.

My grandfather Derrick Keyser rises before me again, and his brother
William and his wife Barbara—I can hear poor demented Leibert Keyser
as he went shouting by—I can remember Uncle Joseph Gorgas and his
wife Sarah Keyser.

All of them came up to the yearly meeting to worship—I have seen
the saints wash each other's feet.

Oh! how dearly I would love to go to meet the remnant of the great
race. The men were noble, and the women fair. * * * * *

I regret that I shall not be in Germantown on the 10th inst., but my
soul, dear Frank, shall be with you that day, and when the Great Day

comes and the name of Keyser shall be called, I trust I may not be absent, but in company with my forefathers go to meet my Lord; and now with a heart full of love for my gathering kinsfolks, let me write my name with theirs, KATE KEYSER FRACKER.

FROM MRS. JUAN G. MATUTE (NÉE MARGARET CANEDO).

GUADALAJARA, Mexico, Nov. 1, 1888.

TO DR. P. D. KEYSER—

MY DEAR COUSIN: After so many years, I must to-day begin my letter, although late, to congratulate you and all the family Keyser on the 200th anniversary the 10th of October last, celebrated in our dear old German-town, and if my memory does not fail me, I believe your country house must be the one your father built, on what was once the woods where we in our youth used to stroll on Sunday afternoon. Oh! how all comes back to my mind, the dear old bench where all the names were cut, from grand-father's down. Oh! what has become of it? the spring,* does it exist, and the friends of my youth where are they? If I could go there and ask, Echo would answer where are they? How sorry I was that Cip. and my son Arnulfo were not able to go and take part in that grand meeting, but I do not lose all hope that some day Arnulfo will be able to go and pay you all a visit; this is one of my greatest desires—that my children could visit my family so dear to me in the United States. Give my love to your wife and only daughter. Good-bye. May God always bless our family! and if we are not to meet again on earth, may we all meet in heaven. With best wishes receive the love of your cousin.

The ceremonies in the Meeting-House concluded with the singing of the Doxology by the family.

After the exercises in the church were concluded, the members of the family wended their way to the residence of Dr. Peter Dirck Keyser, Green street, above Washington lane. The mansion stands back from the street a considerable distance, surrounded by a woods, and the house is reached by a serpentine carriage-way. The moderately mild weather ad-mitted of the house being thrown open for the reception of the guests. A committee of ladies composed of Annie P. Keyser, Margaret C. P. Keyser, Margaret K. Channon, Mrs. Alex. P. Keyser, Jeannette C. Keyser, and Susan Keyser Keyser had decorated the interior of the dwelling with flowers, plants, and flags. Two huge banks of flowers adorned the parlor in the space between the windows; one bank covered the fireplace, and

---

* It was on the carriage road in the grounds leading to the present mansion at the foot of a tree; the spring is still there, filled with fresh, clear, cold water.—C. S. K.

WILHELMUS VAN NASSOUWEN.

Marnix van St. Aldegonde, 1568.

Oorspronglijke Melodij.

Maestoso.

Wil - hel mus van Nas - sou - we ben ick van

Duits - chen bloedt, Het Va - der - land ge - trou - we blijf

ick tot in der doedt. Een Prin - ce van O -

ran - gien ben ick vrij on - ver - veert, Den Kon - inck

van His - paeg nien heb ick al - tijdt ge - eert.

110

one was located at the rear of the room. Silken flags and smilax were suspended from the chandeliers. Every room on the first floor was crowded with the descendants. During the afternoon the family were entertained with vocal and instrumental music. Mr. Frank Keyser sang some of his favorite selections, accompanied by Miss Paris. Mr. Adrian Van Helden sang the national air of Holland, "Wilhelmus van Nassauwsen (William of Nassau)," composed 300 years ago, and the modern national air of the same country, entitled "Wien Neerlandsch Bloed."

Mr. Naaman Keyser, son of Alex. Keyser, photographed a number of the members of Keyser families on the lawn in the rear and front of the Keyser residence.

Fac Simile of the Dinner Ticket.

1688. BI-CENTENNIAL REUNION 1888.

OF THE

Descendants of Dirck Keyser,

AT GERMANTOWN,

WEDNESDAY, OCTOBER 10TH, 1888.

- - -

Dinner at the Keyser Residence,

TULPEHOCKEN STATION,

AT THE CLOSE OF THE EXERCISES,

ONE DOLLAR.

The dinner was prepared and served by Philip A. Roberts, caterer.

Ice blocks with raw oysters, dressed salmon, cold ham, cold tongue, chicken salad, oyster croquettes, fried oysters, boned turkey, ice cream, water ice, cakes, fruit, coffee, and tea.

RELICS EXHIBITED.

The old Bible, brought from Amsterdam by the ancestors of the family, containing births and deaths of the children of Dirck Keyser, owned by Gideon Keyser.

Bible owned by H. B. Bruner, of Germantown, containing the following: "Henry Bruner and Margaret Keyser were married 16th Nov., 1776." Bought this Bible 15th day of Nov., 1776; paid £2, 15s.; Brong Bruner was born in the Canton of Bahl, Switzerland, 1749.

Het Bloedig Tooneel, brought from Holland by Dirck Keyser in 1688.
The book of the land titles of the Keysers in Germantown.
The Bible of Rev. Peter Keyser, owned by Dr. Peter Dirck Keyser.

RELICS EXHIBITED AT THE HOUSE.

Release of rent from Matthew Vanbebber to Dirck Keyser, in the year 1737.

Bond and warrant, signed by Anthony Nice, dated September 30, 1783.

A deed from Dirck Keyser and Alice, his wife, to Jacob Keyser, dated February 13, 1745.

A BREECHES BIBLE.—This translation of the Scriptures, the result of the labors of the English exiles at Geneva, was the English family Bible during the reign of Queen Elizabeth, until the present authorized version of King James. It contains a picture and description of Noah's ark.

On either side of the walls in the hallway, at the entrance of the house, were the figures 1688 and 1888, made of ivy; suspended from the ceiling was an American flag, and a flag of the Netherlands loaned by Mr. Westergaard; the portrait of the present King of Holland, and the portrait of William the Silent, of Rev. Peter Keyser, Joseph Keyser, Hester Fox, William and Benj. Fox, specimens of the handwriting of members of the family, portrait of Peter A. Keyser, Samuel father of Gideon Keyser.

Specimen of the handwriting of Charles Keyser, who during his day was called the Penman of Philadelphia.

A release from Peter Pennypacker and Elizabeth, his wife, born a Keyser; John Pennypacker and Anneke Keyser, Ludwig Horning and Catharine, his wife, born a Keyser, and witnessed by Henry Pennypacker; signed the 16th day of Nov., 1743. These were three of the nine children from which the whole family now living were descended. This was a release of their interest in the estate to Judge Dirck Keyser.

A school-book of Joseph Keyser, father of Charles S. Keyser, containing rules and examples of arithmetic, dated 1778. The Lord's prayer written by Joseph Keyser so small that it was hardly visible to the naked eye. Drawings and pictures of flowers, exhibiting much artistic ability, by members of the family.

An account of the proceedings was given in the Germantown *Independent*, the *Public Ledger* and other Philadelphia papers, and in the *Gazette* and *Telegraph* of Germantown and *Evening Telegraph* of Philadelphia.

The Germantown *Independent* on the day issued an extra edition of the paper of 2000 copies in addition to its regular edition of about 3200 of the *daily* and an extra edition of 800 on the *weekly*, all of which were exhausted. Of this edition of this paper there was furnished by

TIE REUNION.

113

order copies to New Hampshire, Massachusetts, Connecticut, New York, New Jersey, Pennsylvania, Maryland, Virginia, West Virginia, Kentucky, Tennessee, North Carolina, Alabama, Florida, Georgia, Louisiana, Texas, New Mexico, Ohio, Iowa, Illinois, Colorado, California, and Michigan, and to parties to be redirected to the Netherlands and Mexico. The orders were for numbers from 10 to 50. The furthest order west came from Angel Island, California; the furthest east from Nagatauk, Conn.; south, Fernandina, Fla., and Fort Worth, Texas.

NIEUWE ROTTERDAMSCHE COURANT VAN 29 OCTOBER, 1888.

Een van de oudste Amerikaansche geslachten van Nederlandsche afkomst, de familie Keyser, heeft den 10den dezer te Germantown, in Pennsylvanië, waar het hoofd der familie woonachtig is, het tweede eeuwfeest harer vestiging in Amerika plechtig gevierd.

De Keyser's zijn een zeer oud geslacht. Een hunner voorvaders, Leonhard Keyser, was geestelijke in Beieren, werd na het lezen der geschriften van Luther en Zwinglius protestantsch, en behoorde tot de omgeving van den grooten hervormer te Wittenberg. Hij voegde zich later bij de Wederdoopers, werd als zoodanig door den bisschop van Passau gevangen genomen en in 1527 te Scharding verbrand.

Omstreeks 1560 zijn de Keyser's naar Amsterdam uitgeweken. In 1688 verhuisde Dirk Keyser, een zijdehandelaar, naar de Nieuwe Wereld, waar hij den 10den October te Germantown aankwam. Met twee zonen gekomen, liet hij bij zijn overlijden negen klein kinderen na; van dezen zijn de ongeveer duizend Keyser's afgestamd, die in het stamboek der familie zijn ingeschreven. In alle deelen der Nieuwe Wereld vindt men hen tegenwoordig verspreid. Oorspronkelijk behoorende tot de Doopsgezinde broederschap, hebben zij langen tijd zich aan het dragen van wapenen onttrokken en ook geene openbare posten of bedieningen willen bekleeden. Later wordt hun naam echter in alle ambten aangetroffen, en tijdens den burgeroorlog in 1861 dienden twintig leden der familie in het leger, waarvan er vier gesneuveld of in het kamp gestorven en vijf gewond zijn.

De Keyser's zijn verwant aan vele der andere oud-Hollandsche familiën in de Vereenigde Staten. Tot hunne naaste verwanten behooren de Pennypacker's, wier oorspronkelijke naam Pannebakker is geweest.

Bij het feest op den 10den, dat in de oude doopsgezinde kerk te Germantown begonnen en des avonds met een banket van tienhonderd personen besloten werd, zag men al de familie-reliquieën uitgestald, het oude porselein en tafelzilver, het Boek der Martelaren en den Statenbijbel, van hunne voorvaderen afkomstig. Behalve de familieleden waren alleen tot het feest genoodigd de Nederlandsche Consul voor Pennsylvania en

8

Delaware, de heer Lars Westergaard; de heer Van Helden—*a gentleman of Holland*, zooals hij in de plaatselijke bladen genoemd wordt—en Prof. Oswald Seitensticker, van de universiteit van Pennsylvania. De heer van Helden deelde het een en ander mede over de nog in Nederland gevestigde leden der familie Keyser en zong het *Wilhelmus.* Het oudste mannelijke lid der familie, Gideon Keyser, is 82 jaren oud en presideerde het feest.

[TRANSLATION.]

NEW ROTTERDAM GAZETTE OF OCTOBER 29, 1888.

One of the oldest American families of Dutch descent, the Keyser family, celebrated the second centennial of their settlement in America on the 10th inst., at Germantown in Pennsylvania, where the head of that family is living.

The Keysers are of a very old line. One of their ancestors, Leonhard Keyser, was a priest in Bavaria. After reading the writings of Luther and Zwingle, he became a Protestant, and was one of those who surrounded the great Reformer at Wittenberg. Subsequently he joined the Baptists and was made a prisoner by the Bishop of Passau and burned at the stake at Scharding in 1527.

About 1560 the Keysers went to Holland. In 1688 Dirck Keyser, a silk-merchant, emigrated to the New World and arrived at Germantown on the 10th of October. He was accompanied by two sons, and at his death left nine grandchildren. From these have descended about a thousand Keysers who are recorded in the pedigree register of the family. They are now spread over all parts of the New World. Primitively belonging to the Baptist Brotherhood, they for a long time refrained from bearing arms and occupying public offices or positions. Later, however, their name is found in almost every profession, and during the civil war of 1861 twenty members of the family were serving in the army, of whom four were killed in the field or died in camp, and five were wounded.

The Keysers are related to other old Dutch families in the United States. To their nearest relatives belong the Pennypackers, whose original name was Pannebakker.

At the festival on the 10th inst., which commenced in the old Baptist Church of Germantown and closed with a banquet of ten hundred guests, all the family relics were exhibited: old china and table silver, the Book of Martyrs, and the State Bible derived from their ancestors. Outside of the members of the family, the only invited guests to the feast were Mr. Lars Westergaard, Dutch Consul for Pennsylvania and Delaware; Mr. van Helden (*a gentleman from Holland*, as he is called by the local papers), and Prof. Oswald Seidensticker, of the University of Pennsylvania.

Mr. van Helden gave information about members of the Keyser family still living in Holland, and sang the *Wilhelmus.* The oldest male member of the family, Gideon Keyser, 82 years of age, presided at the feast.

The following letter was received from the Island of Texel, North Holland:

TESSEL, Netherland, 28 December, 1888.

DEAR COUSINS: Because we belong undoubtedly to the same stem so we feel us pressed to congratulate you with your Jubilee of the 10th October. Our family is very numerous upon this isle, and with hardly any exceptions they are farmers. Receive with your family the salutations of our family.
AUG. C. KEYSER,
CORNELIS KEYSER, SR.,
LEONARD KEYSER,
DIRK KEYSER,
PIETER KEYSER.

Postmarked TEXEL, 28 Dec., '88, 5–6 N.
Addressed: To the Principal Person of the Family Keyser,
Germantown in Pennsylvanie, N. America.

This letter was suitably acknowledged, and the following letter received:

TEXEL, 10 Feb., 1889.

DEAR COUSINS: We were very glad to receive your letter of the fifteenth of January, and we have learned with much interest and with us many of our family the account of your family. I am sorry that I am not able to show you our relation to-day, notwithstanding I have taken much pains to discover it. Our genealogical tree reaches not beyond 1698. Nevertheless I will endeavor by an examination of our archives and those of Amsterdam to penetrate further into our descent. We had heard of the Keyser reunion by a journal which was sent to me from Passaic. Some Dutch journals also noticed that for your family great historical event. The similarity of the names and those of your family touched us. Your German descent, which we have in common, that we were Anabaptists also, who for their religious opinions were forced to leave Germany, goes far to convince us that we are the same family. We wish to know if your forefather Dirck Keyser left behind him relatives here in Holland when he went to America, which fact if so would facilitate my inquiries. With this letter I send you some photographs: the one is of my niece Anna Keyser, who certainly loses nothing in comparison with the girls of 200 years ago; the second is my wife, dressed in the national costume; the third is my uncle Simon Keyser, and the fourth of my father Cornelis

Keyser; the last portrait is mine. I would be very happy to receive some portraits of your family. Receive our best felicitations.

Truly your cousin,

AUGUST KEYSER.

The letter contained the following photographs: Peter Keyser, son of Sybrand, Burgomaster of Texel; Cornelis Keyser, Sybrand's son living at Texel; Anna Maria Keyser, daughter of Cornelis Keyser, niece of August Keyser; August Keyser, son of Cornelis Keyser, Sybrand's son; E. (Veensta) Keyser, wife of August Keyser; Simon Keyser, son of Sybrand Keyser, born Oct. 30, 1810, d. April 17, 1868, member of Council, President of the Dyke College of Texel, and late member of the Provincial States of North Holland. Cornelis Keyser, son of August Keyser—Cornelis' son; Cornelis Keyser, Pr., member of Council of Texel.*

FROM GONZALES, TEXAS.

GONZALES, 3, 10, 1889.

MR. CHARLES S. KEYSER.

DEAR SIR: Your letter was received some days ago, and I have looked for the family tree but have not yet found it. I will look in every paper, and if found will send it to you. I am the only child of Ezra Keyser, but have two children, the eldest being a boy, Keyser R. Blythe. * * * You can't imagine how much I will appreciate a history of the Keyser family, for I am Keyser from head to foot, and oh! how proud I am of it —and I assure you Ezra Keyser was an honor to the family. * * * He wrote so grandly beautiful—excuse a daughter's pride in her father— but not my opinion only, there have been many who have come here to see his writing again after an absence of many years. * * * But he is dead, gone from us to write in God's beautiful book of life and love. I can write no more now, my heart is too heavy. I will send you what I think will be of use to you. Adieu,

MRS. S. K. BLYTHE,

Gonzales, Texas.

The family will read with much interest the following letter of our relative in the Metropolis to whose munificence I have made allusion; among his numerous life-works was the creation of a home and park which was a pride and pleasure to Norwalk in Connecticut. From this he has recently parted. His reasons for, and feelings on, parting from this island home

* I have sent all the information we have of the family in Holland, which is contained on pages 17 and 19 of this volume.—C. S. K.

are given in answer to a request from the editor of a paper there (*Evening Sentinel*, May 7, 1889). He says:

"You kindly invited me to detail something of my experience at Keyser Island now that it has passed into other hands.

"Thirty years ago, when I purchased the place, I was visited by two of Norwalk's prominent citizens, who asked me in sympathetic kindness if I ever expected to make a home out of this forlorn and rocky island, where no fruit or shade trees could possibly grow, and so far distant from civilization.

"My reply was, 'Wait and see.'

"The trees grew; the shrubbery and flowers became a wilderness of blossoms; the boulders disappeared and formed the sea-walls for the three-quarters-of-a-mile drive that skirted Long Island Sound, and one and a half miles of a four-foot flower border marked the roads and shaded walks over the place, and this within the next succeeding five years. My enjoyment in life has ever sprung from

'Sharing others' sorrows, others' joys.'

Hence it has been very pleasant to me to minister to the pleasure of the many thousands who have enjoyed and appreciated this place, and I am doubly thankful for having been the almoner of so many of nature's bounties.

"It is often asked me if I have no regrets in parting with our island home. 'Oh no! I accept the inevitable cheerfully with thankfulness and no regrets.'

"In early life, with rare and exquisite pleasure, I planted the trees and shrubs, and saw them grow and blossom like so many children; I ministered to the flowers, and they ministered to others' happiness and my own. I drove my horses over the beautiful meadow track before breakfast; a score of friends and relatives sat down to my board. For all these abundant blessings and privileges I am profoundly grateful and thankful.

"Still, I have no regrets, and relinquish the island with the same thankfulness. Like all the experiences of human life, 'change is written upon all.' All our friends, with two or three solitary exceptions, have passed to the spirit side of life, and we are alone. Besides, the cares of a great estate like the island had become a weary burden to us in our declining years, and its relinquishment will give us rest.

"JOHN H. KEYSER."

Charles S. Keyser

THE

Genealogy

OF THE

Keyser Family.

1688—1888.

THE

KEYSER FAMILY

DESCENDANTS

OF

DIRCK KEYSER OF AMSTERDAM.

COMPILED BY

CHARLES S. KEYSER.

PHILADELPHIA:

1889.

THE GENEALOGY OF THE FAMILY.

ORIGIN: THE KEYSER FAMILY OF BAVARIA, MALE;
THE GOVERTS FAMILY OF HOLLAND, FEMALE.

Ancestor: **GERRITS KEYSER, Amsterdam, Male;**
TOBIAS GOVERTSZ VAN DEN WYNGAERT, Amster-
dam, Female.

(1) DIRCK GERRITSZ KEYSER[1], a manufacturer of Amsterdam, son of Gerrits Keyser, married CORNELIA, daughter of TOBIAS GOVERTSZ VAN DEN WYNGAERT, a Mennonite minister.

Children of (1) DIRCK GERRITSZ KEYSER[1] and (2) CORNELIA (GOVERTSZ) KEYSER.

(3) [1]DIRCK KEYSER[2], b. 1635 in Amsterdam; d. Nov. 30, 1714, in Germantown.

(4) [2]GERRITS DIRCK KEYSER, b. in Amsterdam; d. ——, in Amsterdam.

(5) [3]TOBIAS DIRCK KEYSER, b. in Amsterdam; d. Sept. 18, 1655, in Amsterdam.

(6) [4]—— —— ——, b. in Amsterdam; d. July 5, 1655, in Amsterdam.

(7) [5]ANNEKEN KEYSER, b. in Amsterdam; d. June 17, 1681, in Amsterdam.

(3) [1]DIRCK KEYSER[2], m. 22 Nov., 1668, at Buickesloot, Amsterdam, 1st, (8) Elizabet ter Himpel, and 2d, m. 22 Nov., 1682, at Buickesloot, Amsterdam, (9) Johanna Harperts Snoeck.

Children of (3) DIRCK KEYSER[2] and (8)ELIZABET (ter Himpel).*

(10) [1]*Dirck*[3], b. Amsterdam ——; d. Manahataona, Philadelphia county, Jan., 1715.

(11) [2]*Elizabet*[3], b. Amsterdam 23 Aug., 1673; d. Amsterdam, June 23, 1681.

(12) [3]*Pieter Dirck*[3], b. Amsterdam Nov. 26, 1676; d. Germantown 12 Sept., 1724.

Children of (3) DIRCK KEYSER[2] and (9) JOHANNA (Harperts Snoeck).†

(13) [1]*Johanna*[3], b. Amsterdam 5 Sep., 1683; d. Cougenaue, N. J., Sep., 1688.

(14) [2]*Cornelia*[3], b. Amsterdam, 8 Ap., 1685; d. Amsterdam Oct., 22, 1686.

(10) [1]*Dirck, Jr.*[3], m. —— (15) Deborah ——; died without issue.

(12) [3]*Pieter Dirck*[3], m. Anno 1700, Sep. 4, in Germantown, (16) Margaret Souplis,‡ d. of Andrew Souplis, a burgher of New York, and his wife Anneke Souplis.

Children of (12) [3]*Pieter Dirck*[3] and (16) Margaret (Souplis).

(17) [1]**DIRCK KEYSER**[4], b. Sep. 26, 1701; d. Jan. 8, 1756.

(18) [2]**ANDREAS KEYSER**[4], b. July 22, 1703; d. ——; living 1744.

(19) [3]**PETER DIRCK KEYSER**[4], b. July 9, 1705; d. ——.

(20) [4]**JACOB SOUPLIS KEYSER**[4], b. July 13, 1707; d. ——, 1781.

(21) [5]**JOHANNES KEYSER**[4], b. June 25, 1709; d. Sep. 23, 1711.

(22) [6]**ABRAHAM KEYSER**[4], b. May 26, 1711; d. Dec. 30, 1717.

(23) [7]**ELIZABETH KEYSER**[4], b. Jan. 20, 1714; d. ——.

(24) [8]**ANNEKE KEYSER**[4], b. May 23, 1716; d. March 14, 1807.

(25) [9]**KATHELINA KEYSER**[4], b. Oct. 25, 1718; d. ——; living 1744.

(26) [10]**JOHANNES KEYSER**[4], b. July 25, 1721; d. ——; living 1744.

(27) [11]**MARGARET KEYSER**[4], b. Oct. 4, 1723; d. ——; living 1744.

* (8) Elizabet ter Himpel was d. of Peter ter Himpel, a merchant of Amsterdam, and Elizabet van Singel, was b. 12 Nov., 1637, and d. May 12, 1681, aged 43 y. 6 mo., in Amsterdam.

† (9) Johanna Harperts Snoeck, b. ——, 1648, in Amsterdam ; d. Aug. 26, 1686, in Amsterdam, æt. 38 years.

‡ Margaret Souplis was born Ao. 1682; m. after (12) [3]Peter Dirck Keyser's[3] death Michael Eccard, and was living Feb. 11, 1744.

(17) ¹**DIRCK KEYSER⁴**, m. ——, 1725, ⁵Alitje² (Alice) de Neuss*. Ch., ¹**PETER⁵**, b. — 8, 1726; d. young. ²**ELIZABETH⁵**, b. 9, 8, 1728; d. 5, 2, 1812. ³**JOHN⁵**, b. 23, 5, 1730; d. 2, 5, 1813. ⁴**PETER⁵**, b. 18, 8, 1732; d. 11, 3, 1818. ⁵**ALICE⁵**, b. 28, 12, 1734; d. ——. ⁶**DERICK⁵**, b. 2, 4, 1737; d. ——. ⁷**HANNAH⁵**, b. 13, 8, 1739; d. ——. ⁸**ABRAHAM⁵**, b. 8, 7, 1742; d. ——. ⁹**MICHAEL⁵**, b. 30, 8, 1745; d. 5, 10, 1825.

²**ELIZABETH⁵**, m., 16, 11, 1752, Andrew Wood, who d. 28, 5, 1812; ch., ¹GEORGE⁶, b. 29, 11, 1753, d. ——; ²MICHAEL⁶, b. 21, 11, 1755, d. ——; ³MARY⁶, b. 25, 11, 1757, unmd.; ⁴ANDREW⁶, b. 11, 1, 1760, d. ——; ⁵ELIZABETH⁶, b. 12, 2, 1762, m. William Taylor; ⁶JOHN⁶, b. 12, 4, 1765, d. ——; ⁷HANNAH⁶, b. 16, 7, 1767, d. ——; ⁸ANN⁶, b. 22, 3, 1772.

¹GEORGE⁶, m. and removed to Lexington, Ky. ²MICHAEL⁶, m. and removed to Heidelberg, Adams Co., Pa. ⁴ANDREW⁶, m. —— ——; ch., ¹ANDREW⁷.

¹ANDREW⁷, m., 14, 11, 1813, ⁵Ann Keyser⁷; ch., ¹Susan⁸, b. 9, 10, 1814. ²William⁸, 29, 7, 1816; d. 21, 10, 1837. ³Sophia⁸, 10, 8, 1818; d. 9, 2, 1838. ⁴Joseph⁸, b. 1, 11, 1820; d. 4, 2, 1838. ⁵Elizabeth⁸, b. 2, 6, 1823. ⁶Maria⁸, 11, 7, 1825. ⁷Andrew⁸, 4, 12, 1827. ⁸Ann⁸, 17, 1, 1831. ⁹Amelia⁸, 8, 3, 1834.

¹Susan⁸, m., 12, 9, 1854, John C. Channon; ch., ¹Joseph⁹, b. 20, 8, 1855. ²Margaret⁹, 6, 2, 1859.

⁵ELIZABETH⁶, m. William Taylor; l. in Roxboro. ⁶JOHN⁶, m. —— ——; l. in Roxboro. ⁷HANNAH⁶, m. Abraham Rittenhouse, who d.; she removed to Kentucky. ⁸ANN⁶, m. Michael Wills; l. in Norristown.

³**JOHN⁵**,† m., 7, 11, 1752, Elizabeth Rinker; ch., ¹SUSANNA⁶, b. 23, 1, 1753; d. 4, 12, 1833. ²JACOB⁶, b. 18, 9, 1754; d. 17, 12, 1846. ³MARY⁶, b. 2, 1, 1757; d. 20, 11, 1834. ⁴SAMUEL⁶, b. 25, 9, 1760; d. 29, 7, 1773. ⁵——⁶, still-born, 6, 7, 1762. ⁶ABRAHAM⁶, b. 23, 6, 1763; d. — — 1850. ⁷ANN⁶, b. 5, 4, 1765. ⁸——⁶, still-born, 24, 4, 1768. ⁹CHARLES⁶, b. 15, 11, 1770; d. 5, 1, 1852. ¹⁰ELIZABETH⁶, b. 22, 11, 1772; d. 16, 6, 1773.

¹SUSANNA⁶, m. John Weaver, s. of Philip and Susanna Weaver, of G.; went to Frederick Co., Md.; ch. ¹SAMUEL⁷, b. 9, 11, 1777; d. 17, 8, 1778. ²JOSEPH⁷, b. 16, 12, 1779; d. unmd. ³ELIZABETH⁷, b. 29, 12, 1781. ⁴ANN⁷, b. 27, 5, 1784; d. 6, 2, 1870. ⁵SAMUEL⁷, b. 25, 5, 1786. ⁶NATHANIEL⁷, b. 19, 7, 1788. ⁷JOHN⁷, b. 18, 11, 1790. ⁸SARAH⁷, b. 31,

---

* Jan de Neuss¹, b. ——, d. —, 10, 1719; m. Elizabeth ——; ch., Matthias², Cornelius², ³Wynard², ⁴William², ⁵Alitje² (Alice), b. 1702, d. 8, 1, 1756; ⁶Gertrude². ⁵Alitje² (Alice), m. (17) ¹Dirck Keyser⁴.

† John Keyser and Elizabeth (Rinker) Keyser joined the Mennonite Church in 1771.

10, 1793; d. 28, 4, 1816. [9]MARY[7], b 13, 3, 1796. [10]PHILIP[7], b. 18, 2, 1798; d. 10, 3, 1824.

    [3]ELIZABETH[7], m. Harman Yerkes; ch., [1]Miriam[8], [2]Joseph W.[8], [3]Reuben[8], [4]Susan[8], [5]Mary[8], [6]Martha[8], [7]Hiram[8], d. 28, 9, 1836, [8]Nathaniel[8].

    [2]Joseph W.[8], m. Mary Harry; ch., [1]David[9], [2]Annie[9], [3]Mary[9].

    [3]Mary[9], m., 10, 10, 1861, Alan Wood.*

    [4]ANN[7], m., —— 1808, Joseph Hagy, who d. 18, 4, 1817; ch., [1]Mary Weaver[8], b, 6, 1, 1810. [2]Susanna Weaver[8], 10, 6, 1812; d. 21, 10, 1834. [3]Elizabeth[8], b. 4, 2, 1813; d. — 2, 1842. [4]Sarah Weaver[8], b. 16, 10, 1816.

    [1]Mary Weaver[8], m., 2, 4, 1839, Joseph Townsend Mears; ch., [1]Ruth Anna[9], b. 24, 12, 1839. [2]Edward Burrough[9], 20, 12, 1840. [3]Sarah Hagy[9], 23, 6, 1843. [4]Elizabeth[9], 18, 9, 1846. [5]Joseph Townsend[9], 11, 3. 1848. [6]Elmira Atherton[9], 1, 4, 1853; d. 5, 8, 1853.

    [2]Edward Burrough[9], m., 29, 10, 1867, Clara Kollner; ch., Frederick Kollner. [5]Joseph Townsend[9], m., 12, 7, 1876, Nellie C. Hughes; ch., Jennie May, Doris, Theresa.

    [3]Elizabeth[8], m., — 3, 1835, Spencer Roberts; ch. [1]Hugh Oscar[9], [2]Susanna Hagy[9], [3]Charles Rorer[9], [4]Algernon Sidney[9].

    [4]Sarah Weaver[8], m., — 2, 1850, Henry P. Atherton, who d. 27, 1, 1867.

    [2]JACOB[6], m., 16, 10, 1780, Susanna Smith, d. of Peter and Margaret Smith (she d. 20, 5, 1823); ch., [1]MARGARET[7], b. 31, 7, 1781; d. 8, 1, 1864, unm. [2]SAMUEL[7], b. 25, 1, 1783; d. 9, 7, 1868. [3]WILLIAM[7], b. 14, 9, 1785; d. 20, 10, 1853. [4]SARAH[7], b. 11, 9, 1787. [5]ANN[7], b. 18, 7, 1790; d. 4, 11, 1832. [6]JOHN[7], b. 19, 8, 1792; d. 23, 11, 1850. [7]ELIZABETH[7], b. 31, 12, 1795, unm.; d. 39, 12, 1840.

    [2]SAMUEL[7], m., 6, 5, 1807, Mary Miller; ch., [1]Gideon[8], b. 21, 2, 1808; d. 3, 12, 1888. [2]Naaman[8], b. 20, 5, 1810; d. 9, 8, 1867. [3]Reuben[8], b. 4, 4, 1813; d. 22, 7, 1888. [4]Jacob[8], b. 21, 7, 1814; d. 27, 11, 1839. [5]John S.[8], b. 16, 1, 1817; d. 15, 4, 1862. [6]Daniel L.[8], b. 21, 2, 1819; d. 27, 3, 1884. [7]Margaret[8], b. 28, 6, 1821; d. 12, 4, 1829. [8]Elizabeth[8], b. 28, 1, 1824; d. 27, 3, 1858. [9]Sarah[8], b. 8, 11, 1826; d. ——. [10]Still-born[8], 8, 1, 1829. [11]Martha[8], b. 19, 1, 1830; d. 2, 1, 1888.

    [1]Gideon[8], m., 30, 11, 1832, Ann Fryhoffer; ch., [1]Paul[9], b. 29, 11, 1833; d. 23, 8, 1864. [2]George[9], b. 1, 1, 1836; d. 6, 11, 1869.† [3]Jacob[9], ——, ——. [4]Harriet F.[9], b. 19, 11, 1838; d. 22, 4, 1872. [5]William F.[9], ——, ——. [6]Harrison[9], b. 22, 5, 1847; d. 5, 5, 1884.

---

    * Rep. in the 44th Cong. for the 7th Dist. Pa. Prest. 1st Nat. Bk, Conshohocken.

    † He was driving and heard a man, half buried under an embankment on Broad Street, moaning for help. He succeeded, unaided, in rescuing him, but was himself caught by a second fall of the earth and instantly killed.

[7]Naaman[9], b. 17, 9, 1853; d. 27, 4, 1862. [2]Jacob[9], m., 6, 5, 1864, Mary Moore; ch., [1]George[10], m., 7, 11, 1888, Mary L. Hicks. [4]Harriet F.[9], m. Charles Nice; ch., Charles. [5]William F.[9], m., 29, 9, 1874, Addie R. Yake; ch., Helen Ross. [6]Harrison[9], m., 20, 5, 1875, ——.; ch., [1]Harriet Nice[10]; [2]Anna[10].

[2]Naaman[8], m. 13, 4, 1837, Isabella Provest; ch., [1]Charles Provest[9], b. 6, 4, 1838; d. 13, 11, 1839. [2]Alexander Provest[9], b. 7, 11, 1839. [3]Mary Elizabeth[9], b. 5, 3, 1842. [4]Charles Provest[9], b. 7, 10, 1843; d. 1, 7, 1863 (Gettysburg). [5]Henry Clay[9], b. 12, 3, 1845. [6]Margaret Cecilia Provest[9], b. 4, 6, 1850.

[2]Alexander Provest[9], m., 7, 11, 1866, Emma R. Wolf; ch., [1]Naaman Henry, D.D.S.[10]. [2]Isabella Provest[10], m., 21, 3, 1889, Charles F. Idell. [3]Barton Mattis[10]. [4]Francis A. Provest[10]. [3]Mary Elizabeth[9], m., 15, 4, 1862, Cornelius C. Widdis; ch., [1]Cornelius C., Jr.[10]; [2]Edwin Stevens[10]. [3]Susanna Jungkurth[10]. [5]Henry Clay[9], m. Gertie P. Woodbury (lives in Ohio).

[3]Reuben[8], m., 26, 3, 1836, Eliza Van Dyke; ch., [1]Samuel[9], b. 11, 11, 1839; d. 1, 7, 1863 (Gettysburg). [2]Sylvester[9], b. ——; m., 22, 11, 1865, Hannah Ward; ch., [1]Katie Keyser[10], b. 17, 10, 1871; d. 2, 4, 1888. [3]Kate[9], b. ——. [4]Martha[9], b. ——. [5]Edward[9], b. ——. [6]Frank[9], b. ——. [7]Alfred Green[9], b. ——. [8]Jennette Campbell[9], b. ——.

[5]John S.[8], m., 11, 3, 1841, Sarah Ann English; ch., [1]Mary[9]. [2]Horace L.[9] [3]Emma[9], d. 22, 4, 1884. [4]Samuel[9], b. ——. [5]Lucy[9], b. ——. [1]Mary[9], m. John Kulp. [2]Horace L.[9], m. ——; ch., Florence. [5]Lucy[9], m., 3, 3, 1879, Dr. J. K. Wiley, Springfield, Mass.; ch., Joseph Wiley.

[6]Daniel L.[8], m., ——, Susan E. Paul, d. of Henry K. Paul, of Grm., who d. aged 84, and Ann C., who d. aged 79; ch., [1]Dirck[9], b. 9, 2, 1854; d. 16, 8, 1864. [2]Anne Paul[9], b. ——. [3]Romaine[9], b. ——. [8]Elizabeth[8], m., 10, 10, 1844, Daniel Cooledge Bullard; ch., [1]Rufus[9], b. 30, 9, 1845. [2]Charles Keyser[9], b. 3, 4, 1847. [3]Miller[9], b. 20, 12, 1848, in Grm.; d. 3, 4, 1883, in Sedalia, Mo. [4]Eleanor[9], b. 18, 1, 1851. [5]Samuel Keyser[9], b. 23, 4, 1853. [6]Daniel Keyser[9], b. 27, 10, 1855. [7]John Edgar[9], b. 17, 12, 1857; d. 10, 8, 1858, at Niles, Mich. [1]Rufus[9], m., 31, 10, 1867, Ida, d. of Delos Cox; ch., Miller, b. 16, 5, 1871. Gordon, b. 22, 6, 1879. Rufus, Jr., b. 24, 2, 1882. [2]Charles[9], m., 12, 6, 1887, Susan Waterman; ch., Edna, b. 5, 6, 1888. [4]Eleanor[9], m., 25, 5, 1874, Charles McAllister; ch., Frank B., Mattie, Beulah E., Alice M., Daniel C. [5]Samuel[9], m., 20, 1, 1880, 1st, Josie, d. of Wm. G. Moore, who d. 24, 1, 1882; m., 2d,

14, 11, 1888, Minnie Scott, d. of Dr. George H. Scott; ch., of Josie Moore, Mary Elizabeth, b. 1, 11, 1882. [6]Daniel[9], m., 5, 1, 1882, Martha Jane Finley; ch., Mary Elizabeth.

[9]Sarah[8], m., 20, 9, 1853, John Nelson Robinson; ch., [1]Martha B.[9], b. 18, 6, 1854. [2]William R.[9], b. 16, 8, 1855. [3]Martha B.[9], m., 10, 10, 1878, Samuel T. West.

[11]Martha[8], m., 4, 10, 1853, Joseph Button; ch., [1]Samuel Keyser[9], b. 13, 10, 1854; d. 8, 12, 1860. [2]John[9], b. ——; d. 23, 10, 1886. [3]Martha S.[9], [4]Mary Keyser[9], [5]Annie S.[9], [6]Joseph[9], [7]Sarah Keyser[9].

[2]John[9], m., 30, 4, 1879, Annie S. Woddrop; ch., Jennie Woddrop, Helen Roberts, John Conyers. [3]Martha S.[9]; m. Edward Goodall. [5]Annie S.[9], m. Enos Erdman. [6]Joseph[9], m. Lilla Randall.

[3]William,[7] m. Rebecca Derrickson; lived in Swedesboro, N. J.; ch, [1]John[8].

[4]Sarah[7], m. Jno. Geo. Hassinger; lived in Dauphin Co., Pa.; ch., [1]Jacob Keyser[8], b. 28, 7, 1816. [2]Jno. Smith[8], —— 1818. [3]Susan Keyser[8], —— 1820. [4]Samuel Keyser[8], —— 1825.

[1]Jacob Keyser[8], m., 9, 3, 1843, Susan Elizabeth Finney; ch., [1]James Finney[9], [2]Samuel E. Reed[9], [3]William Thomas[9], [4]Mary Anne[9], [5]Sarah Elizabeth[9], [6]Emma Elspy[9].

[1]Jas. Finney[9], m., — 2, 1866, Susan Gilbert. [2]Samuel E. Reed[9], m., 24, 2, 1876, Virginia H. List; ch., [1]Mattie List[10], [2]Samuel Reed[10]. [3]William Thomas[9], m., 19, 5, 1872, Martha A. Coward; ch., [1]William Clarence[10], [2]Clara Elizabeth[10]. [4]Mary Anne[9], m., 26, 11, 1879, William A. Goldsmith; ch.,[1] Jas. Hassinger[10], [2]Elizabeth Finney[10]. [5]Sarah Elizabeth[9], m., 28, 2, 1878, John W. Creider; ch., [1]Mary Hassinger[10], [2]William Claud[10], [3]Charles Wesley[10], [4]Ralph McKinley[10], [5]John W.[10] [6]Emma Elspy[9], m., 19, 6, 1883, Ellsworth L. Smith; ch., [1]Jacob Hassinger[10], [2]Anna Finney[10], [3]Emily[10].

[6]John[7], m. Elizabeth Hackenburg, who was b. 17, 1, 1796, d. 24, 2, 1880; ch., [1]Peter[8], b. 1, 9, 1822. [2]Samuel[8], b. 24, 10, 1823, d. 26, 6, 1860. [3]Jacob[8], b. 5, 3, 1826. [4]Daniel[8], 5, 1, 1828. [5]Mary[8], 23, 5, 1830, d. 17, 4, 1833. [6]Alpheus[8], b. 7, 11, 1832, d. 23, 1, 1888. [7]Joseph[8], b. 24, 5, 1835.

[1]Peter[8], m., —, 7, 1849, Anna Metlar; ch., [1]Roland S.[9], b. 14, 9, 1854. [2]Arthur W.[9], 9, 3, 1854. [3]Linneus E.[9], 27, 7, 1858; m., 12, 7, 1882, Minnie Ball. [2]Samuel[8], m. ——, Mary Neyhart; ch., [1]George[9], [2]Clara[9], [3]Elizabeth[9], [4]Samuel[9].

[2]Clara[9], m. ——, Edward Hannon. [3]Elizabeth[9], m., ——, Edward Powers. [4]Samuel[9], m., ——, ——

[3]Jacob[8], m., 18, 5, 1851, Rachel Neyhart; ch., [1]Mary E.[9], b, 24, 8,

1852, m. Thomas Young. ²Alpheus B.⁹, 19, 9, 1854, m, Elmira Musselman. ³John R.⁹, 4, 9, 1856, m. Amanda Stucker. ⁴Tillie⁹, 24, 20, 1858, m. Frank Cornelius. ⁵William⁹, 24, 1, 1861, m. Anna Summers. ⁶Margaret⁹, 25, 3, 1863. ⁷Charles F.⁹, 1, 6, 1866, m. Maud Hains. ⁸Ward B.⁹, 1, 8, 1868. ⁹Emma⁹, 18, 6, 1872. ¹⁰Ada⁹, 8, 3, 1875.

⁴Daniel⁸, m. Margaret Birckheimer ; ch., ¹William B.⁹, b. 22, 6, 1853. ²John F.⁹, 19, 2, 1857. ³Jacob H.⁹, 12, 7, 1859. ⁴Mary M.⁹, 18, 10, 1861. ⁵Thomas E.⁹, 26, 2, 1865. ⁶Emma A.⁹, 26, 9, 1868. ⁷Nora J.⁹, 1, 1, 1871. ⁸Calvin L.⁹, 17, 5, 1873. ⁹Rosa E.⁹, 4, 11, 1875.

⁶Alpheus⁸, m. Maria Maywell ; ch., ¹Charles F.⁹, ——. ²John⁹, ——. ³Mary⁹, —— decd.

⁷Joseph⁸, m. Maria Garber ; ch., ¹Annie L.⁹, b. 11, 7, 1861, m. William Whaland. ²Maurice⁹, 25, 9, 1863. ³Ada⁹, 21, 4, 1865. Harry, decd., 18, 1, 1884. ⁴Ella⁹, 15, 8, 1870. ⁵Virginia⁹, 28, 11, 1871. ⁶Sadie⁹, 6, 6, 1873. ⁷Norman⁹, 5, 4, 1875. ⁸Augustus G.⁹, 21, 11, 1876. ⁹Joseph⁹, 19, 4, 1879.

³MARY⁶, m., 21, 4, 1777, William Heisler ; ch., ¹ELIZABETH⁷, b. 12, 2, 1778, d. 30, 4, 1778. ²GEORGE⁷, 3, 6, 1779, d. 7, 10, 1804. ³JOHN⁷, b. 31, 10, 1781. ⁴MARY⁷, 11, 2, 1784. ⁵ANN⁷, 29, 12, 1785 (living, 1844, Richmond, Va.). ⁶WILLIAM⁷, 9, 1, 1788, d. 9, 11, 1807 (Alexandria, D. C.). ⁷SUSANNA⁷, 18, 5, 1790. ⁸ELIZABETH⁷, b. 29, 3, 1792, d. 26, 9, 1822. ⁹HANNAH⁷, b. 2, 11, 1793, d. 29, 9, 1822. ¹⁰ABRAHAM⁷, b. 22, 4, 1797, d. 5, 1, 1846. ¹¹SARAH⁷, b. 22, 11, 1798, d. 24, 11, 1798.

²GEORGE⁷, m. Ann Barras ; ch., ¹Joseph⁸, ²Amanda⁸.

³JOHN⁷, m. Elizabeth Knecht (Knight); ch., ¹Geo. M.⁸, decd.; ²William⁸, ³Mary Ann⁸, ⁴Israel Putnam⁸, ⁵Barzillai⁸, decd.; m. Rebecca L. Brown ; ch., ¹Marietta⁹, ²Henry Lawrence⁹, ³B. Roberts⁹, decd.; ⁴Henry E.⁹, ⁵Francis W.⁹, ⁶Reuel Heisler⁸, decd.; m. Mary Taylor ; ch., ¹Laura⁹, ⁸Peter Keyser⁸, ⁹John⁸, ¹⁰Marcus⁸, ¹¹Rebecca⁸, m. —— Sampson.

⁴MARY⁷, m. Israel Roberts ; ch., ¹Martha⁸, ²Israel⁸, ³John⁸, ⁴George⁸, ⁵James⁸, ⁶Elizabeth⁸, ⁷——⁸.

⁵ANN⁷, m. Samuel Carter ; ch., ¹Douglas⁸, ²John⁸, ³Martha⁸, Samuel⁸, ⁴Israel⁸.

⁷SUSAN⁷, m. Jacob Douglas ; ch., ¹Rachel⁸.

⁸ELIZABETH⁷, m. Joseph Kimbrough (Richmond, Va.).

⁹HANNAH⁷, m. Adolph Dill ; ch., ¹Emily⁸, ²William⁸.

⁶ABRAHAM⁶, unm.; died in Germantown.

⁷ANN⁶, m., 19, 8, 1792, Philip Weaver, s. of Richard and Susanna Weaver, of Germantown (he died 10, 3, 1824); one child, d. ——.

⁹CHARLES⁶, m., 4, 10, 1797, Catherine, d. of John and Mary Rees ; ch.,

[1]Mary[7], b. 24, 7, 1798 (lived De Soto Co., Miss.). [2]Elizabeth[7], b. 16, 12, 1799 (lived La Salle Co., Ill.). [3]Rees[7], b. 22, 11, 1801, d. 7, 7, 1826 (Sunbury, Pa.). [4]Matilda[7], b. 21, 10, 1803, d. —— (Murfreesboro, Tenn.). [5]Martha[7], b. 1, 12, 1805, d. —— (Coffee Co., Tenn.). [6]Hiram[7], b. 4, 3, 1808. [7]John L.[7], b. 31, 12, 1809. [8]Charles M.[7], b. 7, 2, 1812, d. 31, 5, 1833 (Maysville, Ky.). [9]Paul[7], b. 23, 12, 1813. [10]Rufus[7], b. 23, 12, 1815 (lived St. Louis). [11]Ezra[7], b. 4, 3, 1820 (lived Murfreesboro, Tenn., and Gonzales, Texas). [12]Catherine[7], b. 4, 3, 1820. [13]Anna[7], b. 24, 1, 1822. [14]Jane Wood[7], b. 15, 11, 1824. [15]Susanna[7], b. 3, 6, 1827.

[1]Mary[7], m. German Baker (lived De Soto Co., Miss.); ch., [1]Samuel A.[8], b. 3, 12, 1821. [2]Martha K.[8], 1, 6, 1823. [3]Hannah,[8] 28, 8, 1824. [4]Catherine K.[8], 20, 2, 1826. [5]Charles K.[8], b. 3, 3, 1827. [6]Joshua[8], 23, 1, 1829. [7]Thomas[8], 20, 11, 1830. [8]Lydia Ann[8], 28, 11, 1832. [9]Sarah Philena[8], 8, 1, 1835. [10]David Phineas[8], 25, 4, 1837. [11]William[8], 16, 4, 1839. [12]Elizabeth Webster[8], 23, 2, 1841, d. 1842.

[2]Elizabeth[7], m. Joshua Brown; ch., [1]Samuel A.[8], 3, 12, 1821. [2]Martha K.[8], b. 1, 6, 1823, d. [3]Hannah[8], 27, 8, 1824. [4]Catherine K.[8], 20, 2, 1826, d. [5]Joshua[8], 23, 1, 1829. [6]Thomas[8], 20, 11, 1830. [7]Lydia Ann[8], 28, 11, 1832. [8]Sarah Philena[8], 8, 1, 1835. [9]David Phineas[8], 25, 4, 1837. [10]William[8], 16, 4, 1839. [11]Elizabeth Webster[8], 23, 2, 1841, d. [12]Catherine Elizabeth[8], 27, 4, 1843.

[4]Matilda[7], m., 4, 3, 1833, G. T. Henderson; ch., [1]William Penn[8], [2]Melville Cox[8], [3]Reese Keyser[8].

[5]Martha[7], m. Geo. Shaw.

[6]Hiram[7], m. Jane ——

[9]Paul[7], m. Mary O'Neill.

[10]Rufus[7], m. Margaret Rupely.

[11]Ezra[7], m. Sophia W. Prior; ch., Sallie Kittie, m. —— Blythe; ch.

[12]Catherine[7], m. Robert S. Morris.

[13]Anna[7], m., ——, 1853, George Jones; ch., [1]Sarah F.[8], [2]Lydia[8], m., ——, 1885, Charles C. Haines; ch., Anna J.

[14]Jane Wood[7], m., 5, 9, 1850, Alpheus Channon; ch. [1]Charles Keyser,[8] m., 8, 1, 1883, Ella Kirk.

[15]Susanna[7], m. Joseph King, Jr.; ch., [1]Charles Keyser[8], b. 28, 8, 1846. [2]Susanna[8] 4, 4, 1849.

[1]PETER[5], m., 1st, 5, 5, 1756, Hannah Levering, d. of William Levering, who d. 19, 8, 1775; m., 2d, 14, 10, 1787, Mary Mechlin (who died 14, 4, 1810). Ch. of Hannah Levering: [1]WILLIAM[6], b. 29, 12, 1757, d. 23, 2, 1842. [2]DERICK[6], b. 28, 3, 1760, d. 24, 2, 1839. [3]ELIZABETH[6], b. 30, 1, 1763, d. 24, 9, 1826. [4]PETER[6], 9, 11, 1766, d. 21, 5, 1849. [5]SARAH[6], b. 9, 6, 1771, d. 5, 8, 1835.

¹WILLIAM⁶, m., 21, 9, 1781, Barbara Leibert, d. of Peter and Mary Leibert, of Germantown; ch., ¹JOHN⁷, b. 25, 6, 1782, d. 12, 10, 1785. ²PETER⁷, b. 30, 10, 1783, d. 28, 9, 1788. ³SARAH⁷, b. 17, 7, 1786. ⁴MARY⁷, b. 9, 2, 1788. ⁵WILLIAM⁷, b. 16, 1, 1790, d. 12, 4, 1825. ⁶JOHN⁷, b. 8, 11, 1791, d. 24, 9, 1793. ⁷LEIBERT⁷, b. 20, 5, 1794. ⁸KEZIAH⁷, b. 20, 5, 1794, d. 22, 6, 1794.

³SARAH⁷, m., 20, 2, 1803, Robert William Kirk (Alexandria, D. C.); ch. ¹James⁸, b. 20, 1, 1804, d. 9, 10, 1844.

⁴MARY⁷, m., 11, 8, 1806, Joseph L. Thomas; ch., ¹William Keyser⁸, b. 21, 6, 1807. ²James⁸, 16, 12, 1808. ³Gustavus⁸, 29, 9, 1810. ⁴James Keyser⁸, 11, 4, 1818. ⁵Joseph⁸, 7, 8, 1821, d. 7, 8, 1821. ⁶Joseph⁸, b. ——.

²DERICK⁶, m., 1st, 25, 4, 1782, Elizabeth Clemens, d. of Garrit and Keturah Clemens; 2d m., 1821, Rebecca Brown.

Ch. of Elizabeth Clemens: ¹ABRAHAM⁷, b. 9, 5, 1783, d. 18, 8, 1829. ²GEORGE⁷, b. 17, 9, 1784, d. 19, 9, 1837. ³HANNAH⁷, b. 13, 9, 1786, d. 29, 7, 1787. ⁴PETER⁷, b. 25, 8, 1788, d. 2, 9, 1789. ⁵SARAH⁷, b. 16, 12, 1789. ⁶RACHEL⁷, b. 19, 4, 1791, d. 19, 6, 1796. ⁷PETER⁷, b. 8, 2, 1793, d. 1, 10, 1814. ⁸WILLIAM W.⁷, b. 20, 1, 1795, d. ——, 1863. ⁹KETURAH⁷, b. 29, 3, 1797, d. ——, 1867. ¹⁰CHARLES MARIS⁷, b. 6, 12, 1799. ¹¹Still-born⁷, 7, 10, 1802. ¹²JAMES⁷, b. 15, 12, 1806, d. ——, 1863.

²GEORGE⁷, m., 1st, 18, 2, 1823, Elizabeth Chenowith; ch., ¹Ann Maria⁸, b. 24, 1, 1803, d. 24, 8, 1812. ²Unnamed⁸. ³Eliza Caroline⁸, b. 7, 6, 1807, d. 13, 1, 1811. ⁴Adaline Sophia⁸, b. 19, 12, 1810, d. 2, 6, 1820. ⁵George Warren⁸, b. 1, 11, 1812, d. 1, 7, 1816.

m., 2d, 13, 5, 1822, Frances Ann Walters; ch., ¹Philip Walter⁸, b. 11, 4, 1824, m. Amelia Shoemaker, who d. ——. ²Benjamin Howard⁸, b. 3, 7, 1827, d. ——. ³Charles Augustus⁸, b. 9, 11, 1829, m., 6, 12, 1865, Mary E., d. of Charles Maris Keyser; ch., Alverda Armstrong.

⁵SARAH⁷, m., 22, 1, 1805, Asabel Hussey; ch., ¹Elizabeth K.⁸, b. 5, 2, 1806. ²Jane⁸, b. 5, 2, 1807. ³Hannah S.⁸, b. 8, 6, 1810. ⁴Edith⁸, b. 16, 10, 1812.

¹Elizabeth K.⁸, m., 5, 8, 1835, Edward Crew. ²Jane⁸, m., 8, 12, 1832, Ephraim Robbins. ³Hannah S.⁸, m., 21, 2, 1831, Isaac Dillon.

⁸WILLIAM W.⁷, m., 9, 7, 1818, Elizabeth Fort; ch., ¹Derick W.⁸, b. 26, 5, 1819. ²Charles Clinton⁸, 25, 6, 1821, d. 17, 5, 1867. ³Keturah Benson Keyser⁸, b. 15, 2, 1824. ⁴Elizabeth Fort⁸, 16, 1, 1827.

¹Derick W.⁸, m., 1, 2, 1844, Laura A. McComas; ch., ¹Mary Elizabeth⁹, b. 24, 11, 1844. ²Ellen Fort⁹, b. 27, 9, 1849.

¹Mary Elizabeth,⁹ m., 19, 12, 1867, Theodore Clayton; ch., ¹John Laws¹⁰, b. 22, 11, 1868. ²Roy¹⁰, 3, 5, 1874. ²Mabel Fort¹⁰, 9, 12, 1880. ⁴Emily Clark¹⁰, 24, 11, 1882.

²Charles Clinton⁸, m., 15, 11, 1866, Anna E. Callow; d. without issue.

³Keturah Benson Keyser⁸, m., 7, 5, 1840, John Tileston Fracker, of Zanesville, Ohio; ch., ¹Elizabeth Keyser⁹, b. 18, 4, 1842. ²Keturah Benson⁹, 19, 9, 1843. ³Harry F.⁹, 8, 11, 1846. ⁴Sarah Kauffman⁹, 3, 1, 1848. ⁵John Tileston⁹, 24, 2, 1850. ⁶Frank Fayette⁹, 16, 6, 1852. ⁷Charles Derick Keyser⁹, 16, 8, 1850; d. 31, 8, 1858. ⁸Laura Keyser⁹, 16, 8, 1859. ⁹Mary Keyser⁹, b. 13, 4, 1862. ¹⁰Anna Hildreth⁹, b. 13, 4, 1862; d. 24, 7, 1862.

¹Elizabeth Keyser⁹, m., 26, 10, 1865, David Abbot Chambers; ch., ¹Tileston Fracker¹⁰, b. 28, 12, 1869. ²Mary Beard¹⁰, 26, 4, 1872. ³David Laurance¹⁰, 12, 1, 1879. ²Keturah Benson⁹, m., 2, 11, 1880., James D. Wheeler; ch., ¹Walter Keyser¹⁰, b. 24, 7, 1881. ³Harry⁹, m., 2, 3, 1883, K. C. Miller; ch., ¹Amanda Miller¹⁰, b. 6, 3, 1884.

⁴Sarah Kauffmann⁹, m., 29, 4, 1884, Paul Arnold.

⁵John Tileston⁹, m., 19, 9, 1876, Emma Gibson; ch., ¹Harry Chambers¹⁰, b. 20, 9, 1877. ²William Gibson¹⁰, 4, 2, 1879. ³John Smeltzer¹⁰, 15, 9, 1880. ⁴Frank Wheeler¹⁰, 12, 2, 1882. ⁵Laura Arnold¹⁰, 24, 5, 1884. ⁶Anna May¹⁰, 15, 2, 1887.

⁶Frank Fayette⁹, m., 2, 11, 1878, Frances Linton; ch., ¹Clarence¹⁰, b. 20, 11, 1880. ²Elizabeth Chambers¹⁰, 28, 1, 1886. ³Sarah Kauffman¹⁰, 12, 5, 1888.

⁸Laura Keyser⁹, m., 12, 22, 1883, John W. Macartney; ch., ¹Kate Keyser¹⁰, b. 4, 11, 1885. ²James Wilkinson¹⁰, 21, 10, 1888.

¹Elizabeth Fort⁷, m. John Valentine Smeltzer.

⁹KETURAH⁷, m., 14, 11 1815, Robert Benson, of Baltimore; d. childless.

¹⁰CHARLES MARIS⁷, m., 1st, 22, 6, 1831, Mary Ann, d. of James Armstrong, widow of —— Munro; ch., ¹Mary Elizabeth⁸, 31, 7, 1832, d. 14, 5, 1887. ²James Armstrong⁸. m., 2d, Mary Eliza Wilson, d. of William Wilson, of Balt.; ch., ¹Martha Wilson⁸, ²Anna Smith⁸, ³Wilson⁸, ⁴Margaret Ireland⁸, ⁵Charles Maris, Jr.⁸, ⁶Newberry Allen Smith⁸, M. D., ⁷Grace Gilmore⁸.

¹Martha Wilson⁸, m. Joshua Levering, of Balt.; ch., ¹Wilson K.⁹, ²Minnie K.⁹, ³Joshua⁹, ⁴Margaret⁹, ⁵Martha W.⁹, ⁶Ernest⁹, ⁷Hannah Louisa⁹.

²Anna Smith⁸, m. Jas. R. Edmunds, of Balt.; ch., ¹Mary K.⁹, ²Charles K.⁹, ³Anna S.⁹, ⁴Grace G.⁹, ⁵Helen⁹.

⁵Charles Maris, Jr.⁸, m. Julia A. Poulson, d. of A. W. Poulson, of Balt.; ch., ¹Hannah Louise⁹, d.; ²Charles Maris⁹.

⁷Grace Gilmore⁸, m. Frank E. MacIntire, of Phila.

¹²JAMES⁷, m., 1, 7, 1829, Eleanor Cecelia McNulty; ch., ¹Elizabeth Clemens⁸, b. 6, 4, 1830. ²George⁸, 27, 1, 1832, 19, 7, 1866, no issue.

³Charles Derick⁸, b. 5, 1, 1834, d. 8, 7, 1834. ⁴William Wilson⁸, b. 25, 6, 1835. ⁵Sarah Hussey⁸, 15, 10, 1839. ⁶Keturah Benson⁸, 5, 12, 1841. ⁷James Robert⁸, 20, 11, 1844. ⁸Charles Maris⁸, b. 27, 8, 1847, d. ——. ⁹Edward Crew⁸, b. 8, 4, 1850 ¹⁰Richard Fuller⁸, 11, 4, 1853. ¹¹Martin Fink⁸, 18, 9, 1855.

¹Elizabeth Clemens⁸, m., 1st, 8, 4, 1856, Martin L. Fink; ch., ¹James Keyser⁹, b. 20, 2, 1857; m., 2d, Walden Worley, 15, 12 1867, no issue.

¹James Keyser⁹, m., 15, 3, 1881, Frances M. Toner; ch., ¹John Roy¹⁰, b. 23, 1, 1882. ²James¹⁰, 15, 2, 1883. ³Martin L.¹⁰, 29, 4, 1886. ⁴Annie Elizabeth¹⁰, 21, 8, 1887.

¹William Wilson⁸, m., 14, 6, 1862, Alice Walker; ch., ¹Alice⁹, b. 21, 4, 1865. ²Ella⁹, 25, 11, 1869. ³Mary Elizabeth⁹, 29, 7, 1871. ⁴Elizabeth Walker⁹, 21, 10, 1874. ⁵Helen Linthicum⁹, 21, 8, 1880.

⁵Sarah Hussey⁸, m., 15, 10, 1839, John C. Hay; ch., ¹Roxana⁹, b. 21, 7, 1860. ²George Keyser⁹, 26, 5, 1862, d. 26, 7, 1863. ³Eleanor⁹, b. 8, 5, 1864. ⁴Sarah Elizabeth⁹, 12, 8, 1866. ⁵John Carrol⁹, 21, 9, 1868, d. 10, 3, 1870. ⁶William Edward⁹, b. 7, 9, 1870. ⁷Mary Louisa⁹, 8, 8, 1872, d. 18, 4, 1874.

¹Roxana⁹, m., 24, 11, 1880, S. Clifford Mansfield; ch., ¹Clifford Hay¹⁰, b. 18, 9, 1881. ²Ella Broumel¹⁰, 5, 10, 1883.

⁴Sarah Elizabeth⁹, m., 14, 1, 1885, George R. Beman; ch., ¹Bessie¹⁰, b. 21, 12, 1885. ²Ransom Hay¹⁰, 8, 11, 1887.

⁶Keturah Benson⁸, m., 4, 12, 1860, Edwin Walker; ch., ¹Charles Wagner⁹, b. 29, 11, 1863, m., 3, 12, 1883, Cornelia W. Dobles⁹. ²Edwin Walker⁹, b. 4, 8, 1866, d. 11, 10, 1883. ³Sarah Hay⁹, b. 8, 9, 1868. ⁴Joshua⁹, 21, 7, 1871. ⁵William Keyser⁹, 6, 10, 1873, d. 31, 7, 1874. ⁶John Carrol⁹, b. 29, 9, 1875. ⁷Kate Keyser⁹, 10, 10, 1877. ⁸Eugene Levering⁹, 9, 7, 1879, d. 14, 7, 1879.

⁷James Robert⁸, m., 15, 10, 1870, Louisa King; ch., ¹William Robert⁹, b. 1, 3, 1872. ²Lucy King⁹, 24, 2, 1874. ³Barry King⁹, 12, 6, 1876. ⁴Annie Ruth⁹, 24, 8, 1877. ⁵Eleanor Cecelia⁹, 19, 12, 1879. ¹⁰Richard Fuller⁸, m., 15, 6, 1881, Virginia Clark Raborg; ch., ¹Robert Levering⁹, b. 21, 12, 1884. ²Helen Virginia⁹, 10, 7, 1887. ³—— b. —— 1889.

³ELIZABETH⁶, m., 29, 1, 1784, Benjamin Lehman; ch.,¹WILLIAM LEHMAN⁷, b. 4, 2, 1785, m. Mary Bringhurst. ²PETER K.⁷, b. 16, 6, 1787, m. a d. of John Crane. ³BENJAMIN⁷, b. 22, 8, 1789, m., 24, 12, 1825, Catherine A. Rex. ⁴HANNAH K.⁷, b. 30, 10, 1791, unm'd. ⁵ELIZA⁷, b. 8, 5, 1794, m. Piscator Langstroth ; ch., ¹James⁸, m. Harriet Ashmead. ²Ben-

jamin", m. —— Maule. [3]Eliza",* m. —— Figuera. [4]Hannah Jane[6], m. Francis A. Drexel,† d.

[6]JOSEPH F.[7], b. 8, 10, 1796. [7]JAMES[7], b. 24, 5, 1799, d. 19, 12, 1801. "SYLVANUS[7], b. 28, 2, 1805, d. 3, 10, 1835.

[4]PETER[6], m., 30, 3, 1790, Catherine Clemens‡ (she d. 6, 6, 1854); ch., [1]ELHANAN WINCHESTER[7], b. 23, 2, 1791, d. 7, 2, 1860. [2]MARY[7], b. 16, 1, 1793, d. 27, 5, 1870. [3]NATHAN LEVERING[7], b. 8, 4, 1795, d. 12, 5, 1869. [4]CHARLES[7], b. 29, 6, 1797, d. 12, 7, 1798. [5]ELIZABETH[7], b. 9, 9, 1798, d. —— 4, 1878. [6]HANNAH[7], b. 10, 12, 1800, d. —— 12, 1856. [7]CLEMENTINE[7], b. 11, 9, 1803. [8]SUSANNA[7], b. 11, 9, 1803, d. 8, 7, 1856. [9]PETER AUGUSTUS[7], b. 3, 9, 1805, d. 2, 3, 1869. [10]WILLIAM EDWARD[7], b. 1, 11, 1807, d. 3, 12, 1844. [11]SARAH ANN[7], b. 31, 10, 1810, d. 15, 6, 1815. [12]MARGARETTA[7], b. 10, 4, 1813, d. 1, 6, 1841.

[1]ELHANAN WINCHESTER[7], m., 21, 12, 1819, Maria, d. of Michael Fox (she d. 1, 4, 1834); ch., [1]Katherine Frances", b. 20, 10, 1820, d. 18, 3, 1888. [2]George Fox", b. 15, 7, 1822. [3]Emily", b. 29, 7, 1824, d. 20, 2, 1826. [4]Frank", b. 11, 7, 1826. [5]Sally Ann", b. 6, 5, 1828, d. 12, 3, 1886. [6]Harry", b. 6, 9, 1830. [7]Benjamin Urner", b. 22, 8, 1832.

[1]Katherine Frances", m., 16, 2, 1843, William Henry Wallace; ch., [1]William Henry, Jr., M. D.[9], b. 28, 5, 1844. [2]Frederick Rodman[9], 25, 9, 1847. [4]Emily Frances[9], 13, 1, 1856. [3]Bertha[9], 8, 3, 1859.

[1]William H., Jr., M. D.[9], m., 28, 5, 1873, Annie M. Lynn; ch., [1]Katherine[10], 15, 5, 1874. [2]Mary E.[10], 25, 6, 1875. [3]Annie Lynn[10], 28, 12, 1876. [4]Elizabeth[10], 8, 6, 1878.

[2]Frederick R.[9], m., 17, 10, 1876, Elizabeth Todd Ashby; ch., [1]Frederick Ashby[10], 21, 6, 1881.

[4]Bertha[9], m., 15, 12, 1888, Henry Lee Tatnall.

[2]George Fox", m. Elizabeth Kimmey; ch., Kate.

[4]Frank", m. Louisa Calvert.

[5]Sally Ann", m., 26, 12, 1854, John R. Savage; ch., Jennette m. Robt. Levick, Mahlon Levis, Kate, John R., Jr.

[6]Harry", m., 11, 2, 1863, Isabel Ross.

[7]Benjamin Urner", m., 25, 10, 1859, Esther A. Todd; ch., [1]William B. Todd[9], b. 9, 9, 1862. [2]Elhanan W.[9], b. 10, 5, 1864. —— —— —— ——

---

* Now the Baroness da Conceicao; her daughter Bessie is Mrs. Nuno Jardini, living at Funchal, Madeira; her daughter Anna, the Vicountess da Andaluz Largo di Milagre, Santarem, Portugal.

† The Banker of Philadelphia.

‡ Her sister Elizabeth m. [2]Derick Keyser[6]; and her sister Rachel m. Geo. Gorgas; of Rachel Gorgas' 13 children, three survive, Mrs. Newberry Smith, Mrs. William Wayne, and Mrs. Elizabeth Pierie w. of Wm. S. Pierie, the father of George Gorgas Pierie.

²MARY⁷, m., 19, 11, 1818, Christopher S. Langstroth ; ch., Clementine⁸,
b. 27, 9, 1819, m., 20, 11, 1851, William D. Fobes.*

³NATHAN LEVERING⁷, m., 21, 11, 1822, Maria, d. of John Geyer ; ch.,
¹Sarah Elizabeth⁸, b. 18, 9, 1823. ²William Geyer⁸, b. 29, 9, 1825 ; d.
12, 8, 1848. ³Peter A., Jr.⁸, b. 24, 8, 1827 ; d. 7, 11, 1874. ⁴John Geyer⁸,
b. 26, 10, 1829. ⁵Catherine Clemens⁸, b. 9, 4, 1832.

  ¹Sarah Elizabeth⁸, m., 5, 5, 1841, John D. Blanchard ; ch., ¹Maria K.⁹,
b. 21, 4, 1843 ; m. Edwin A. Landell. ²Adelaide⁹, b. 26, 10, 1844 ;
d. 30, 6, 1886. ³Katherine⁹, b. 2, 4, 1847 ; m. C. Henry Roney.
⁴Sally Geyer⁹, b. 2, 10, 1849.

  ³Peter A., Jr.⁸, m., 1, 10, 1848, Martha Thomas ; ch., ¹Sallie Geyer⁹,
²Nathan Levering⁹, ³A. Louisa⁹.

  ⁴John Geyer⁸, m., 8, 7, 1858, Mary Ann Haines ; ch., ¹William Geyer⁹,
b. 6, 8, 1859 ; d. 19, 11, 1887. ²John Geyer⁹, b. 3, 7, 1864. ³Nathan
Levering⁹, b. 10, 6, 1869.

  ⁵Catherine Clemens⁸, m., 29, 4, 1832, Thomas R. Alexander ; ch.,
¹Thomas A.⁹, b. 2, 6, 1862.

⁵ELIZABETH⁷, m., 24, 10, 1825, Benjamin Urner; ch., ¹Catherine⁸, b. 15,
9, 1826 ; d. 20, 9, 1826. ²Peter A.⁸, b. 9, 12, 1827 ; d. ——. ³Henry
Clay⁸, b. 29, 1, 1830. ⁴Benjamin⁸, b. 9, 9, 1832. ⁵Edward Hall⁸, b.
13, 8, 1834 ; d. 25, 7, 1836. ⁶Nathan⁸. ⁷Edward⁸, b. 12, 1, 1838.

⁶HANNAH⁷, m., 18, 8, 1825, John Riehle ; ch., ¹Edith⁸, b. 14, 7, 1826.
²Catherine⁸, b. 24, 3, 1828 ; d. 10, 4, 1832. ³J. Sigismund⁸, b. 27, 10,
1831. ⁴Henry⁸, b. 26, 11, 1833. ⁵Clementine⁸, b. 24, 11, 1835.

⁷CLEMENTINE⁷, m., 31, 3, 1825, Michael K. Lynd (who d. 17, 11, 1832);
ch., ¹James⁸, b. 10, 3, 1826. ²Peter Keyser⁸, b. 24, 11, 1827.

⁸SUSANNA⁷, m., 15, 8, 1826, Frederick R. Backus ; ch, ¹William Rod-
man⁸, b. 15, 1, 1828. ²Catherine Clemens⁸, b. 21, 9, 1831. ³Frederick
Bayard⁸, b. 27, 12, 1833. ⁴Mary E.⁸, b. 8, 3, 1838.

  ²Catherine Clemens⁸, m., 1, 10, 1850, Joseph B. Shewell ; ch., ¹Edith
D.⁹, b. 26, 6, 1851. ²Kate Rodman⁹, b. 8, 1, 1854. Helen Mary, b.
7, 4, 1856. Alice, b. 25, 5, 1861 ; m. 2d Joseph Price.

  ³Frederick Bayard⁸, m., 8, 6, 1858, Caroline Harris Moore ; ch.,
¹Frederick Rodman⁹, ²Mary⁹.

  ⁴Mary E.⁸, m., 15, 10, 18—, William S. Noble ; ch., ¹Mary E.⁹,
²Frederick Charles⁹, ³Agnes⁹, ⁴Mary⁹, d. 1860. ⁵William W.⁹, b.
1865. ⁶Maud⁹, b. 1867 ; m., 2d, Dr. Thaddeus Leavett.

⁹PETER AUGUSTUS⁷, m., 9, 8, 1832, Martha, d. of George Eyre ; ch.,
¹Eyre⁸, b. 1, 7, 1833. ²Peter Dirck⁸, b. 8, 2, 1835.

---

  * William Dana Fobes, President of the Buffalo Historical Society.

²Peter Dirck⁸, M.D., m., 25, 2, 1858, Sallie E., d. of Jacob Steiner, of Philadelphia; ch., ¹Sallie Steiner⁹.

¹Sallie Steiner⁹, m., 26, 4, 1886, Louis Mardenbrough French, of Connecticut.

¹²MARGARETTA⁷, m., 12, 9, 1830, Cipriano Cañedo, of Guadalaxara, Mexico; ch., ¹Cipriano⁸, b. 2, 5 1831. ²Margaretta⁸, 7, 1, 1833. ³Catherine⁸, 30, 4, 1835; d. 10, 8, 1881. ⁴Louis⁸, 9, 7, 1840, d. 26, 9, 1840.

²Margaretta⁸, m., 25, 12, 1856, Juan Y. Matute; ch., Margarita Y., b. 5, 11, 1857. Juan José, 31, 3, 1860. Arnulfo M., 15, 8, 1862. Catalina, 24, 2, 1865. Maria Eugenia, 5, 11, 1868; d. 18, 4, 1883. Regnalda, 23, 3, 1869. Elena, 6, 7, 1871.

Juan José, m., 15, 6, 1885 (in lower California), Teresa de la Toba; ch., Arturo Matute, b. 28, 5, 1886. Maria Eugenia 3, 10, 1887.

Juan José⁹, m. —— ——; ch., Arthur¹⁰, Maria Eugenia¹⁰.

³Catherine⁸, m., 23, 9, 1852, Samuel B. Bond; ch., ¹William Vincent⁹, b. 31, 8, 1853. ²Cipriano Cañedo⁹, b.——; d. 10, 10, 1880, in the City of Mexico. ³Henry Davis⁹, —— ——; d. 10, 7, 1862. ⁴Margarita Y. C.⁹, b. —— ——; d. 8, 2, 1869.

¹William Vincent⁹, m. Alice Saxton Goodyear; ch., Samuel Cañedo, b. 10, 2, 1877. Richard Watson, 14, 8, 1882. William Goodyear, 7, 6, 1884.

⁵SARAH⁶, m., ——, ——, 1794, Joseph Gorgas, who was b. 24, 4, 1773; ch., ¹PETER KEYSER⁷, b. 9, 1, 1795; d. 15, 6, 1856. ²MARTHA⁷, b. 10, 10, 1796; d. ——. ³CHARLES⁷, b. 6, 3, 1799; d. 26, 8, 1800. ⁴WILLIAM⁷, b. 17, 7, 1801; d. 7, 7, 1803. ⁵HANNAH⁷, b. 13, 5, 1804. ⁶RACHEL⁷, b. 24, 7, 1807; d. 28, 2, 1849. ⁷ELIZABETH⁷, b. 8, 11, 1811.

¹PETER KEYSER⁷, m., 10, 3, 1822, Lydia Lentz Weaver, who was b. 30, 11, 1797; d. 30, 12, 1872; ch., ¹William Weaver⁸, b. 8, 12, 1822; d. 5, 6, 1842. ²Eliza Jane⁸ and ³Sarah Ann⁸, b. 28, 11, 1824; d. 28 and 29, 1, 1825. ⁴Emma Matilda Thomas⁸, b. 3, 3, 1826; d. 13, 1, 1883. ⁵Cornelia Hart⁸, b. 28, 2, 1828. ⁶Anna Thomas⁸, b. 10, 11, 1829. ⁷Sarah Keyser⁸, b. 9, 12, 1831; d. 6, 1, 1885. ⁸Charles Keyser⁸, b. 26, 11, 1833; d. 22, 10, 1862. ⁹Joseph⁸, b. 10, 4, 1836; d. 5, 4, 1856.

⁴Emma Matilda Thomas⁸, m., 1, 1, 1840, Daniel Charles Elliott Brady, who was b. 9, 3, 1821; d. 27, 5, 1878; ch., ¹Cornelia⁹, b. 28, 8, 1846; d. 18, 10, 18—. ²Anna Gertrude⁹, b. 3, 1, 1848. ³Charles Patrick Angus⁹, 29, 5, 1850. ⁴Mary⁹, 4, 1, 1852; d. 8, 1, 1852. ⁵William Weaver⁹, b. 28, 12, 1853; d. 29, 5, 1856. ⁶William Wea-

ver⁹, b. 30, 8, 1857 ; d. 30, 8, 1857. ⁷Thomas Forrest⁹, b. 3, 12, 1858 ; d. 3, 12, 1858. ⁸Sarah Elizabeth⁹, b. 28, 12, 1859. ⁹Emma Belle⁹, 17, 10, 1861 ; d. 20, 10, 1861. ¹⁰Wilhelmina Weaver⁹, b. 17, 4, 1863. ¹¹Elliot Thomas⁹, 8, 1, 1865. ¹²George⁹, 13, 9, 1867 ; d. 27, 10, 1867.

³Charles Patrick Angus⁹, m., 1, 6, 1882, Marie Townsend, who was b. 18, 1, 1852 ; ch. ¹Douglas Elinipsico¹⁰, b. 16, 5, 1883. ²Cornelia Gorgas¹⁰, 6, 10, 1885 ; d. 21, 2, 1888.

⁸Sarah Elizabeth⁹, m., 25, 6, 1884, Frank P. Lynch ; ch., John William, b. 12, 3 1886. Emma Brady, 2, 10, 1888.

¹⁰Wilhelmina Weaver⁹, m., 30, 4, 1889, Charles Shafer Updike.

⁵Cornelia Hart⁸, m., 1st, 12, 11, 1850, Thomas Forrest Fraley, who was b. 3, 10, 1834 ; d. 5, 3, 1862 ; ch., ¹Lydia Gorgas⁹, b. 29, 5, 1854 ; d. 30, 1, 1882, unmd ; m., 2d, 27, 4, 1865, Theodore Trewendt, who was b. 18, 2, 1811 ; d. 12, 12, 1883.

⁶Anna Thomas⁸, m., 1, 12, 1853, James Manderson, who was b. 12, 1, 1812, d. 24, 12, 1886.

⁷Sarah Keyser⁸, m., 13, 5, 1851, John Hanson Michener ;* ch., ¹Harry Gorgas⁹, b. 1, 8, 1852. ²Frank Leslie⁹, 10, 2, 1854. ³Joseph Gorgas⁹, b. 28, 11, 1855, d. 20, 11, 1883 ; ⁴Nelson Fitzgerald⁹, b. 28, 11, 1855, d. 21, 9, 1879. ⁵William Weaver⁹, 3, 11, 1857. ⁶Charles Gorgas⁹, 17, 12, 1861. ⁷John Hanson, Jr.⁹, 13, 6, 1865.

¹Harry Gorgas⁹, m., 15, 11, 1877, Lydia Atherton Middleton; ch., ¹Susan Bell¹⁰, b. 22, 8, 1880. ²Frances Hanson¹⁰, 7, 7, 1885. ²Frank Leslie⁹, m., 25, 3, 1879, Ella Hansell Bullock ; ch., ¹Sarah Keyser, b. 5, 6, 1882. ⁷John Hanson, Jr.⁹, m., 24, 4, 1889, Martha Salena Truitt.

²MARTHA⁷, m. ——, ——.

⁶RACHEL⁷, m., 7, 6, 1834, John Foulk Bullock, who was b. 22, 9, 1806, and d. in Mexico, ——, 9, 1856 ; ch., ¹Joseph Gorgas⁸, b. 12, 9, 1835 ; d. 26, 10, 1864. ²Charles Keyser⁸, 25, 2 1837.

²Charles Keyser⁸, m., 14, 2, 1861, Anna Matilda Bowman, who was b. 11, 9, 1840 ; ch., ¹Lillie Gorgas⁹, b. 16, 6, 1863. ²Anna Matilda⁹, 16, 6, 1867 ; d. 28, 2, 1872. ³Charles Keyser⁹, b. 18, 10, 1873 ; d. 18, 7, 1874. ⁴Mabel⁹, b. 13, 10, 1875 ; d. 16, 3, 1889. ⁵Joseph Gorgas⁹, b. 4, 2, 1878.

¹Lillie Gorgas⁹, m., 1, 12, 1887, Henry Halderman Wentz.

⁷ELIZABETH⁷, m. L. Lehman.

⁵ALICE⁵, m., 24, 2, 1757, Christian Duy† ; ch., ¹ELIZABETH⁶, b. 6, 10,

---

* John Hanson Michener, President of the Bank of North America.

† Christian Duy, b. Oberhausen, Germany, 31, 4, 1734, d. 23, 9, 1798.

1757, d. 24, 10, 1757.   ²MARY⁶, b. 22, 11, 1758, d. 8, 2, 1764.   ³JACOB⁶, b. 9, 7, 1761.   ⁴CHRISTIAN⁶, b. 4, 2, 1764, d. 18, 2, 1764.   ⁵GEORGE⁶, b. 11, 4, 1765.   ⁶ELIZABETH⁶, 13, 7, 1768.   ⁷CHARLES⁶, 15, 12, 1770, d. 10, 2, 1771.   ⁸JOHN KEYSER⁶, b. 2, 5, 1772, d. 12, 9, 1828.   ⁹HAN-NAH⁶, b. 29, 8, 1775.

⁸JOHN KEYSER⁶, m. Margaret Gilbert, who d. 18, 6, 1831; ch., ¹CARO-LINE⁷, ²REBECCA⁷, ³LAMBERT⁷, b. 15, 12, 1799, d. 24, 2, 1871.   ⁴ELIZA-BETH⁷, ⁵JOHN KEYSER⁷, ⁶MARGARET⁷, ⁷ALICE⁷.

³LAMBERT⁷, m. Louisa E. Oat, who was born 2, 8, 1802, d. 31, 3, 1883; ch., ¹Albert William⁸, b. 9, 4, 1823, d. 19, 4, 1846.   ²Charles Augustus⁸, b. 24, 2, 1826.   ³Adeline Margaret⁸, 9, 10, 1827.   ⁴George Christian⁸, 30, 8, 1830.   ⁵Louisa Caroline⁸, 15, 12, 1833.   ⁶G. Bedell⁸, 11, 7, 1836.

⁶DERICK⁵, m., ——, 1763, Rachel Ottinger, who d. 1, 2, 1826*; ch.,¹PETER⁶, b. 7, 1, 1764, d. 8, 7, 1773.   ²CHRISTOPHER⁶, b. 6, 7, 1765.   ³AARON⁶, b. 19, 10, 1766.   ⁴CHRISTOPHER⁶, 10, 10, 1768.   ⁵HANNAH⁶, 20, 6, 1770, d. 8, 10, 1779.   ⁶SARAH⁶, b. 8, 7, 1773, d. 12, 10, 1785.   ⁷NATHAN⁶, b. 6, 7, 1774, d. 8, 6, 1817.   ⁸JOSEPH⁶, b. 15, 9, 1776, d. 21, 9, 1785.   ⁹WILLIAM⁶, b. 11, 3, 1778, d. 18, 5, 1837.   ¹⁰MOLLY⁶, b. 1, 2, 1781.   ¹¹RACHEL⁶, b. 20, 11, 1782, d. 28, 2, 1791.   ¹²SARAH⁶, b. 27, 3, 1784.

³AARON⁶, m. Margaret Hallman; no ch.

⁴CHRISTOPHER⁶, m.,——, Catherine Donat†, who was b. 30, 8, 1772; d. 20, 4, 1847; ch., ¹JOSEPH⁷, b. 29, 7, 1792.   ²ANN⁷, 12, 5, 1795.   ³WIL-LIAM⁷, 21, 5, 1797; d. 24, 9, 1857.   ⁴CHRISTOPHER⁷, 3, 9, 1799.

¹JOSEPH⁷, m., ——, Mitchener.   ²ANN⁷, m., ——, Joseph Lauer.   ³WIL-LIAM⁷, m., 1st, 25, 2, 1819, Ann Williams, who d. 30, 10, 1829; ch., ¹Mary Ann⁸, b. 27, 1, 1821.   ²Edmund⁸, 21, 4, 1823.   ³Catherine Eliza⁸, 5, 9, 1825.   m., 2d, 13, 10, 1836, Mary Ann Shields, who was b. 27, 6, 1812; d. 10, 4, 1838; ch., ¹William Allen⁸, b. 24, 3, 1838.   m., 3d, 20, 6, 1839, Sarah Miller; no chil.

¹Mary Ann⁸, m. Geo. Young; ch., ¹Charles W⁹.

⁴CHRISTOPHER⁷, m., 29, 8, 1822, Priscilla Tyson, who was b. ——, 1795; ch., ¹Eliza⁸, b. 18, 10, 1823.   ²Daniel⁸, 25, 11, 1824.   ³E. Tyson⁸, 5, 1, 1826.   ⁴Rebecca⁸, ——, 2, 1827.   ⁵William Donat⁸, 26, 4, 1828.   ⁶Charles Donat⁸, 19, 11, 1829.   ⁷Margaret Ann Tyson⁸‡, 24, 4, 1831; d.   ⁸Augustus⁸, 13, 3, 1833.   ⁹Catherine K.⁸, 23, 9, 1836.   ¹⁰Camille Ross⁸, 17, 11, 1837.   ¹¹Frank Wilson⁸, 27, 11, 1842; d.

---

* Rachel Ottinger, d. of Christopher and Rachel Ottinger, of ——, Austria.   Their house, built in Flourtown, 1743, is still in complete preservation.

† The Donats were French emigrés,—George, the g. g. f., Christian, g. f. of the descendants now living at Chestnut Hill.

‡ Ass. Librarian of the Merc. Lib. of Philada., the first woman that filled this position, as far as we have knowledge, in any public library of the city.

[1]Eliza[8], m., 13, 9, 1860, Mahlon Reeder; ch., Frank Keyser, b. 4, 7, 1861.

[2]Daniel[8], m., 2, 4, 18, ——, Elizabeth Kramer; ch., Emily Sanger, b. 30, 7, 1846. Rebecca, 1, 3, 1848. Laura Foulk, 21, 5, 1849. Tyson, 13, 1, 1851. Mary, 11, 7, 1852. Edward Elrod, 24, 11, 1854. William Henry, 21, 10, 1856. John Detwiler, 13, 1, 1859. Anna, 6, 6, 1861. Camille, 18, 6, 1863. Geo. W., 30, 1, 1865, Emma, 7, 3, 1867. Clara Detwiler, 4, 3, 1869. Maggie, 14, 11, 1871. Frank W., 2, 5, 1873.

[3]E. Tyson[8]*, m., —, —, ——, Angeline, Strobel; ch., George (lives in California).

[4]Rebecca[8], m., ——, Edward R. Elrod; ch., [1]Lawrence Leroy,[8] Emma (live in Nevada).

[5]William Donat[8],† m., Louisa Mott; ch., Henry, Charles, May (live in Nevada).

[6]Charles Donat[8],‡ m., ——, in England; ch., —— —— —— —— —— —— —— ——.

[8]Augustus[8], m., —— ——, in California.

[9]Catherine[9], m., 26, 5, 1859, John S. Detwiler; ch., Thomas Wittney, b. 11, 3, 1860; d. 18, 3, 1863. Alfred Howard, b. 3. 6, 1861. Edwin A. Landell, 6, 5, 1863. Clara Virginia, 23, 6, 1864. Benjamin, 30, 11, 1865; d. 22, 1, 1872. Kate D., b. 14, 11, 1867. Maggie Keyser, 20, 6, 1869. Mamie A., 16, 1, 1872. Gertrude M., 16, 5, 1873; d. 22, 7, 1874. Blanche, 9, 1, 1875. Mabel, 10, 12, 1876.

[10]Camille Ross[9], m., 23, 11, 1859, Frank Siddall§; ch., Frank Siddall, Jr., b. 19, 5, 1864,

[7]NATHAN[6], m. ——.

[8]WILLIAM[6], m. ——; ch., [1]AARON[7]. [2]NATHAN[7], b. 25, 9, 1802; d. 16, 1, 1886. [3]JOHN[7].

[2]NATHAN[7],|| m., 28, 1, 1828, Eliza Heilerman ; ch., [1]William[8]. [2]Charles[8], unmd. [3]Mary J.[8], unmd. [4]Elizabeth[8]. [5]Caroline[8]. [6]Anna[8]. [7]Belle[8], unmd.

* One of the 1st settlers in California ('49).

† Member of the 1st Legislature of Nevada.

‡ One of the pioneers in Australia.

§ Of the family of Richard Siddall, merchant of Woodhay, Cheshire, England, who died in Philadelphia, 1742, leaving a large estate in securities held by the Bank of England. James and Joseph Siddall, father and son, emigrated from England in 1810, and settled at Philadelphia. Frank Siddall was candidate for the legislature in 1877, and long associated politically with the compiler of this volume.

|| Nathan Keyser was comm. Justice of the Peace of Mtgry. township, Ap. 14, 1846, for five years. He celebrated his golden wedding in 1878.

[1]William[5], m. Rebecca Holdridge, who d.

[4]Elizabeth[5], m. E. W. Haws; ch., William, m. Anna Taylor; ch., Harry; Anna, m. Henry Smith; ch., Mabel, Gladys.

[5]Caroline[5], m. Jas. K. Stevenson; ch., Clara, Ida.

[6]Anna[5], m. William Forrest.

[10]**MARY**[6] (Molly), m., 1, 2, 1781, Matthias Knorr; ch., [1]**RACHEL**[7], b. —
—, 1802. [2]**SUSAN**[7], b. 12, 5. 1805; d. 25, 2, 1881. [3]**MATTHIAS**[7], b. —,
1807; d. 13, 10, 1837. [4]**MARY**[7]. b. 26, 9, 1809. [5]**JOHN KEYSER**[7], b. —,
1811; d. — 2, 1888. [6]**SARAH**[7], b. —, 1813; d. 2. 12, 1830. [7]**LYDIA
DOROTHEA**[7], b. —, 1817. [8]**NATHAN KEYSER**[7], b. —, 1819; d. ——,
1851.

[1]**RACHEL**[7], m., ——, Dr. Isaac N. Marselis*; ch., [1]Maria Marielle[8],
[2]Henry Nicholas[8], [3]Rachel Anna[8], [4]Rosa[8], [5]Helen[8].

[1]Maria Marielle[8], m. Joseph Loughead; ch., Maria Marielle, Isaac
Marselis, Cornelia, Rachel.

[2]Henry Nicholas[8], m. Virgilia Broome; ch., [1]Bessie Marselis[1], [2]Harry
Marselis[9], [3]Charles Marselis[9].

[3]Rachel Anna[8], m., 1st, Dr. William H. Squires; 2d, Albert Hew-
son; ch., Isaac Marselis Squires[9], d.

[4]Rosa[8], m. Theodore Arms; ch., [1]Lucy[9], [2]Helen[9], [3]Theodore[9].

[5]Helen[8], m. Rev. Charles Van Dyne.

[2]**SUSAN**[7], m., 1st, J. Samuel Passmore; ch., [1]Thos. S. Passmore[8], M.D.,
decd., [2]Rachel Susan[8]. m., 2d, John Dyer.

[2]Rachel Susan[8], m. Dr. Bernard Berens; ch., [1]Anna Maria[9], [2]Joseph[9],
[3]Louise Otto[9], [4]Olivia[9], [5]Lydia Dorothea[9], [6]Bernard[9], [7]Conrad[9], [8]Susan
Agnes[9], [9]Thomas Passmore[9].

[3]Louise Otto[9], m. Frank Frishmuth; ch., Bertha Louise, Harriet
Whitney, Lydia Dorothea, Edmund, d.

[4]Olivia[9], m. Samuel Rulon; ch., Samuel Rulon, Jr.

[5]Lydia Dorothea[9], m. Howell Jones.

[6]Bernard[9], m. —— Moorehead, of N. Y.

[6]Conrad[9], m. —— Brockett, of Conn.

[3]**MATTHIAS**[7], m., 1807, Mary Tyson (now Grafly); ch., [1]Sarah[8], m.
Erastus Hill.

[1]**MARY**[7], m., 15, 12, 1833, William H. Slingluff; ch., [1]Sarah[8], ——
[2]Mary Moore[8], b. 15, 2, 1837. [3]John[8], 3, 8, 1839; [4]Clara[8], 6, 9, 1846;
[5]William Fry[8], 11, 10, 1851.

[1]Sarah[8]. m. Jacob Lents Rex; ch., Mary Slingluff, b. 12, 2, 1856;
William Slingluff, 24, 12, 1857; John, 15, 12, 1859.

[2]Mary Moore[8], m., 8, 12, 1859; Hon. A. Brower Longaker; ch.,

* Dr. Isaac Marselis d. 1881.

[1]Leila[9], b. — 7, 1862. [2]Rosalie[9], 3, 4, 1873; Morris Slingluff, 15, 6, 1876.

[1]Leila[9], m., 18, 8, 1884, H. H. Kurtz; ch., W. Wesley, Leila.

[3]John[8], m. Wilhelmina Gilbert; ch., [1]Mary Slingluff[9], b. 20, 6, 1863. [2]William Herman[9], 31, 8, 1865. [3]Helen Gilbert Slingluff[9], 13, 2, 1869.

[1]Mary Slingluff[9], m., —, 9, 1882, Howard Boyd; ch., James Slingluff, John Howard.

[4]Clara[8], m., 1st, D. H. Pawling. m., 2d, 12, 2, 1885, Colonel H. H. Fisher.

[5]William Fry[8], m. Annie Virginia Streeper; ch., [1]William H. Slingluff[9], [2]Charles Carrol Slingluff[9].

[5]JOHN KEYSER[7], m., 18, 5, 1837, Kate Keen; ch., [1]Matthias[8], b. 16, 8, 1838. [2]Mary Thompson[8], 27, 8, 1840, d. 16, 8, 1867. [3]Andrew Keen[8], 13, 12, 1842, d. 8, 11, 1865. [4]John Keyser[8], 1, 1, 1846. [5]James Keen[8], 7, 2, 1848, d. 11, 3, 1848. [6]Kate Keen[8], 7, 6, 1849.

[1]Matthias[8], m., 27, 1, 1874, Julia Wildes.

[2]Mary[8], m., 9, 4, 1861, George Thompson; ch., Kate Knorr, Charles, George.

[4]John Keyser[8], m., 3, 1, 1869, Maggie Baker; ch., Matthias, Kate, John.

[6]Kate Keen[8], m., 13, 11, 1873, D. Webster Grafly.

[7]LYDIA DOROTHEA[7], m. Charles Magarge*; ch., [1]Emma Cecelia[8], b. 6, 8, 1845.

[1]Emma Cecelia[8], m. ——, Lewis Hassinger; ch., Charles Magarge Hassinger.

[12]SARAH[6], m. Jacob Neff, ——.

[7]HANNAH[5], m., ——, 1761, Jacob Knorr, who d. 3, 2, 1805; ch., [1]GEORGE[6], b. 11, 12, 1761. [2]CATHERINE[6], b. 30, 10, 1765, m. John Funk†, d. 2, 3, 1812. [3]SARAH[6], b. 17, 4, 1768 (m. William Kulp‡), d. 23, Feb., 1837. [4]HANNAH[6], b. 1, 12, 1770 (m. William Hallman), d. 14, 9, 1808 [5]ELIZABETH[6], b. 1, 12, 1770, d. 5, 10, 1844, m. John Engle§. [6]SUSANNA KNORR[6], b. 25, 10, 1772 (m. Dr. Lange), d. 6, 1, 1846. [7]BARBARA[6], b. 20, 4, 1775, d. 21, 9, 1776. [8]BARBARA[6], b. 29, 7, 1777, d. 24, 9, 1785. [9]JACOB[6], b. 3, 10, 1780 (m. Elizabeth Peters), d. 24, 9, 1812.

[9]MICHAEL[5], b. 30, 8, 1745, m., 25, 11, 1767, Catherine Knorr, who d. 28, 7, 1828; ch., [1]HANNAH[6], b. 22, 3, 1769, d. 8, 1, 1841. [2]PETER[6], b. 24, 9, 1770, d. 13, 3, 1771. [3]JOHN[6], b. 8, 1, 1772, d. 5, 4, 1840. [4]ALICE[6], b. 10, 1, 1773. [5]CATHERINE[6], b. 17, 8, 1774. [6]MICHAEL[6], b. 19, 10,

---

* Charles Magarge d. 1883. † John Funk, s. of Jacob Funk.
‡ William Kulp, s. of Isaac Kulp. § John Engle died 5, 10, 1844.

1775, d. 20, 12, 1778. ⁷SAMUEL⁶, b. 3, 12, 1778, d. 6, 11, 1839.
⁸SARAH⁶, b. 4, 1, 1780, d. 1, 9, 1847.
³JOHN⁶, m., Mary Wilt ; ch., ¹NATHAN⁷, d. inf. ²MICHAEL⁷, d. 5, 4, 1871.
³ALICE⁷, d. 28, 5, 1872, unmd. ⁴SILVESTER⁷, b. 15, 8, 1806, d. 11, 2, 1889.
⁵ELKANAH⁷, unmd.

²MICHAEL K.⁷, m., Ann Campbell; ch., Edwin J., d. 21, 3, 1875.
Leander, d. inf. Emma K., m. Geo. E. Britton. Elmira, m. Robert S.
Dugan. Virginia, m. Samuel Cregan. Mary, d. inf.
⁴SILVESTER⁷, m. Mary A. Phillips, d. of John Phillips; ch., ¹Aline L.
A.⁸, d. 30, 12, 1864. ²Louis A.⁸, ³Alice Cordelia⁸, m. Edward A,
Gaskill, ⁴Evelina C.⁸, d. ; ⁵Josephine P.⁸, m. Jas. H. Clark, ⁶James M.⁸.
⁷Algernon Sidney⁸, m. Anne E. Kelly. ⁸Leora Marion⁸, m. John Wise.
⁵CATHERINE⁶, m., 17, 8, 1795, James Lynd ; ch., ¹SAMUEL W.⁷, b. 17,
12, 1796; d. —, 1876. ²HANNAH⁷, b. 22, 10, 1798. ³ALICE⁷, 22, 10,
1798. ⁴ELIZABETH WHITE⁷, 21, 10, 1800. ⁵MICHAEL K.⁷, 1, 10, 1802 ; d.
17, 11, 1832. ⁶CATHERINE K.⁷, 24, 6, 1804. ⁷SARAH S.⁷, 11, 8, 1806.
⁸JAMES⁷, 17, 5, 1808. ⁹JAMES⁷, 25, 9, 1810. ¹⁰ANN LOUISA⁷, 14, 9, 1812.
¹¹ELIJAH WARING⁷, 28, 12, 1813. ¹²HIRAM⁷.

¹SAMUEL W.⁷, m., 18, 9, 1823, Leonora Staughton, d. of Dr. Staughton;
ch., ¹George⁸, ²James⁸, ³Robert⁸, —— —— ——.
²HANNAH⁷, m., 4, 4, 1822, Elijah Mitchell ; ch., ¹Sallie⁸, m. Rev.
Malachi Taylor. ²Anna Louisa⁸, m. Rev. E. G. Taylor, ³Ellen⁸, m.
James Flint. ⁴Eliza⁸, m. Samuel Davis.
⁴ELIZABETH WHITE⁷, m., 14, 9, 1820, Joseph E. McIlhenny. ¹Catherine L.⁸, m. Chas. M. Jackson; ch., Katie Jackson. ²Jas. L.⁸, m.
—— Paris. ³Joseph E.⁸, m. —— McCanly. ⁴Eliza W.⁸, m. ——
Stephens. ⁵Virginia⁸, m. —— Ponte. ⁶Edward⁸, m. Amy R. Peters.
⁷Helen B.⁸, m. Frank Paris.
⁵MICHAEL K.⁷, m., 31, 3, 1825, Clementine Keyser⁷; ch., ¹James⁸,
b.10, 3, 1826; d. 30, 6, 1876. ²Peter Keyser⁸, 24, 11, 1827, m. Susan
Brown.
⁶CATHERINE K.⁷, m. 3, 8, 1837, Dr. William Schmoele ; ch., ¹Catherine
Lynd⁸, ²Caroline Marie⁸, ³Dr. William⁸.
¹Catherine Lynd⁸, m., 8, 12, 1864, David H. Wolfe ; ch., William
Schmoele, Bella, Kate Lynd, Katie Marie.
²Caroline Marie⁸, m. Albert B. Jarden ; ch., Katie J., Albert B.,
Caroline M.
³Dr. William⁸, m. Mary Walker ; ch. William, Jr., Marie, Rebecca,
Catherine K. L., Harry, Frederick Joseph.
⁷SARAH S.⁷, m. William L. Smith.

⁹JAMES, JR.⁷, m., 11, 9, 1837, Olivia F. Walters, d. of Colonel Jason Walters (Valley Forge) ; ch., —— ——.

¹⁰ANN LOUISA⁷, m. Edwin P. Frick, d. 18, 7, 1851 ; ch., ¹Mary L.⁸, m. William Cookshott, ²Jacob⁸, m. Elizabeth Neveil, ³Edwin P.⁸, m. —— McIntire.

¹¹ELIJAH WARING⁷, m., 23, 8, 1846, Letitia Whitaker d. of John Whitaker; ch., ¹James⁸, —— ²Lilie⁸, ³Estelle⁸, m. —— Jackson.

⁷SAMUEL⁶, m. 1st, Mary,* d. of John Stouffer, of Baltimore; ch., ¹SAMUEL STOUFFER⁷, b. 18, 2, 1805 ; d. 18, 2, 1871 ; m. 2d, Hetty Polk; ch., ¹MICHAEL F.⁷, b. 4, 11, 1806; d. 27, 9, 1855. ²SOPHIA E.⁷, b. 10, 4, 1808; d. ——. ³INDIANA⁷, b. 1, 1, 1810; d. 24, 10, 1854, unmd. ⁴HETTIE JANE⁷, b. 17, 2, 1816; d. 12, 2, 1844.

¹SAMUEL STOUFFER⁷, m., 1834, Elizabeth, d. of William Wyman,† of Lowell, Mass. (she d. 18, 2, 1886); ch., ¹Samuel⁸ and ²William⁸, b. 23, 11, 1835. ³Henry Irvine⁸, b. 16, 12, 1837 ; d——. ⁴Sarah Elizabeth⁸, b. —— ; d. ——.

¹Samuel⁸, m., 1868, Julia Theresa, d. of Genl. Henry A. Thompson ; ch., ¹Selina Elizabeth⁸, b. 13, 4, 1869. ²Samuel Stouffer⁸, b. 26, 6, 1870. ³Julia Theresa⁸, b. 22, 3, 1875.

²William⁸, m., 10, 11, 1858, Mary H., d. of Robert J. Brent, of Baltimore; ch., ¹Robert Brent⁹, b. 5, 8, 1859. ²John Wyman⁹, b. 25, 5, 1861 ; d. inf. ³Mary Brent⁹, b. 21, 7, 1862 ; d. inf. ⁴Mabel Wyman⁹, b. 30, 12, 1867; d. inf. ⁵Mathilde Lawrence⁹, b. 26, 2, 1870. ⁶William⁹, b. 25, 11, 1871.

¹Robert J. Brent⁹, m., 14, 6, 1888, Ellen Carr, d. of James Howard McHenry, of Sudbrook, Balt. Co.

⁴Sarah Elizabeth⁸, m., 3, 1, 1863, John W. Williams, of Phila.; ch., ¹Elizabeth⁹, b. 5, 6, 1864 ; d. 6, 4, 1868. ²Anne Keppele⁹, 7, 7, 1866. ³Samuel⁹, 11, 5, 1869; d. inf. ⁴Sarah⁹, 30, 12, 1872.

¹MICHAEL F.⁷, m. Catherine B. Thomas, of Frederick Md.; ch., ¹Samuel⁸, b. 1848; d. —, —, 1850. ²Mary Parker⁸, b. —, 8, 1850. ³Harry Thomas⁸, b. —, 9, 1851 (residents of New York City).

²SOPHIA E.⁷, m., 27, 10, 1829, Dr. Samuel Boyd, of New York.

³HETTIE JANE⁷, m. Henry J. Drayton, of S. C.; d. without issue, 12, 2, 1844.

⁸SARAH⁶, m., 23, 2, 1804, Newberry Smith, of Philadelphia: ch., ¹EDWARD A.⁷, b. 6, 6, 1805: d. —, 9, 1832, single.

---

* One sister m. Mr. Robert Garrett, f. of the late John W. Garrett, for 25 years Pres't of the B. & O. R. R.; another m. Mr. John King; the youngest m. Mr. John Kimmel, f. of Hon. Wm. Kimmel, del. to Congress from Baltimore.

† One of the original settlers of Lowell, Mass.; the Wyman Exchange bears his name.

[2]NEWBERRY, A.[7], b. 24, 4, 1807; d. 25, 10, 1877.
[3]CORNELIA A.[7], b. 4, 3, 1811; d. 25, 7, 1844, single.
[2]NEWBERRY, A.[7], m., —, —, 1832, Ann A. Gorgas; ch., [1]Sarah Keyser[8], b. 29, 11, 1832. [2]Emma W.[8], b. 13, 6, 1838; d. —, —, 1863. [3]Anna M.[8], b. 27, 6, 1841; d. in infancy.

[1]Sarah Keyser[8], m., 1st, 11, 6, 1862, Edward A. Turpin. m., 2d, Geo. C. Harvey; ch., [1]Emma S. Turpin[9], b. 17, 12, 1864.

[2]Emma W.[8], m., —, 6, 1856, Edward C. Stockton; ch., [1]Newberry, A.[9], b. 22, 10, 1859. [2]Constance[9], b. 3, 10, 1861.

[1]Newberry, A.[9], m., —, 6, 1887, Christine S. Hare; ch , [1]Mary Hare[10], b. 3, 9, 1888.

(18) **²ANDREAS KEYSER⁴**, m. Hannah ——. Ch., **¹JACOB⁵**, b. ——;
d. —, 9, 1786. **²MATTHIAS⁵**, b. —— ; d. —, 11, 1766. **³WILLIAM⁵**, b. —— ;
d. prior to 1786. **⁴MARY⁵**, b. —— ; d. —, 1, 1814.
¹JACOB⁶, m. Elizabeth ; ch., none living 1786.
²MATTHIAS⁵, m. Hester —— ; ch., **¹SARAH⁶**. **²HANNAH⁶**. **³LYDIA⁶**.
m. ——. **⁴ELIZABETH⁶**. **⁵ANDREW⁶**.
　²HANNAH⁶, m. —— Jones ; ch., **¹CHRISTOPHER⁷**. **²MARY⁷**.
　³LYDIA⁶, m. Jacob Roop; ch., **¹ELIZABETH⁷**. **²ANN⁷**.
　⁴ELIZABETH⁶, m. ——.
³WILLIAM⁵, m. Mary —— ; ch., **¹ANDREW⁶**.

(9) **JACOB SOUPLIS KEYSER**[4], m., prior to 1744, Margaret —— (who was living 1793); ch., **JACOB**[5], b. —— : d. —, 5, 1781. **BENJAMIN**[5], b —,—, 1746; d. 11, 8, 1808. **JOSEPH**[5], b. —— ; d. 16, 9, 1793, unmd. **JOHN**[5].

JACOB[5], m., prior to 1771, Hannah, d. of Wichard Miller; ch., **ENOCH**[6], b. 28, 3, 1771; d. —, —, 1861, unmd. **ANN**[6], b. —— ; d. ——.

ANN[6], m. Conrad Redheffer, who d. —, 10, 1813; ch., **ELIZABETH**[7], b. —— : d. ——, unmd. **HANNAH**[7], b. 1, 1, 1795 (living 1889).

HANNAH[7], m. —— —— —— Nice; ch. —— —— —— —— —— ——.

BENJAMIN[5], m. —— —— prior to 1776, Ann Nice *; ch., **JOSEPH**[6], b. 18, 3, 1777; d. 6, 6, 1836. **HESTER**[6], b. 16, 3, 1779; d. 25, 12, 1847. **MOLLY**[6], b. 19, 2, 1781 ; d. 8, 1, 1846, unmd. **JACOB**[6], b. 26, 7, 1784; d. 20, 8, 1784. **THIRZA**[6], b. 6, 8, 1785; d. 13, 5, 1857. **JACOB**[6], b. 6, 10, 1788; d. 6, 2, 1859. **ANN**[6], b. 28, 10, 1792; d. 3, 8, 1867.

JOSEPH[6], m., 11, 5, 1824, Susan Shearer, d. of Jacob Shearer, of Moreland †; ch., **CHARLES SHEARER**[7], b. 18, 6, 1825. **WILLIAM FOX**[7], b. 12, 8, 1827; d. 11, 2, 1885. **CAROLINE**[7], b. 11, 8, 1829. **ANNA JANE**[7], b. 12, 8, 1832 ; d. 5, 1, 1833. **JOSEPH BENJAMIN**[7], b. 9, 11, 1836; d. 6, 11, 1864.

CHARLES SHEARER[7], m., 12, 6, 1866.‡ Sophronia MacKay (Norris); ch., **Susan Keyser**[8], b. 1, 10, 1873. **Ann Childs**[8], b. 2, 3, 1876; d. 12, 11, 1885.

CAROLINE[7], m., 21, 8, 1855, William Cowper, s. of John Auchinclos Inglis, S. C.; ch., **Anne Childs**[8], b. 28, 8, 1856; d. 4, 5, 1875.§ **John Auchinclos**[8], b. 3, 8, 1859.

* Hans de Neus's[1] g. d. Hans de Neus[1] (brother of Jan de Neus[1], p. 123), b. —— : d. 19, 7, 1736; m. Jannetje, who d. 11, 9, 1742: ch. **Cornelius**[2], b. —— ; d. —, —, 1734. **John**[2], b. —, —, —; d. —, —, 1743. **Elenor**[2], b. —, —, ——. **Anthony**[2], b. —, —, —— ; d. —, 2, 1762.

Cornelius[2], m., 30, 5, 1725. Mary Durlnro; ch., **William**[3], **John**[3], who died —, 6, 1793. **John**[3] m., —— —— ——, Jane Northrop; ch., Susanna, m. —— Heritage; Mary, m. —— Isdell; Cornelia, m. —— Van Booskerk; Jane, m. —— Harker; Rachel, m. Jacob Shearer, of Moreland; ch., Susan, m. **JOSEPH KEYSER**[6], she was b. 15, 5, 1802; d. 10, 12, 1874.

Anthony[2], m., 1st, Jane —— ; ch., **John**[3] (Judge of O. C., Philadelphia, 1785), **William**[3], d. single, **George**[3]. m., 2d, 23, 1746, Mary Packer; ch., **Richard**[3], **Mary**[3], **Ann**[3], b. 10, 6, 1754; d. 19, 9, 1822; **Susanna**[3], **William**[3], **Jacob**[3] (*alias* Jesse), **Anthony**[3].

John[3], m. Mary Cauffman; ch , **John**[4], **George**[4], **Jane**[4], b. 8, 7, 1763; d. 2, 11, 1850. **Jane**[4] m. Michael Baker; ch., Mary, dec'd, George Nice, dec'd, m., **ANN KEYSER**[6], Michael, dec'd, Sarah, dec'd, Jacob, dec'd, Joseph, dec'd, William, dec'd; Benj., dec'd, Hannah (living, 1889).

Richard[3], m. —— Coleman: **Mary**[3], m. —— Dover: **Ann**[3], m., ——, ——, **BENJAMIN KEYSER**: **Susanna**[3], m., 1st, 16, 2, 1767, Joseph Turner, and 2d, —— Leutz. Mary Packer Nice m., 2d, in 1772, Benj. Davis.

† Member of House of Rep., 1806-14, State Senator, 1814-18, and soldier of the Revolution.

‡ In the Protestant Chapel, Rome, Italy.

‡ The Home for Incurables had its origin in the heart of this member of our family, who was herself an incurable from paralysis in her childhood.

[2]John Auchinclos[3], m., 21, 10, 1885, Minnie Uhle DeCan; ch., Muriel Ralston, b. 22, 9, 1886.

[2]HESTER[6], m. John Fox; ch., [1]WILLIAM LYBRAND[7], [2]BENJAMIN[7], [3]ANN[7], b. ——, 1808, d. 22, 7, 1856. [4]EDWARD JOHN[7].

[1]WILLIAM LYBRAND[7], m., ——, Marian Holahan. [2]BENJAMIN[7], m. Louisa Batson. [3]ANN[7], m. —— Cephas G. Childs. [4]EDWARD JOHN[7], m. Martha Chew Johnson; ch., [1]John Michael[8], b. 25, 10, 1832. [2]William Lybrand[8]. [3]Thomas Robb[8]. [4]Esther[8]. [5]Edward Wayne[8].

[1]John Michael[8], m., 9, 2, 1859, Mary J. Simpson; ch., [1]Anna Childs[9]. [2]Marian R.[9].

[1]Anna Childs[9], m., 23, 4, 1884, George Lorraine Dunn.

[2]Marian R.[9], m., 9, 1, 1889, Thomas Seward Gay.

[5]THIRZA[6], m., 15, 10, 1807, Richard Engle; ch., [1]ELIZA[7], b. ——, d. ——. [2]CAROLINE[7], b. ——, d. ——. [3]SYLVANUS[7], b. ——, d. ——. [4]GUSTAVUS[7], ——. [5]RICHARD[7], b. ——. [6]CHARLES[7], b. ——.

[4]GUSTAVUS[7], m., 1, 9, 1854, Sarah F. Arrison; ch., Caroline R[8].

[5]RICHARD[7], m., 13, 6, 1888, Elizabeth Keyser.

[6]JACOB[6], m., —, —, ——, Catherine Snyder; ch., [1]JOSEPH[7]. [2]BENJAMIN[7]. [3]AMELIA SNYDER[7]. [4]JACOB[7]. [5]ALBERT[7]. [6]WILLIAM[7], [7]RICHARD[7] (twins). [8]WILLIAM[7]. [9]GEORGE[7].

[1]JOSEPH[7], m., —, —, ——, Harriet Manpay; ch., [1]Elizabeth[8]. [2]Clara[8]. [3]Albert[8]. [4]Byron[8]. [5]Marian[8]. [6]Benjamin[8].

[1]Elizabeth[8], m. [5]RICHARD ENGLE[7]. [2]Clara[8], m.

[4]JACOB[7], m. Sarah Ettinger; ch., [1]Annie[8]. [2]Harry[8].

[5]Marian[8], m. John Kisterbock, s. of Josiah Kisterbock, Pres't of the City Nat, Bank.

[7]ANN[6], m., 11, 2, 1817, George Nice Baker*; ch., [1]MYRA[7], b. 18, 11, 1817. [2]JANE NICE[7], b. 16, 7, 1819; d. 18, 8, 1866, unmd. [3]ANNA KEYSER[7], b. 9, 10, 1821; d. 14, 4, 1877, unmd. [4]WILLIAM SPOHN[7], b. 17, 4, 1824.

[4]WILLIAM SPOHN[7], m., 12, 5, 1853, Eliza Downing Rowley; ch., [1]George Nice[8], b. 18, 6, 1854; d. 24, 10, 1881, unmd. [2]Laura[8], b. 30, 9. 1856. [3]Richard Rowley[8], b. 19, 10, 1858.

[2]Laura[8], m., 21, 10, 1875, Henry Whelen, Jr.; ch., [1]William Baker[9]. [2]Laura[9]. [3]Elsie[9].

[3]Richard Rowley[8], m., 20, 10, 1886, Clara Mary Small; ch., William Spohn Baker, Jr.

⁴**JOHN**⁵*, m., prior to 1758, Rebecca Nedrow,† d. of Ann Nedrow; ch., ¹THOMAS⁶, b. 22, 2, 1765; d. ——. ²MARGARET⁶, b. ——, 1758; d. ——, 1836. ³MARY⁶, b. ——, d. ——. ⁴ANN⁶, b. ——, d. —— (living 1793).

¹THOMAS⁶, m., 14, 9, 1788, Susanna Weaver; ch., ¹REBECCA⁷, b. 19, 4, 1790; d. ——. ²JULIA ANNA⁷, b. 19, 2, 1792. ³DEBORAH⁷, b. 31, 12, 1793. ⁴BARTHOLOMEW⁷, b. 24, 11, 1798; d. ——. ⁵MIRIAM⁷, b. 12, 3, 1801. ⁶SALOME⁷, b. 25, 10, 1802. ⁷JOHANNA⁷, b. 8, 11, 1804; d. ——. ⁸WILLIAM MAKENSIE⁷, b. 4, 2, 1808. ⁹JOHN KEYSER⁷, b. 1, 9, 1810.

¹REBECCA⁷, m. Rynard Fry; ch., ¹Jacob⁸, ²Thomas⁸, ³William C⁸., ⁴Rynard⁸.

　　³William C.⁸, m. Elizabeth Robinson; ch., ¹William H.⁹, ²Rynard⁹, d., ³Frank H.⁹, ⁴Edwin⁹.

²JULIA ANNA⁷, m., —, 2, 1812, Samuel Hammer; ch., ¹Elkanah⁸, b. 15, 9, 1815. ²Reuben⁸, b. 5, 10, 1816. ³Keturah⁸, b. 29, 9, 1819, d. 2, 12, 1861. ⁴William⁸, b. 4, 3, 1821, d. —, —. ⁵Samuel⁸, b. 3, 10, 1823. ⁶Joseph⁸, b. 6, 7, 1825. ⁷Emeline⁸, b. 22, 4, 1827. ⁸Philip, b. 6, 3, 1829.

　　³Keturah⁸, m., 14, 6, 1838, Charles Longstreth Orum ;‡ ch., ¹Rachel⁹, m. Russel E. Moon. ²Julia A.⁹, ³Myra⁹, ⁴Morris⁹, m. Ella Mariner. ⁵Ellen⁹, m. John H. Campbell.

³DEBORAH⁷, m. Peter Hammer; ch., ¹Jesse⁸, ²John⁸.

⁵MIRIAM⁷.

⁷JOHANNA⁷, m. —— Anderson.

²MARGARET⁶, m., 16, 11, 1776, Henry Bruner ;§ ch., ¹MARY⁷, b. 20, 9, 1777. ²JOHN⁷, b. 26, 9, 1779. ³BARBARA⁷, b. 19, 5, 1781. ⁴MARGARET⁷, 10, 3, 1783. ⁵JACOB⁷, 8, 2, 1785. ⁶REBECCA⁷, 9, 8, 1789. ⁷ANN⁷, b. 15, 7, 1790. ⁸SARAH⁷, 7, 10, 1791, d. 1867. ⁹ESTHER⁷, b. 24, 9, 1793. ¹⁰BENJ. GEORGE⁷, 2, 10, 1796, d. 26, 10, 1840. ¹¹HANNAH⁷, b. 30, 5, 1798, d. —, 1836.

⁸SARAH⁷, m., —, 1809, Isaac M. Kulp, who d. 1835 ; ch., Elizabeth B., m. —— Pierson.

¹⁰BENJ. GEORGE⁷, m., 20, 9, 1819, Sarah Sutter, who d. 10, 5, 1865 ; ch., ¹Sarah⁸, ²Mary⁸, ³Henry Benjamin⁸, now of the Department of Highways, Philadelphia.

---

* ⁴John⁵ was Bunker Hill John. (Hannah Nice, 1888.)

† Rebecca Nedrow d. 23, 2, 1788.

‡ Charles Longstreth Orum, b. 24, 10, 1814, d. 11, 9, 1884.

§ Henry Bruner was one of four children of Henry and Barbara Bruner, of the Canton of Basle, Switzerland, who settled in Germantown prior to 1750. The father died in 1768, Aug. 26, aged 52 y. 8 m. 15 d. The son died Oct. 4, 1828. He was a soldier in the Revolution, elder of the Presbyterian church, Germantown, and a universally respected citizen.

(22) [7]**ELIZABETH KEYSER**[4], m., 1733, Peter Penebacker; ch., [1]**JOHN**[5],
b. 11, 2, 1733. [2]**HENRY**[5], b. 2, 7, 1736. [3]**JACOB**[5], b. 16, 8, 1738. [4]**WILLIAM**[5],
26, 8, 1740, d. 9, 11, 1815. [5]**MARGARET**[5], b. 8, 11, 1742. [6]**CATHERINE**[5],
8, 10, 1744. [7]**SAMUEL**[5], 4, 11, 1746, d. —, 1837. [8]**ELIZABETH**[5], 4, 1,
1749. [9]**BARBARA**[5], 25, 12, 1752.

[1]**JOHN**[5], m. ——; ch., [1]**DANIEL**[6], b. 22, 12, 1761. [2]**SUSANNA**[6], m.
Peter Bicker. [3]**ELIZABETH**[6], m. John Sharp. [4]**HANNAH**[6], m. John
Hill.

[1]**DANIEL**[6], m. Mary Musser; ch., [1]**WILLIAM**[7], [2]**MAGDALENA**[7], [3]**SUSANNA**[7],
[4]**DANIEL**[7], b. 29, 8, 1791. [5]**SAMUEL**[7], 15, 8, 1794. [6]**JOHANNES**[7], 17, 4,
1797. [7]**ELIZABETH**[7], 30, 6, 1800. [8]**MARY**[7], 30, 4, 1803. [9]**JESSE**[7], 27, 11,
1805.

[1]**WILLIAM**[7], m., 6, 6, 1814, Elizabeth Schnader; ch., [1]**Elizabeth**[8], [2]**Mary**[8],
[3]**Hannah**[8], [4]**William**[8], [5]**Lydia**[8], [6]**Sarah**[8], [7]**Samuel**[8], [8]**Jesse**[8], [9]**Susannah**[8],
[10]**Israel**[8].

[2]**MAGDALENA**[7], m., 1, 5, 1816, John Lausch.

[3]**SUSANNA**[7], m. Michael Martin.

[4]**DANIEL**[7], m. Barbara Hartman.

[5]**SAMUEL**[7], m. Susanna, d. of Geo. Rupp.

[6]**JOHANNES**[7], m. Elizabeth Reem.

[7]**ELIZABETH**[7], m. John Schwartz.

[8]**MARY**[7], m. Jacob Schwartz.

[9]**JESSE**[7], m., 23, 2, 1830, Catherine Rishel.

[4]**WILLIAM PANNEBACKER**[5], m. —— Hause; ch., [1]**SALOME**[6], [2]**SUSAN**[6],
[3]**JESSE**[6], b. 5, 4, 1773. [4]**JONAS**[6], 22, 2, 1776. [5]**ELIZABETH**[6], 25, 12,
1777. [6]**JESSE**[6], 1, 2, 1783.

[4]**JONAS**[6], m. Mary, d. of Caspar Schneider; ch., [1]**NATHAN**[7], b. 12, 4,
1805. [2]**HANNAH**[7], 12, 2, 1807. [3]**ELIZABETH**[7], 7, 12, 1809. [4]**MARY**[7], 7,
12, 1809. [5]**SUSAN**[7], 1, 7, 1812. [6]**JONAS**[7], 5, 12, 1814. [7]**SARAH**[7], 17, 8,
1818. [8]**JOHN**[7], d. 1821.

[1]**NATHAN**[7], m. Lydia S., d. of Henry Brownback; ch., [1]**William Pierce**[8],
b. 26, 11, 1845, m. Emma Olivia Christman. [2]**Mary Catherine**[8], 30, 9,
1849. [3]**Preston Nathan**[8], d. 15, 8, 1849. [4]**Emma Cora**[8], b. 11, 3, 1853,
m. Granville Stauffer.

[2]**HANNAH**[7], m., 12, 2, 1807, William Walters.

[4]**MARY**[7], m. Jacob S. Worman.

[5]**SUSAN**[7], m. Peter Mowry.

[7]**SARAH**[7], m. Joel S., s. of George and Veronica Fink.

[5]**SAMUEL PANNEBECKER**[5], m., 15, 5, 1768, Hannah Gesbert, who was b.
26, 3, 1747, d. 1837; ch., [1]**DANIEL**[6], b. 17, 2, 1769. [2]**BENJAMIN**[6], 24,
12, 1770. [3]**WILLIAM**[6], 19, 9, 1772. [4]**JACOB**[6], 11, 8, 1775. [5]**SAMUEL**[6],

8, 2, 1770. [6]JOHN[6], 11, 11, 1781. [7]JOSEPH[6], 6, 2, 1785, d. 1807.
[8]ABRAHAM[6], 11, 2, 1787.

[1]DANIEL[6], m. Susanna Paul.

[2]JACOB[6], m. ——.

[3]SAMUEL[6], m., 23, 2, 1802, Catherine, d. of Henry Wireman, who d.
13, 1, 1800.

[4]JOHN[6], m. Mary, d. of Jacob Snyder.

[5]ABRAHAM[6], m. Hannah Hill.

(5) ANNEKE KEYSER[4], m., 25, 3, 1736, John Pennebacker; ch.,
[1]DIRCK[5], b. 1, 1, 1737. [2]HENRY[5], 1, 3, 1738. [3]MARGARET[5], 11, 1, 1742.
[4]ELIZABETH[5], 12, 7, 1743. [5]JACOB[5], b. 1, 5, 1746. [6]CATHERINE[5], 26, 12,
751, unmd. [7]HANNAH[5], 25, 2, 1754. [8]SAMUEL[5], 23, 5, 1760.

[1]DIRCK[5], m., ——, Hannah de Haven, b. 1737, d. 1825; ch., [1]BENJA-
MIN[6], b. 20, 9, 1760, d. 31, 12, 1820. [2]REBECCA[6], [3]ABRAHAM[6],
[4]ELIZABETH[6], [5]JOHN[6], b. —, 8, 1768, d. 28, 2, 1834. [6]HANNAH[6],
[7]CATHERINE[6], unmd., [8]MARY[6], [9]DERICK[6].

[1]BENJAMIN[6], m., 13, 3, 1787, Sarah, d. of Green B. Samuels (she was b.
10, 2, 1768, d. 9, 7, 1825); ch., [1]GEO. MAYBERRY[7], b. 31, 12, 1787.
[2]ANN[7], 8, 7, 1789. [3]NATHAN[7], 19, 10, 1791. [4]JOEL[7], 9, 8, 1793, d. 5, 4,
1862. [5]CHARLOTTE H.[7], b. 29, 9, 1795, d. 3, 7, 1851. [6]JOHN[7], b. 15, 4,
1798. [7]MARY[7], 21, 8, 1800. [8]MARK[7], 1, 4, 1801.[9] REBECCA M.[7], 26,
3, 1803, d. unmd. 1849. [10]ISAAC SAMUELS[7], b. 3, 9, 1805. [11]SARAH[7], 2,
3, 1808. [12]BENJAMIN[7], 9, 10, 1809, d. 8, 7, 1811. [13]SAMUEL HUNT[7], b.
11, 10, 1812; d. 15, 6, 1850, unmd.

[1]GEO. MAYBERRY[7], m., 1835, Anne Crim; ch., [1]Benjamin[8], b. 24, 10,
1835, d. 5, 9, 1861. [2]Ann[8].

[2]Ann[8], m. Adam Douglas; ch., [1]Benj. Pennebacker[9], [2]Dorcas[9], [3]Mary[9],
[4]Samuel Hunt[9].

[4]JOEL[7], m., 27, 5, 1823, Margaret Perry Stribling, who d. 18, 7, 1861;
ch., [1]Mary Crawford Stribling[8], b. 22, 3, 1824. [2]Sarah Ann[8], 4, 1,
1826, d. 5, 5, 1842. [3]Caroline[8], b. 21, 2, 1828, d. 30, 3, 1829. [4]Geo.
Mayberry[8], b. 2, 2, 1830. [5]Wilhelma Tate[8], 28, 4, 1832. [6]Rebecca
Jane[8], 12, 4, 1834. [7]Margaret M.[9], 12, 6, 1836.* [8]Joel[8], 7, 9, 1838.
[9]Francis Stribling[8], 26, 9, 1840.

[1]Mary Crawford Stribling[8], m., 24, 10, 1844, Lemuel, s. of Rhesa
and Catherine Allen; ch., [1]Frances Taliaffero[9], b. 29, 7, 1848, d. 24,
10, 1872. [2]Joseph Rhesa[9], b. 26, 1, 1850. [3]Lemuel Ethan Allen[9],
12, 10, 1851. [4]Florence Wilhelma[9], 17, 8, 1856.

[4]George Mayberry[8], M. D., m., 7, 11, 1854, Julia Egbertine Wortham,

* It was in this descendant of Anneke Keyser the endurance of our lineage was so notably mani-
fested, in a time of its most extreme trial, p. 63.

who was b. 31, 10, 1834, d. 1, 9, 1873 ; ch., [1]Percy Vivian[9]*, b. 17, 2, 1856, m. Anna J. Hardwicke. [2]Maria[9], 19, 8, 1857. [3]Julian[9], 28, 3, 1862, m. Jennye Stevens. [4]Nina[9], 27, 1, 1864, m. Leslie C. White. [5]Adele[9], 2, 12, 1866, m. Benj. C. Epperson.

[5]Wilhelma Tate[8], m., 25, 11, 1852, Solomon K. Moore ; ch., [1]Margaret Stribling[9], [2]Arthur Lewis[9], b. 10, 11, 1856. [3]Mary Egbertine[9], 21, 1, 1859, d. 12, 3, 1861.

[8]Joel[8], m., ——, 1866, Eliza Powers ; ch., [1]Edgar[9], [2]Frances[9], [3]Magdalena[9].

[5]CHARLOTTE H.[7], m., 20, 8, 1818, Walter Newman ; ch., [1]Sarah C.[8], [2]Ann Rebecca[8], d. unmd. [3]Benjamin Pennybacker[8], b. 24, 1, 1823. [4]Mary Caroline[8], d. unmd. [5]Elizabeth[8], d. young. [6]Henrietta Charlotte[8].

[1]Sarah C.[8], m. Jacob Gaw ; ch., [1]Henrietta Charlotte[9], [2]Robert Newman[9], [3]Ann Rebecca[9], [4]Benjamin Pennybacker[9], m. Elizabeth, d. of John T. Hickman, who was b. —, 9, 1822 ; ch., [1]Walter Hickman[10], b. 17, 7, 1852. [2]Edgar Douglas[10], 26, 3, 1854. [3]John Thomas[10], 12, 10, 1856. [4]Charles Henry[10], 12, 9, 1859, d. 18, 7, 1861. [5]Caroline Mary[10], b. 23, 7, 1862.

[8]MARK[7], m., 26, 1, 1823, Catherine Kratzer.

[10]ISAAC SAMUELS[7], m., —, 5, 1832, Sarah A., d. of Col. Zebulon Dyer ; ch., [1]John Dyer[8], b. 20, 3, 1833. [2]Isaac Samuels Pennybacker[8], 20, 3, 1833. [3]James Edmund[8], 29, 4, 1844. [4]Mary L.[8], decd. [5]Fanny B.[8], [6]Frank L.[8], decd. [7]Benjamin C.[8], decd.

[1]John Dyer[8], m., 24, 8, 1865, Elizabeth Maupin ; ch., Mary Lee Pennybacker[9], b. 28, 8, 1866. [2]Kate Abigail Pennybacker[9]. 30, 5, 1868. [3]John George Pennybacker[9], 30, 11, 1870.

[2]Isaac Samuels[8], m. Susan Eliza Funk, who was b. 5, 1, 1850.

[3]James Edmund[8], m. Laura R. Van Pelt, who was b. 27, 9, 1847 ; ch., Carrie McCoy[9], b. 16, 5, 1872. Lucy Sheltman[9], 9, 5, 1874, d. ——, ——. Isaac Samuels[9], b. 19, 7, 1875.

[2]REBECCA[6], m. Geo. Mayberry ; ch., [1]REBECCA[7], [2]BENJAMIN[7], [3]SYLVANUS[7], decd., [4]ISAAC[7], decd., [5]CATHERINE PENNYBACKER[7], b. 9, 4, 1795, m. Joseph H. Samuels. [6]JOHN PENNYBACKER[7].

[1]REBECCA[7], m. Henry L. Prentiss ; ch., [1]Mary A.[8], m. Henry Goodno. [2]Lucy[8], [3]Patrick Adair[8], [4]Benjamin Mayberry[8],† b. 23, 11, 1819. [5]Henry Clay[8], [6]Henrietta[8], decd.

[2]BENJAMIN[7], m. Nancy Samuels.

[6]JOHN PENNYBACKER[7], m. Lucy Faring ; ch., [1]Lucy[8], m. Geo. Kincheloe. [2]George Mayberry[8], m. Fanny Kincheloe ; ch., [1]Henry W.[9], [2]Robert[9], [3]Lucy[9].

---

* Superint. Pub. Schools, Tyler, Texas.   † Benj. Mayberry Prentiss, p. 61.

³ABRAHAM⁶, m. Elizabeth Ruffner; ch., ¹ISAAC⁷, ²ELIZABETH⁷, ³JOHN⁷, ⁴ABRAHAM⁷, ⁵MOUNCE BYRD⁷, ⁶REBECCA⁷, ⁷MARY A.⁷

  ¹ISAAC⁷, m. Elizabeth Alkin.

  ²ELIZABETH⁷, m. James Gill; ch., ¹James⁸, ²Elizabeth⁸.

  ³JOHN⁷, m. Catherine Duncan; ch., ¹Mounce Byrd⁸, ²Coleman⁸, ³Charles⁸, ⁴——⁸.

  ⁴ABRAHAM⁷, m. Rebecca Mitchell; ch., ¹Mounce Byrd⁸, ²Benjamin⁸, ³John⁸, ⁴Edgar⁸.

  ⁵MOUNCE BYRD⁷, m. Amanda Pennybacker; ch., ¹Penelope⁸, m. Dr. Jas H. Owens. ²Cora⁸, m. Jas. H. Spencer. ³Lewis⁸, ⁴Medora⁸.

  ⁶REBECCA⁷, m. Harrison Miller.

  ⁷MARY A.⁷, m. Samuel Buffington.

⁴ELIZABETH⁶, m. Isaac, s. of Green B. Samuels; ch., ¹JOSEPH H.⁷, ²ABRAHAM⁷, ³JOHN⁷. d. 25, 12, 1860. ⁴REBECCA⁷, ⁵ISAAC⁷, ⁶NANCY⁷, ⁷RUTH⁷, ⁸GREEN BERRY⁷, ⁹ELIZABETH⁷.

  ¹JOSEPH H.⁷ m., 10, 5, 1813, Catherine Pennybacker Mayberry; ch., ¹Stark⁸, ²Sylvanus⁸, ³Benjamin⁸, ⁴George⁸, ⁵Green⁸, ⁶Mary⁸, ⁷Lucy⁸, m. John J. Ayer. ⁸Elizabeth⁸.

  ²ABRAHAM⁷, m. Hannah Neal.

  ³JOHN⁷, m., 17, 6, 1824. Emily, d. of Joseph Gardiner; ch., ¹Henry Jefferson⁸, b. 12, 7, 1825. ²Joseph⁸, 18, 9, 1826. ³Lafayette⁸, 16, 6, 1828. ⁴Alexander H.⁸, 8, 3, 1830. ⁵Eliza⁸, 24, 11, 1831. ⁶Mary Theresa⁸, 25, 8, 1833. ⁷Eveline⁸, 31, 11, 1834. ⁸Emily⁸, 23, 7, 1836. ⁹John⁸, 31, 3, 1839. ¹⁰America Eugenia⁸, 16, 6, 1841.

  ¹REBECCA⁷, m. Abraham Byrd; ch., ¹Perry⁸, ²Abraham⁸, ³Sylvanus⁸, ⁴Mary⁸, ⁵Maggie⁸, ⁶Annie⁸, ⁷Erasmus⁸.

  ⁷RUTH⁷, m. John Haas; ch., ¹Charles E. Haas⁸.

  ⁸GREEN BERRY⁷, m. Mary Coffman; ch., ¹Margaret⁸, ²Isaac⁸, ³Anna⁸, ⁴Green B.⁸, ⁵Samuel⁸.

⁵JOHN⁶, m. Phœbe Paget; ch., ¹HANNAH⁷, decd., ²MARY⁷, b. —, —, 1796. ³DERRICK⁷, 25, 9, 1797. ⁴REBECCA⁷, 1799. ⁵JOHN⁷, 1801. ⁶WILLIAM⁷, 1803. ⁷HIRAM⁷, 1805. ⁸ALBERT⁷, 1806, decd. ⁹JOSEPH SAMUELS⁷, 1810. ¹⁰CATHERINE⁷, 1812. ¹¹AMANDA⁷, 4, 8, 1814, m. M. B. Pennybacker. ¹²BENJAMIN RUSH⁷, 20, 6, 1817.

  ²MARY⁷, m. Samuel Hupp; ch., ¹Hiram⁸, ²Elizabeth M.⁸, b. 24, 10, 1820, ²Caroline⁸, ³Derrick⁸, ⁴Isaac⁸, 1825, ⁵Samuel⁸, 1827, ⁶Anne⁸.

  ³DERRICK⁷, m., 13, 12, 1832, Amanda M. Strayer; ch., ¹John S.⁸, b. 25, 11, 1834. ²Thomas Jefferson⁸, 15, 8, 1837; d. 1862. ³Joseph S.⁸, b. 8, 10, 1838. ⁴Derrick D.⁸, 5, 11, 1841. ⁵Albert D.⁸, 1, 12, 1843. ⁶Mary V.⁸, 19, 11, 1846. ⁷Henrietta S.⁸, 22, 10, 1848.

[4]Derrick D.[8], m., 5, 4, 1866, Elizabeth Bowman; ch., [1]John[9], [2]Thomas[9], [3]Charles[9], [4]Samuel Samuels[9], [5]Mary[9], [6]Abigail[9].

[6]Mary V.[8], m., 27, 4, 1866, Hiram K. Devier; ch., [1]Mary Beulah[9], [2]Henrietta Leila Susan[9], [4]Annie Hupp[9], [4]Emily Strayer[9].

[7]Henrietta S.[8], m., 12, 3, 1867, Charles J. Brock; ch., [1]Owen Bertram[9], [2]Mary Irene Virginia[9], [3]Lurema Maud[9], [4]Cora Evans[9], [5]Mabel[9], [6]_____ _____[9].

[4]REBECCA[7], m. Martin Hupp; ch., [1]William[8], [2]Virginia[8], [3]Mary[8].

[5]JOHN[7], m. Jane Beckwith; ch., [1]Benjamin[8], [2]Jeanette[8], [3]Derick[8], [4]Virginia[8].

[6]WILLIAM[7], m. Susan Duncan; ch., [1]James[8], [2]John[8], [3]Amanda[8], [4]Elizabeth[8], [5]Abigail[8], [6]Virginia[8], [7]America[8], [8]Joseph[8], [9]William H.[8], [10]Charles[8].

[7]HIRAM[7], m. Ann Mitchell; ch., [1]Benjamin Rush[8], [2]Amanda[8], m. William Hardwick, [3]John Byrd[8], [4]Perry[8], [5]Caroline[8], [6]Mary Ann[8], [7]Alfred[8], [8]Hiram[8].

[3]John Byrd[8], m. Rebecca ——.

[9]JOSEPH SAMUELS[7], m., 1st, Elizabeth Morgan; ch., [1]John Morgan[8]; m., 2d, Sarah A., widow of [10]Isaac Samuels Pennybacker[7]. P. 149.

[10]CATHERINE E.[7], m. James W. Mitchell; ch., [1]Hiram P.[8], [2]Joseph S.[8], [3]John Mark[8], [4]Mary Ann[8], m. Samuel Hupp, [5]Isabella[8], [6]Adelia[8], [7]Rebecca[8], [7]Amanda[8], [9]Lucy[8].

[3]John Mark[8], m. a dau. of [5]Mark Pennybacker[7]; ch., [1]Ida May[9], [2]Ora Kate[9], [3]Emory[9], [4]Lulu E.[9]

[12]BENJAMIN RUSH[7], m., 28, 1, 1847, Penelope, d. of Barnes Beckwith; ch., [1]Willelma[8], [2]Morgan[8], [3]Jeanette[8], [4]Georgia Maybury[8], [5]Nebraska[8], [6]Jessie[8].

[1]Willelma[8], m. William Crooks.

[6]HANNAH[6], m. Mounce Byrd.

[9]DERRICK[6], m., —, 4, 1815, Elizabeth, d. of John Neal.

[1]HANNAH[7], m., 13, 5, 1837, George Kincheloe; ch., [1]Lucy F.[8], [2]Jane[8].

[1]Lucy F.[8], m., 12, 2, 1864, James M. Jackson.

[3]Jane[8], m., 11, 12, 1860, P. D. Gambler.

[3]MARGARET[5], m., 1st, Henry Acker; 2d, —— Eyster.

[5]JACOB[5], m. Ann, d. of John Pawling; ch., [1]NATHAN[6], b. 2, 3, 1771.

[2]ELIZABETH[6].

[1]NATHAN PENNYPACKER[6],* m., —, 3, 1802, Frances Brower, who was b. 1, 6, 1783; ch., [1]Jacob[7], [2]Joseph B.[7], [3]Ann[7].

[2]JOSEPH B.[7], m., 28, 10, 1828, Jane Walker; ch., [1]Margaret C.[8], [2]Nathan[8], [3]Elizabeth B.[8], [4]Ann[8], [5]Thomas W.[8], [6]Francis B.[8], [7]Sarah Jane[8], [8]Mary Emma[8], [9]Isaac W.[8], [10]Maria C.[8], [11]Jacob[8], [12]Hannah M.[8]

* He was the first to adopt the name Pennypacker.

³Elizabeth B.ˣ, m. Edwin M. Supplee.

⁴Ann ̄, m. Robert Grover.

⁶Frances B.ˣ, m., 18, 1, 1859, Richard Stephens.

¹¹Jacob ̄, m., 3, 9, 1872, Kate S. Bowman.

¹²Hannah M.ˣ, m., 12, 4, 1873, Oliver P. Ludwig.

³Ann⁷, m., 25, 11, 1830, Jas. A. Pennypacker; ch., James Francis, b. 10, 1, 1832; d. 15, 5, 1837. Nathan Anderson,* 20, 10, 1835. Mary E., 24, 7, 1838.

²ELIZABETH⁶, m. John Francis; ch., ¹Ann,⁷ ²Rebecca⁷, ³Deborah⁷, ⁴Eliza⁷, ⁵Felix⁷.

¹Ann⁷, m. Geo. Highly; ch., ¹Henry⁸, ²Hannah⁸, ³Eliza⁸, ⁴Thomas⁸, ⁵Felixˣ, ⁶Maryˣ, ⁷Deborahˣ.

²Rebecca⁷, m., 1st, Joseph Crawford; ch., ¹Ann⁸, ²Albert⁸, ³Amandaˣ; m., 2d, Jacob Kulp; ch., ¹Josephˣ, ²Emmaˣ.

³Deborah⁷, m. Henry Loacks; ch., ¹Ann Elizabethˣ, ²John Henryˣ.

⁴Eliza⁷, m. Thos. Sheppard; ch., ¹Angelinaˣ, ²—— ——ˣ.

⁷HANNAH⁶, m., 29, 5, 1774, Michael Reiser, or Rayser; ch., ¹JOHN⁶, ²NATHAN⁶, ³NANCY⁶, ⁴ENOCH⁶, ⁵AMOS⁶.

* Nathan A. Pennypacker, M.D., was Captain in the 4th Reserves, Brevet Col. on General Hoyt's staff, for three years member of the Assembly, Commissioner for the building of the Insane Asylum, President of the School Board, Chester Co. He m. Eliza, d. of Capt. Samuel Davis, who survives him.

(21) **⁵JOHANNES⁴**, m. Barbara Funk (circa 1744); ch., **¹JOHN⁵**, **²CHRIS-TIAN⁵**, **³MICHAEL⁵**, b. —, d. 1794, **⁴CHARLES⁵**.

¹**CHARLES⁵**, m. —— Shelly, d. of Dr. Shelly, Philada., moved from Germ. to Page Co., Va., prior to the Revolution; ch., **¹JOSEPH⁶**, **²——⁶**, **³JOHN⁶**.

²——⁶, m. and left one son, ¹CHARLES⁷, b. 1793, and living 1889.

³JOHN⁶, m. Catherine Rhinehart; ch., **¹ALEXANDER⁷**, **²ELIZABETH⁷**, **³CHRISTOPHER⁷**, b. 19, 3, 1799; d. 8, 9, 1869.

³CHRISTOPHER⁷ m. —— Urner; ch., ¹Mary Catherine⁸, b. 6, 2, 1822. ²Elizabeth Ann⁸, b. 10, 3, 1823. ³Susan Rebecca⁸, b. 29, 11, 1824. ⁴Sarah Ann⁸, 30, 11, 1829. ⁵John Anderson⁸, 30, 11, 1829. ⁶Abigail⁸, 30, 3, 1831. ⁷Frances M.⁸, 6, 10, 1832. ⁸Henry Marsellus⁸, 24, 1, 1835. ⁹Barbara Allen⁸, 11, 3, 1838. ¹⁰Emily Jane⁸, 21, 4, 1839. ¹¹Family Margaret⁸, 23, 1, 1841.

¹Mary Catherine⁸, m. Jas. Wright; ch., Irene, William, John, Cecil, Jennette.

²Elizabeth Ann⁸, m. Samuel Skidmore; ch., Calvin, Marsellus, Rebecca, Frank, Family, Charles, Thomas.

³Susan Rebecca⁸, m. Rev. Martin Urner; ch., Anne, Charles Keyser, Clarence, Fannie, Maggie.

⁶Caroline Abigail⁸, m. Milton Taylor; ch., Jennie, Hiram.

⁷Francis M.⁸, m. Joseph Bumgarden; ch., Annie Lizzie.

⁸Henry Marcellus⁸, m. Nannie Kite; ch., Carrie, William, Ernest, Thomas, Virgie, Otis, Annie, Maggie.

¹⁰Emily Jane⁸, m., 1st, Jouette Gaily; ch., William, Annie, Olie, Charles; m., 2d, Thaditus Mayes; ch., ——.

²**CHRISTIAN⁵**, m. Barbara Evans (Conrad); ch., CHRISTIAN.

¹CHRISTIAN⁶, m. Elizabeth Conrad; ch., ¹JACOB C.⁷, ²JOSEPH⁷, d. without issue; ³CHARLES C.⁷, d. without issue; ⁴SAMUEL C.⁷, ⁵RACHEL⁷, ⁶MARY⁷, ⁷ANN⁷, who m. Charles Warner; ⁸JOHN⁷.

⁵RACHEL⁷, m. —— Nace; ch., Margaret, who m. —— Young; Ann, who m. —— Fritz.

⁶MARY⁷, m. Conrad Wolfe.

⁸JOHN⁷,* m. ——; ch., ¹John II.⁸, ²Christopher⁸, ³Joseph⁸, ⁴Samuel⁸.
¹John II.⁸, m. Elizabeth Judah, d. of David and Elizabeth Judah; ch., ¹William J.⁹, ²John II.⁹,† ³Elizabeth⁹. ¹William J.⁹, m. Harriet Swift; ch., Nelly Everett m. P. W. Atkin, Elizabeth J., d. William Swift, of Pensacola, Fla. ²John II.⁹, m. Jessie Farquharson.

---

* John built the first dock in Pensacola.

† John II., his grandson, built the first dock in California, foot of Jay Street, Sacramento City, 1850. He is the author of "Reason and Revelation," in reply to Ingersoll; and interested and actively employed on work for the progress of humanity (see p. 70).

³**MICHAEL**⁵, m. Catherine ——, who d. — 7, 1811; ch., ¹ANNA GER-TRUDE⁶, b. 2, 3, 1788; d. 21, 4, 1863. ²ANDREW⁶, b. 1, 7, 1790; d. 7, 1, 1866. ³DANIEL⁶, b. ——; d. ——, unmd., at Baton Rouge.

¹ANNA GERTRUDE⁶, m. John Peoples, who d. 27, 11, 1854; ch., ¹CATHERINE⁷, b. 10, 8, 1804; d. 18, 1, 1886. ²WILLIAM⁷, 13, 6, 1806; d. 27, 8, 1884. ³ANDREW⁷, b. 8, 3, 1808; d. 8, 3, 1808. ⁴MARY ANN⁷, b. 3, 11, 1810; d. 29, 2, 1844. ⁵ROBERT⁷, b. 31, 7, 1812; d. 28, 11, 1884. ⁶JOHN⁷, b. 12, 1, 1815; d. 26, 12, 1885. ⁷ELIZABETH⁷, b. 25, 12, 1817; d. ——. ⁸DANIEL⁷, b. 27, 6, 1820; d. 10, 6, 1889. ⁹RE-BECCA⁷, b. 26, 2, 1823; d. 25, 12, 1885. ¹⁰DAVIS⁷, b. 27, 11, 1826; d. 27, 11, 1826.

¹CATHERINE⁷, m. 11, 6, 1826, Andrew Dunlap; ch., ¹Hannah⁸, b. 27, 6, 1827. ²Isabella⁸, b. 4, 11, 1828; d. 4, 11, 1828. ³Mary A.⁸, b. 17, 11, 1829. ⁴Elizabeth R.⁸, b. 6, 8, 1831. ⁵Hugh⁸, b. 12, 1, 1833. ⁶Catherine R.⁸, b. 26, 3, 1834. ⁷John P.⁸, b. 6, 3, 1836. ⁸William T.⁸, b. 4, 2, 1838. ⁹Martha J.⁸, b. 10, 3, 1840; d. 22, 12, 1845. ¹⁰Margaret Wil-hemina⁸, b. 23, 2, 1842. ¹¹Deborah J.⁸, b. 12, 12, 1844; d. 27, 11, 1884. ¹²Almira A.⁸, b. 27, 3, 1846; d. 6, 8, 1858.

¹Hannah⁸, m., 27, 3, 1866, David Colgan.

³Mary A.⁸, m., 19, 12, 1854, Hugh McCorkle.

⁴Elizabeth R.⁸, m. 12, 1, 1864, Harvey Tollinger; ch., ¹William⁹, b. 13, 5, 1865. ²Mary H.⁹, b. 28, 12, 1866. ³Raleigh M.⁹, b. 5, 7, 1869. ⁴Cassandra⁹, b. 5, 7, 1871. ⁵Minnie E.⁹, b. 28, 4, 1876; d. 9, 7, 1877.

⁵Hugh⁸, m., 2, 11, 1865, Margaretta Doan; ch., ¹John D.⁹, b. 25, 8, 1866. ²Charles H.⁹, b. 12, 12, 1867. ³Lilian J.⁹, b. 1, 11, 1869. ⁴How-ard A.⁹, b. 23, 10, 1871. ⁵Robert C.⁹, b. 19, 11, 1873. ⁶Emma R.⁹, b. 9, 9, 1876. ⁷David H.⁹, b. 25, 7, 1878. ⁸William T.⁹, b. 2, 7, 1880. ⁹Louisa M.⁹, b. 8, 9, 1882. ¹⁰Frank T.⁹, b. 9, 9, 1884.

⁶Catherine R.⁸, m., 17, 11, 1853, William Tollinger; ch., ¹Andrew⁹, b. 31, 10, 1854. ²Thomas⁹, 9, 2, 1857; m. Margaret Ligget. ³Cath-erine⁹, b. 18, 6, 1859. ⁴Jane E.⁹, b. 18, 8, 1861. ⁵Ulysses S.⁹, d. —. ⁶David C.⁹, b. 9, 7, 1869. ⁷Josephine⁹, 22, 1, 1872.

⁷John P.⁸, m. 15, 12, 1859, Lydia A. Trout; ch., ¹Wilton M.⁹, b. 19, 8, 1860. ²Lydia C.⁹, 2, 2, 1862. ³Nicholas V.⁹, 24, 8, 1863. ⁴John A.⁹, 10, 6, 1866. ⁵Mary Hannah⁹.

⁸William T.⁸, m., 19, 1, 1870, Mary J. McAllister.

¹⁰Margaret Wilhemina⁸, m., 9, 3, 1875, James Wiley; ch., ¹Hugh⁹, ²Ann⁹, ³David H. C.⁹

¹¹Deborah J.⁸, m., —, —, 1866, William Hamilton; ch., ¹Robert A.⁹, b. ——, 1867. ²George N.⁹, ——, 1868. ³Catherine D.⁹, ——; d. 30, 4, 1888. ⁴Hannah C.⁹, ——, 1871. ⁵Johoheba C.⁹,

——, 1873. [6]Rutherford B.[9], ——, 1876. [7]Mary E.[9], ——, 1880; d. 12, 4, 1882.

[1]MARY ANN[7], m. James Dunlap; ch., [1]Anna Catherine[8], b. 7, 12, 1832, [2]John James[8], b. 1, 10, 1834; d. 15, 4, 1837. [3]William Andrew[8], 20, 7, 1836. [4]Martha Elizabeth[8], b. 18, 3, 1838; d. 2, 1, 1863. [5]Hugh Knox[8], b. 24, 4, 1840; d. 13, 11, 1844. [6]Margaret Isabella[8], b. 26, 6, 1842.

[1]Anna Catherine[8], m. Charles Dulin; ch., [1]Mary A.[9], b. 28, 10, 1857. [2]Sarah C.[9], 17, 8, 1859. [3]John H.[9], 15, 10, 1861; d. 24, 5, 1862. [4]Anna E.[9], b. 15, 3, 1863. [5]Charles H., Jr.[9], 15, 4, 1865. [6]Thomas C.[9], 25, 3, 1867. [7]Martha E.[9], 26, 11, 1869; d. 26, 11, 1869. [8]Cora M.[9], b. 20, 2, 1871. [9]William F.[9], 10, 7, 1873. [10]James C. R.[9], 8, 1, 1877; d. 29, 8, 1877. [11]Elwood E.[9], b. 1, 12, 1878; d. 9, 10, 1883.

[6]Margaret Isabella[8], m. John Dulin; ch., [1]Alifair E.[9], b. 21, 1, 1862. [2]Martha E.[9], 12, 2, 1863. [3]Margaret J.[9], 9, 6, 1865. [4]William P.[9], 31, 3, 1870. [5]John F.[9], 26, 5, 1875. [6]Mary F. L.[9], 24, 5, 1883. [7]Hannah F.[9], 16, 4, 1885.

[7]ELIZABETH[7], m. William B. Wilen; ch., [1]Mary A.[8], b. 31, 3, 1842. [2]Sylvania[8], 18, 11, 1843. [3]Anna C.[8], 1, 2, 1846; d. 27, 1, 1875. [4]Will. Ida[8], b. 27, 2, 1854. [5]Harmona[8], 4, 4, 1858; d. 27, 6, 1862. [6]William B., Jr.[8], b. 23, 1, 1860; d. 12, 6, 1860. [7]Elizabeth[8], b. 10, 8, 1862; d. 9, 8, 1863.

[1]Mary Ann[8], m., 7, 1, 1871, F. A. Hall; ch., [1]Elmer R.[9], b. 4, 12, 1873. [2]Ida May[9], 17, 2, 1883.

[2]Sylvania[8], m. 29, 3, 1865, George S. McKee; ch., [1]William[9], b. 4, 5, 1866. [2]Ella[9], 20, 7, 1867. [3]Lizzie[9], 12, 1, 1869; d. 3, 4, 1884. [4]Frank[9], b. 28, 2, 1870; d. 26, 1, 1869. [5]Bertha[9], b. 27, 4, 1874; d. 29, 9, 1884.

[3]Anna C.[8], m., 4, 4, 1867, Moses S. Cochran; ch., [1]William Wilen[9], b. 1, 1, 1868. [2]Ida[9], 18, 1, 1875; d. 20, 1, 1875.

[4]Will. Ida[8], m., 22, 12, 1870, Jas. W. Scanlan; ch., [1]Elizabeth May[9], b. 17, 12, 1872; d. 28, 6, 1875. [2]Mary Florence[9], 17, 10, 1877; d. 17, 11, 1881.

[9]REBECCA[7], m. Thomas Mullan; ch., John Edward, Elizabeth Ellis (Cornbrooks), Washington, d. Thomas, Jr., of Wilmington, Del.

[2]ANDREW[6], m., 10, 2, 1818, Rebecca Jarvis, g. d. of Melchoir Meng, of Germantown (she was b. 10, 2, 1792, in Germantown); ch., [1]JAMES DAVIS[7], b. 13, 1, 1819; d. 18, 2, 1889. [2]DANIEL[7], 17, 11, 1820; d. 7, 6, 1858. [3]REBECCA JANE[7], 14, 11, 1822. [4]MARY D.[7], 22, 10, 1824; d. 25, 11, 1830. [5]ANNA CATHERINE[7], 5, 8, 1826; d. 18, 11, 1830. [6]DAVID[7], 10, 3,

1828. [7]WILHEMINA[7], 7, 11, 1829; d. 13, 5, 1884. [8]ANDREW[7], 4, 9, 1831.
[9]MARY ANN[7], 6, 5. 1833. [10]ANNA CATHERINE[7], 8, 12, 1838.

[1]JAMES DAVIS[7], m., 6, 10, 1852, Ann T. Webster; ch., [1]Elizabeth Webster[8], b. 10, 8, 1853. [2]Andrew Davis[8], 1, 4, 1858. [3]Rebecca Jane[8].

[1]Elizabeth Webster[8], m., 7, 12, 1876, George Johnes De Armond; ch., [1]James Keyser[9], b. 21, 12, 1877. [2]William Webster[9], 20, 7, 1880; d. 28, 4, 1882.

[3]Rebecca Jane[8], m., 1st, Charles Shepherd Smith; ch., [1]Edgar Keyser[9], d. [2]Clara Kate[9], —, 9, 1852. [3]Linda[9], ——; m. 2d, 13, 11, 1861, Franklin G. Smith.

[2]Clara Kate[9], m., 5, 1, 1875, Charles E. Hires; ch., [1]Linda S.[10], b. 24, 9, 1878. [2]Rebecca K.[10], 14, 10, 1883; d. 29, 1, 1884. [3]John Edgar[10], 8, 2, 1885. [4]Harrison S.[10], 31, 5, 1887.

[6]DAVID[7], m., 1st, Rebecca Stevenson; ch., —— Stevenson, b. 21, 7, 1854; d. 6, 9, 1885. [2]Laura[8]; m., 2d, —, 2, 1874, Margaretta Richards; ch., [1]Herbert, b. —, 11, 1874.

[8]ANDREW[7], m., 1st, Harriet Brown; ch., [1]Harriet[8], 31, 1, 1862. [2]Edith May[8], d. [3]Charles Edgar[8]. [4]George[8], d. [5]Harriet[8]; m. 2d, 22, 11, 1873, Lynd Saxton; ch., ——.

[9]MARY ANN[7], m., ——, 1861, Sanford P. Campbell; ch., Sanford, b. ——, 1862. Anna Catherine, 12, 9, 1864. Edward Wilson, 27, 4, 1868. Mayland Cuthbert, 1, 10, 1872.

[10]ANNA CATHERINE[7], m. Mark Burkwell, ch., Frank, ——, d. 1875. Catherine, ——, 1876.

———

POSTFACE.—The compilation of the genealogy ends here. Its sources are, the papers preserved in the family Bible of our ancestor; Charles Keyser—the teacher's genealogic trees, three of which remain; Peter A. Keyser's MS. books of the families and land titles, with the additions by Dr. Peter Dirck Keyser; the Hon. Samuel W. Pennypacker's MS. Vol. of the genealogy and biographies of the Pannebecker line; Romaine Keyser's MS. volume; the Hon. Hor. Gates Jones' Levering family; and individual contributions of members of the family.

With the genealogy, also, the whole work of compilation ends; while very incomplete—nihil conceptum est, et perfectum—it is yet, as far as it is written, a reliable relation of the characteristics and the environment of our family line, for now over three centuries.

CHARLES S. KEYSER.

INDEX OF HISTORY.

THE FAMILY LINES.

www.ingramcontent.com/pod-product-compliance
Lightning Source LLC
Chambersburg PA
CBHW030832270326
41928CB00007B/1020

www.ingramcontent.com/pod-product-compliance
Lightning Source LLC
Chambersburg PA
CBHW030832270326
41928CB00007B/1020